Western Education and
Political Domination in Africa

WESTERN EDUCATION AND POLITICAL DOMINATION IN

AFRICA

A Study in Critical and Dialogical Pedagogy

Magnus O. Bassey

BERGIN & GARVEY
Westport, Connecticut • London

Library of Congress Cataloging-in-Publication Data

Bassey, Magnus O.
　　Western education and political domination in Africa : a study in critical and dialogical pedagogy / Magnus O. Bassey.
　　　p.　　cm.
　　Includes bibliographical references and index.
　　ISBN 0-89789-622-X (alk. paper)
　　1. Politics and education—Africa—History.　2. Education—Africa—Western influences.　3. Africa—Civilization—Western influences.　4. Elite (Social sciences)—Africa.　5. Critical pedagogy—Africa.
　　I. Title.
LC95.A2B37　1999
379.6—dc21　　　　99-12712

British Library Cataloguing in Publication Data is available.

Copyright © 1999 by Magnus O. Bassey

All rights reserved. No portion of this book may be reproduced, by any process or technique, without the express written consent of the publisher.

Library of Congress Catalog Card Number: 99-12712
ISBN: 0-89789-622-X

First published in 1999

Bergin & Garvey, 88 Post Road West, Westport, CT 06881
An imprint of Greenwood Publishing Group, Inc.
www.greenwood.com

Printed in the United States of America

The paper used in this book complies with the Permanent Paper Standard issued by the National Information Standards Organization (Z39.48-1984).

10 9 8 7 6 5 4 3 2

Copyright Acknowledgment

The author and publisher gratefully acknowledge permission for use of the following material:

Statistical data from *Statistical Profile of Education in Sub-Saharan Africa*, Association for the Development of Education in Africa (ADEA, 1994), are reprinted with permission of ADEA.

In order to keep this title in print and available to the academic community, this edition was produced using digital reprint technology in a relatively short print run. This would not have been attainable using traditional methods. Although the cover has been changed from its original appearance, the text remains the same and all materials and methods used still conform to the highest book-making standards.

This book is dedicated to my wife and children.

Contents

	Tables	ix
	Acknowledgments	xi
1.	Introduction	1
2.	Traditional African Education	15
3.	Christian Missionary/Colonial Education in Africa	27
4.	Western Education and the Rise of Educated Elites in Africa	51
5.	Western Education and Political Socialization in Africa	61
6.	Educated Elites and Political Domination in Africa	73
7.	Schools in Africa as Sites of Cultural and Structural Inequalities, Disempowerment, Sexism, Domination and Hegemony	83
8.	Education in the Service of Apartheid in South Africa, 1802–1993	99
9.	Education of Most Worth for Africa in the Twenty-First Century	105

Notes	125
Bibliography	145
Index	159

Tables

1.1	Student Flows, Selected Sub-Saharan Countries, 1990	5
1.2	Public Recurrent Expenditure per Student, Selected Sub-Saharan Countries	10
7.1	Gross Enrollment Ratios by Gender and Level, Sub-Saharan Africa, 1970–1990	92
7.2	Gross Primary Enrollment Data for Selected Countries in Sub-Saharan Africa, 1960, 1970, 1980 and 1990	94
7.3	Field of Study, Females as a Percentage of Total Secondary Enrollment, Selected Sub-Saharan Countries, 1980 and 1990	96
7.4	Field of Study, Females as a Percentage of Total Tertiary Enrollment, Selected Sub-Saharan Countries, 1990	98

Acknowledgments

Even a cursory look at the footnotes and bibliography in this book will reveal the extent of my indebtedness to authors and scholars too many to enumerate here. However, I wish to express my gratitude collectively to all those from whom I have learned as acknowledged throughout the length of this book. But I must thank the World Bank and the Association for the Development of Education in Africa specifically for granting me permission to reproduce statistical data from their publications.

I am particularly grateful to the acquisitions editor at Greenwood Publishing Group, Ms. Jane Garry for her guidance; to Ms. Gillian Beebe for supervising the publication of this work and to the copy editor, Arlene Belzer, for reading the manuscript so meticulously. I am thankful to my father-in-law, Mr. Alexander Evans for reading the manuscript and making useful suggestions for improvement. I am most grateful to members of my family for their interest in this project. To my friends and well-wishers—I thank them all.

1

Introduction

The contribution of Western education to the making of the present African political elites is well documented.[1] What is not as well documented is how the Western educated elites have used their education for political domination in Africa. James Coleman argues that Western education had unintended consequences because it prepared the minds of African political elites who were able to demand and eventually obtain independence from the colonialists in Africa. These educated elites also wrestled power from the traditional rulers. James Coleman makes this point:

> The introduction of a modern educational system in colonial areas had significant political consequences. It was the single most important factor in the rise and spread of nationalist sentiment and activity. From the modern educational system emerged an indigenous elite which demanded the transfer of political power to itself on the basis of the political values of the Western liberal tradition or the ethical imperatives of Christianity, both of which had been learned in the schools. ... Designed essentially to serve only evangelizing or imperial purposes, Western education became a prime contributor to the emergence of new independent nations.[2]

And Sir Eric Ashby noted: "From the graduates of the universities the currents of nationalism flowed." This means that Western education created the new educated African elites who were able to take political leadership in their various countries as well as oppose European rule in Africa.

J. F. Ade Ajayi described these events:

The Christian missionaries introduced into [Africa] the ideas of nation-building of contemporary Europe. They also trained a group of [Africans] who accepted those ideas and hoped to see them carried out, and later began to use those ideas as a standard by which to judge the actions of the [European] administration. In doing this, the Christian movement sowed the seeds of [African] nationalism.[3]

Mission-run schools, therefore, produced the bulk of African political leaders who later assumed the responsibility for self-government. These educated elites were able to oppose Europeans in both the political and religious spheres by establishing printing presses like the *Lagos Weekly Record* and the *Lagos Daily News* that were used to ferment anti-European sentiments in Lagos, Nigeria. From the 1940s, secondary school education became a mechanism for sorting and selecting young Africans for rapid upward mobility based almost exclusively on their academic abilities. These people were able to use their education to gain power both at the state and national levels, and thereafter also used their power to obtain the best education for their children at the secondary and university levels.[4] The Ajayi Commission appointed by the western Nigerian government in 1963 made this point:

The standard of living of Nigerians is becoming increasingly differentiated. But the average Nigerian at the moment apparently does not worry too much about this because with good secondary education his child could rise to the top and he will at once become associated with the higher standards. If increasingly the average person begins to find this passport beyond his means, the class structure will fossilise and discontent will grow.[5]

Writing in 1966, Peter Lloyd affirmed that: "In Africa at the present, the elite is characterized by the number of its members who have come from humble homes." But, "the well-educated and wealthy elite is tending to become a predominantly hereditary group."[6] Similarly, James Coleman maintains that the "academic traditions inherited from England and the other countries of Western Europe . . . were markedly elitist in their concept of the social function of education."[7] He goes on to argue that "colonial policies and practices fostered an elitist mentality by sharply differentiating the educated elements from the illiterate masses."[8] A Nigerian made this point rather clearly when he said: "Those who had savings spent them to send their children to schools and colleges, because they saw that only salaried people were secure even in spite of salary cuts and stabilization. . . . It was then that I began to look at education as a commodity that does not fall in price."[9] Indeed, it has been said that the life chances of an individual in Africa for achieving political elite status are enormously enhanced if he or she belongs to, or can rise into, the upper levels of the stratification system. Education is the major determining factor for social mobility because it is only through education that an individual can achieve higher occupational enhancement, higher income, higher status and higher prestige in Africa. In other words, education is about the only major determinant for moving into elite status in Africa.[10] But educational policies in Africa were and still are designed to perpetuate elite power. It is for this reason that a man wrote in a Nigerian newspaper, "One cannot help getting the impression that the policy of awarding scholarships is to make the rich even richer and the poor, poorer, thus enabling the former to continue to lord it over the latter." This being the case, during colonial days, development unions, families, clans and communities contributed money to send their sons abroad to receive an education in order to represent them in the sharing of the national pie. Almost all the early political leaders in Africa were beneficiaries of these types of efforts and arrangements. But in Buganda, the early beneficiaries of Western education in Africa were those who were marginalized in African society and those who were at the periphery of the traditional social structure.

However, the fact that these new elites have used their education as a means of political domination in Africa has not been thoroughly researched and documented. How have educated elites been able to do this in Africa? As controllers of all major political and social institutions, these elites make sure that their power is never threatened because they deny the poor the necessary knowledge to protect the political and economic rights that would enable the poor to advance in society. Lucian W. Pye writes that "those who have been exposed to modern forms of knowledge are often precisely the ones who are most anxious to obstruct the continued diffusion of the effects of that knowledge; they desperately hold that which they have and avoid all risks."[11] Educated elites have also protected their powers and privileges through the imprisonment as well as the outright killings of political opponents and through military dictatorships in Africa. Other methods include thuggery, house arrests, protective custody, and the perpetuation of political rule through the rigging of elections, the use of brute force against political opponents and the unwillingness to abdicate power. On the other hand, schools in Africa are used to produce ideologies that support the dominant group's authority to rule. Hence, schools have indeed become places that produce not only subjects but subjectivities. In addition, the educated elites have assumed total control of the ideology, religion and philosophy of education and schooling, and as Karl Marx once noted: "Ideologies express interests and needs of the dominant groups in any epoch but in terms that have universal applicability."

African political elites inject certain political attitudes into the curriculum. And as Paulo Freire has argued education is one sure way that individuals in society are assigned positions of power, esteem, rank and wealth. Through the control of education, elites impose a "culture of silence" on the masses, thereby keeping the people not only perpetually "alienated" but in a position of "marginality."[12] Freire defined people in a position of marginality as "people in a position of hunger, disease, despair, mental deficiencies, pain, promiscuity, and the impossibility of being."[13] According to Freire, certain types of education (e.g., banking education) perpetuate such an existing order. This type of education transmits privileges and allocates and instills respect for the existing order. Though established to transmit knowledge, "banking education," as Freire called it, contributes to perpetuating status cleavages. Freire maintained that modern democracies rely on indirect coercion and resort to less direct physical violence to assure control. The widespread belief in equality makes it difficult for the ruling class to grant ascriptive status overtly. Hence, new and more discreet means must be found. This role is now assigned to education.

According to Freire, elites, as a matter of deliberate policy, encourage the use of what is called narrative education "to make the majority adapt to the purpose the minority prescribe for them, thereby depriving them of the right to their own purpose."[14] Freire reasoned that schools, particularly in the Third World, "contain attempts to silence, to rationalize the irrational and to gain acceptance for structures that are oppressive."[15] Such colonization of the mind does not require imperialism because it is possible for one class of citizens to colonize others, men to colonize women, whites to colonize blacks and one ethnic group to colonize another. Freire defined a colonized person as an individual who "accepts readily the economic exploitation or cultural domination by the colonizer." Nowhere is this more true than in Africa.

As I will show in this book, schooling most cruelly and harshly affects the poor and the educationally disadvantaged in Africa. Class-determined characteristics put children of the poor at a competitive disadvantage in the schools even when they are not academically handicapped. Although education is used to assign people to positions of power, esteem, rank and wealth, in most countries in Africa a large percentage of the population cannot afford the cost of education (see Table 1.1).

Schools in Africa work to "silence, marginalize, and control as well as construct forms of cultural containment, conformity, discrimination, and socio-economic inequality," for the poor.[16] During colonial rule, for ex-

Table 1.1
Student Flows, Selected Sub-Saharan Countries, 1990

Country	Percent of first grade entrants completing the primary level	Primary entrants proceeding to secondary schooling (percent)
Benin	40	15
Botswana	80	36
Burkina Faso	71	23
Burundi	77	8
Cameroon	69	21
Cape Verde	51	23
Central Africa Republic	62	19
Congo	54	33
Côte d'Ivoire	71	16
Djibouti	88	24
Gabon	44	16
Guinea	67	39
Lesotho	50	51
Madagascar	38	14
Malawi	42	3
Mali	50	22
Mauritania	68	18
Mozambique	40	14
Niger	82	25
Rwanda	50	2
Swaziland	73	51
Togo	59	16

Source: World Development Report 1994. (Oxford: Oxford University Press, 1994). Cited in Adhiambo Odaga and Ward Heneveld, *Girls and Schools in Sub-Saharan Africa: From Analysis to Action* (Washington, DC: The World Bank, 1995), 81.

ample, there was uneven acquisition of education between ethnic groups or regions within particular parts of Africa. This was due either to a policy of protecting one group as in northern Nigeria or favoring one group over others as in Rwanda or by the "differential adaptive capacity, or receptivity to education on the part of indigenous cultural groups."[17] Whatever the case, these imbalances have led to underrepresentation of some groups in party leadership, the bureaucracy, the army and the police force, which, in turn, have led to a series of crises and confrontations within independent African countries like Nigeria, Algeria, Liberia, Sierra Leone, Sudan, Morocco, Chad, Somalia, Rwanda and Zaire, just to mention but a few.

Writing on the inequality of educational opportunity in Kenya, David Court notes: "The political vulnerability of Kenyan educational policy lies in the extent to which opportunity is manifestly unequal. As educational opportunities are not equally available and present selection devices tend to reinforce initial regional and individual advantages . . . the degree and extent of inequality in Kenya pose an imminent threat to Kenya's much vaunted social stability."[18]

Education in contemporary Africa has created the "marginality" of those who are not educated because schools have served as tools for keeping wealth and power in the hands of the educated elites. Statistics in Africa show that the more educated a person is, the more money he or she makes. Even though research has shown that expansion of educational opportunities would reduce inequality in Africa, African elites are very reluctant to embrace this policy. John Knight and Richard Sabot have argued that "the academic advantages conferred by family background mean that it is primarily the children of the poor and uneducated who are excluded by the qualitative restrictions imposed by the government."[19] Indeed, Peter Lloyd found in his study that educational attainment of African men was a predictor of their socioeconomic status and that socioeconomic attainment of sons tended to be the same as those of their fathers. This means that status in contemporary African societies is inherited and not transcended. In this study, Lloyd also found that there was a link between schooling and opportunities, and a link existed between schooling and inequality because schools in Africa stratify and rank-order opportunity. Schools reproduce not only the ideologies of the educated elites but also their class structure. Power of the ruling elites is reinforced within the schools through academic selections and socioeconomic stratification. Also, educated elites are more able to give their children a head start by sending them to private nursery schools and providing them with the best elementary and secondary school education. Studies conducted by Remi Clignet and Philip Foster in Ivory Coast, Philip Foster in Ghana and David Abernethy in southern Nigeria show that children of managerial and clerical workers are overrepresented at the secondary school level while children of farmers are proportionately underrepresented. Indeed, Barbara B. Lloyd maintains that "children of the educated elite are taller, heavier, healthier, and begin schooling earlier and with more skills than the products of illiterate or traditional [African] homes. These are the most obvious results of superior housing, diet, medical care—in fact, of privilege."[20] She goes on to say that perhaps more so than in industrial nations, the educated [African] seeks his career in the professions or in the governmental bureaucracy. Unlike Western middle-class suburban-dwelling children, . . . these youngsters are not ignorant of their fathers' occupations. Due in part to the residential patterns set down during the colonial era, officers are housed near their work. . . . [T]oday, [African] university staff live on university grounds, senior government officials in residence areas near their offices, graduate teachers on their school compounds, and even among private lawyers it is common for the family to live on the first floor of a two-story building which houses the father's chambers on the ground floor.[21]

Lloyd illuminates the effects of parental elite status on students' life experiences, self-esteem, and academic achievement and notes:

The children may go to school by car, together with their parents, who leave home for work at the same time in the morning, and in the early afternoon return together for dinner. On Sundays a busy father sometimes takes the children with him when he goes to work in his office for a few hours in the afternoon. Thus, elite children become familiar with the work of government officials, lawyers, professors, and teachers, and through observation learn the requirements of the roles they may expect one day to perform.[22]

Through government regulation of the curricular and teaching modes, the educated elites in Africa are able to impose their own cultural values on the masses.

As the saying goes, "As is the state, so is the school," and "What you want in the state, you must put into the school." The example of South Africa comes to mind here. In South Africa during apartheid, for example, the Afrikaners developed their own philosophy of education called fundamental pedagogics—a unique South African development whose main doctrine was that the "child must, as a function of his or her educational experience, be made morally defensible against ideologies such as liberalism, pragmatism, [and] communism through the inculcation of the Christian Philosophy of Life."[23] Contemporaneous with this philosophy was the use of technical jargons to justify and reify simple educational concepts, thereby obscuring understanding by the common people. By so doing, South African minority ruling elites were able to remove educational discourse from the sphere of the general public into the hands of the so-called experts. Another lesson to learn here is that the minority white elites in South Africa used education to legitimize their illegal stay in power and to justify the separate but unequal systems of education. The Afrikaners achieved these objectives through the use of fundamental pedagogics that stated that "different cultural groups have different philosophies of life, and that, in turn, appropriate educations for different cultural groups must therefore be grounded in significantly different philosophies of education."[24] Indeed, fundamental pedagogics further provided the intellectual and religious justification for the perpetuation of apartheid and racism in South Africa by stating that "different ethnolinguistic, cultural, and racial groups have different philosophies of life and 'worldviews' " and therefore blacks and whites should not be educated together.[25]

Fundamental pedagogics also endorsed absolute domination by teachers in the teaching-learning processes—an antithesis to critical pedagogy. However, Timothy Reagan reminds us that: "We too, live in a society in which academics, and even philosophers of education, contribute to the maintenance of fundamentally unjust and inequitable social relations."[26] Hence, although the South African example is unique, other nations in Africa are known to have manipulated their educational systems to suit their ideologies. Indeed, Michel Foucault argued: "Truth is linked in circular relation with systems of power which produce and sustain it, and to effects of power which it induces and which extend it."[27] He went on to explain that:

Each society has its regime of truth, its "general politics" of truth: that is, the types of discourse which it accepts and makes function as true; the mechanisms and instances which enable one to distinguish true and false statements, the means by which each is sanctioned; the techniques and procedures accorded value in the acquisition of truth; the status of those who are charged with saying what counts as true.[28]

Perhaps nowhere in the world is this more true than in Africa (see chapter 6). However, Foucault continues that, "it is in discourse that power and knowledge are joined together."[29] He concludes that knowledge and power are connected. "Power and knowledge directly imply one another," Foucault argues, "There is no power relation without the correlative constitution of a field of knowledge, nor any knowledge that does not presuppose and constitute at the same time power relations."[30] He goes on to explain the connection between power and knowledge by saying that "There is an administration of knowledge, a politics of knowledge, relations of power which pass via knowledge and which, if one tries to transcribe them, lead one to consider forms of domination designated by such notions as field, region and territory."[31] Henry Giroux makes a similar point about how a class-based society is reproduced:

Reproduction refers here to texts (language and communication patterns) and social practices whose messages, inscribed within specific historical settings and social contexts, function primarily to legitimate the interests of the dominant social order. I want to argue that these can be characterized as texts, as social practices about pedagogy, and refer primarily to categories of meaning constructed so as to legitimize and reproduce interests expressed in dominant ideologies.[32]

Among others, South Africa under apartheid was an excellent example of this.

Also, education has provided the elites in Africa the tools to exploit their less fortunate countrymen and women. For example, as government employees, educated elites often take advantage of their less fortunate citizens. David B. Abernethy makes this point very succinctly about the attitudes of some educated elites during the colonial era in Africa:

Education provided a man with the tools to exploit as well as to serve others, and the first literates, employed by government and by European business firms, often took advantage of their unique position as intermediaries between the white man and the African to exploit their own countrymen. An interpreter might threaten to distort an illiterate's story unless offered a bribe; a commercial agent might undervalue a farmer's produce, knowing that the farmer could not check the offered price against the list price in the agent's notebook.[33]

Since women and the poor do not always control schools in Africa, schools have become instruments for the oppression of women and the poor. Indeed, schools are established for the poor and women only to teach them how to become good consumers of goods and how to participate in the world of work (see Table 1.2). In Africa, children of the rich attend schools for leadership and spend more time on intellectual activities, but children of the poor spend most of their time on vocational training. The type of education designed for the poor has led to dependency that in turn has kept the poor masses in their respective places.

Schools in Africa also perpetuate sex-role stereotypes regarding behavior, emotion and occupation between boys and girls. Girls are educated to take their places in the homes. They are told that they will be housewives and mothers and are taught to be dependent on men and to nurture their families. Schools, therefore, serve to legitimate the relations of domination as demonstrated by inequality and uneven educational development and opportunities between boys and girls. Indeed, a recent study conducted in Africa showed that the determinants of occupational attainment are education, race, sex, employment experience and family background. Bonnie Cook Freeman argues that "wittingly or unwittingly, the family has had an impact on shaping the young child to his or her appropriate sex role."[34] But she concludes that "for the most part, the school, as a public caretaking institution and socializing agent, tends not to counter the forces of parental socialization but becomes implicated in reinforcing traditional sex roles introduced by the family."[35]

Schools in Africa disenfranchise poor students in other ways too. For example, poor students do not understand the language of the school because formal instruction in African schools are undertaken in European languages. Perhaps Africa should learn from Paulo Freire who

Table 1.2
Public Recurrent Expenditure per Student, Selected Sub-Saharan Countries
(*Constant 1990 U.S. dollars*)

	Primary		Secondary		Tertiary	
Country	*1980*	*1990*	*1980*	*1990*	*1980*	*1990*
Botswana	174	219	779	1302	7999	7218
Burkina Faso	71	61	319	201	9114	4007
Burundi	45	27	417	245	2780	2280
Central Africa Rep.	100	45	126	88	3135	1726
Ethiopia	26	51	90	77	1749	851
Kenya	52	46	113	162	3322	2347
Lesotho	43	37	361	223	3141	987
Malawi	16	15	289	192	2973	1782
Mali	96	107	243	830	2751	2618
Mauritania	167	86	972	406	2875	2020
Rwanda	41	54	415	182	3329	4050
Senegal	191	116	530	258	3676	2681
Sierra Leone	31	6	122	35	3672	777
Swaziland	74	70	268	246	1053	2316
Tanzania	11	12	193	132	1809	1412
Togo	45	46	180	189	4858	1398
Zambia	56	16	321	138	3084	865
Zimbabwe	143	126	761	233	2398	806

Source: Association for the Development of Education in Africa. *Statistical Profile of Education in Sub-Saharan Africa*, 1994. Cited in Adhiambo Odaga and Ward Heneveld, *Girls and Schools in Sub-Saharan Africa: From Analysis to Action* (Washington, DC: The World Bank, 1995), 82.

stated: "(C)olonized persons and colonial nations never seal their liberations, conquer or reconquer their cultural identity, without assuming their language and discourse and being assumed by it."[36] Also, it must be said that the use of European languages in the educational systems and for official business in Africa works in favor of those who are well acquainted with the foreign language and qualifies them for high civil and public service appointments as well as for lucrative positions in industries. It is therefore safe to say that, in Africa, serious inequalities are created by the educational system itself.[37]

Although, schools in Africa perpetuate inequalities, teachers in Africa do not realize that schools perpetuate such inequalities. Teachers still limit their learners to a "passive role in the meaning-making process, and therefore fail to produce a type of political knowledge that can expose and challenge the production and reproduction of oppressive relationship."[38] Teachers in Africa are not transformative intellectuals. A transformative intellectual is one who uses the language of critique to challenge social, economic and political inequalities in society and also challenges the way the dominant elites oppress and exploit the masses. Indeed, Henry Giroux argues that teachers "need to analyze how cultural production is organized within asymmetrical relations of power in schools."[39] He goes on to add that teachers "need to construct political strategies for participating in social struggles designed to fight for schools as democratic public spheres."[40] This means, teachers should be involved in what Barry Kanpol calls "cultural politics"—those voices that "challenge dominant, oppressive values in society."[41]

This book offers a critical analysis of the behavior of African educated elites and argues that educated elites in Africa have used their education and the schools to perpetuate their dominance over their less fortunate countrymen and women. Indeed, as in the words of Henry Giroux, "school as a vehicle for social justice and public responsibility has been replaced by other imperatives." According to him the result, therefore, is a "notion of schooling that has a great deal to do with oppression and too little to do with [education]."[42]

This book has eight other chapters. Chapter 2 discusses traditional African education. The chapter argues that, although without formal educational institutions, African societies had developed some means of transmitting their cultures from one generation to the next. Chapter 3 discusses the contribution of European missionaries to the development of Western education in Africa. The chapter, however, argues that although education for the missionaries was an essential part of their "civilizing" mission because it was a way of winning converts, training African catechists and workers and creating an African middle class, the rapid expansion of education in Africa was actually the accidental outcome of missionary and church rivalry rather than the result of altruistic policy to provide expanded educational opportunities for the African populace. The chapter concludes, therefore, that missionaries in Africa were making a virtue of necessity. In chapter 4 I argue that until the 1960s the establishment of schools—and indeed, Western education itself in many parts of Africa—was virtually a monopoly of the Christian missions. The missions' interest in education evolved from the missionaries' perceptions of schools as important avenues for conversion. According to Bishop Shanahan, one of the pioneer Catholic missionaries in eastern Nigeria, "Those who hold the school, hold the country, hold its religion, hold its future."⁴³ Father Wauters, a Catholic missionary in Ondo and Ekiti divisions in Yorubaland put the point rather bluntly:

We knew the best way to make conversions in pagan countries was to open schools. Practically all pagan boys ask to be baptized. So, when the district of Ekiti-Ondo was opened (in 1916) we started schools even before there was any church or Mission house.⁴⁴

What made educational work even more compelling for missionaries in Africa was that, except for small pockets of acceptance, missionaries were neither accepted nor tolerated in most parts of Africa. Consequently, missionaries turned their attention to youths and schools as sources of conversion because they soon realized, to their utter dismay and puzzlement, the futility of trying to convert men of good standing in African society. Indeed, as one Roman Catholic missionary lamented:

For a man of social status to accept Christianity in this country . . . is to expose himself to poverty for the rest of his life; it is to renounce, as the Lord asks of the Religious only, his fortune, his future and even his family.⁴⁵

As Felix Ekechi argues, "Formal education became the bait with which the young generation was enticed to Christianity."⁴⁶ Good education, it was believed, would enable young African men to earn a good living as well as enable them to exert their own influence and that of their adopted religious denomination upon the society at large.

Chapter 5 examines the place of Western education in the making of modern African political elites. It argues that Western education was responsible for the emergence of the indigenous African elite who demanded and wrestled power from traditional rulers and European colonialists on the basis of European liberal tradition and Christian principles; it was directly responsible for the rise and spread of nationalism in Africa. Western education also formed the foundation for the development of a national language that made effective political communication possible. Indeed, James Coleman argues that, although Western education was not intended as a forum for political recruitment, "it in fact called forth and activated some of the most upwardly mobile and aggressively ambitious elements of the population—elements most determined to acquire political power, most confident in the rightness of their claim, and most convinced of their capacity to govern."⁴⁷ The chapter concludes that Western education was therefore the most important factor in the evolution of modern nation-states in Africa.

In chapter 6 I have presented some examples to support my position that Western educated elites have used their education as a means of political domination in Africa. My examples are drawn from Ghana, Nigeria, Kenya, Ivory Coast, Guinea, Liberia, Sierra Leone, Libya, Uganda and a few other countries. I have argued that educated minorities in Africa had used their education to wrestle power from the colonialists and from traditional rulers in their various countries but have perpetuated their stay in power by limiting access to education through corruption, imprisonment, military dictatorships and the outright killings of political opponents. These elites have also exploited and oppressed subordinate groups through their ill-gotten wealth.

In chapter 7 I argue that schools in Africa are sites of cultural and structural inequalities, disempowerment, sexism, domination and hegemony. The chapter highlights the problematic relationship between African societies at large, teachers, students and schooling as exemplified by structural and cultural inequalities, unequal power relations, domination, sexism and hegemony in schools in Africa. Examples here include how educated elites in Africa have made opportunities available to its members to the exclusion of the poor through selective ordering, legitimization of certain language forms in schools, legitimization of certain thinking types and legitimization of elite codes and experiences to the exclusion of the histories, experiences and world-views of the poor.

Chapter 8 shows how the whites in South Africa gave blacks an inferior education as a means of keeping themselves in power. Chapter 9 discusses education that would be of the most worth for Africa in the twenty-first century, which is the type of education that teaches students to see schools as places that produce not only subjects but subjectivities. This type of education should teach students that learning is as much about the acquisition of knowledge as it is about the production of social practices that provide students with a sense of identity, self-worth, value and place. In other words, education should prepare students to be active, critical and risk-taking citizens.[48] In order for schools to perform these feats, teachers must be transformative intellectuals. Teachers should be involved in cultural politics—those actions that challenge dominant, oppressive values in society—and teachers must see the language of critique and possibility as mutually inclusive. Teachers must produce the types of pedagogy that highlight the problematic relationship between the society at large, teachers, students and schooling as exemplified by structural inequality, unequal power relations, domination, exploitation, sexism and hegemony in Africa. Education must empower the powerless by enabling those traditionally silenced and denied the opportunity to participate fully in the making of educational decisions to become critical subjects in the learning process—that is, people who will be able to exercise power over the conditions of knowledge production and acquisition.

Finally, teachers must produce the type of pedagogy that raises students' consciousness and critical thinking skills to enable them to "delve into their own histories and systems of meaning, to learn about the structural and ideological forces that influence and restrict their lives."[49] However, the starting point for producing these types of teachers who will place emphasis on democratic and critical citizenship is in teacher education preparation. Teacher education curricula in Africa, therefore, must incorporate the language of critique and possibility. Teacher candidates should be provided with the critical knowledge, terminology and the necessary conceptual frameworks to enable them to "critically analyze the political shortcomings of schools."[50] Such an education should also enable would-be teachers to learn the skills needed to enhance respect for democracy and for building an ethical society.

2

Traditional African Education

Though without schools as formal institutions, traditional African societies had developed the means of creating and transmitting their cultures from one generation to the next. This is so because in order to survive, a society must have a way of creating useful citizens and preparing its youth for the lives they must lead in adult society by providing them with basic skills and transmitting such skills from one generation to the next. Education is about the only known way of performing this task. R. M. Ruperti argues: "The ... education of the youth of a community is part and parcel of the culture of the community; without culture, ... there is no education; and without education, ... no culture ... and no community. When one talks of education, therefore, one is also inevitably talking of community culture and cultural communities."[1]

It is against this background that we must understand the concept, methods and practice of traditional African education. The system of education practiced in Africa in precolonial times is known as traditional education. Traditions are the sum total of the beliefs, opinions, customs, cultural patterns and other ways of life that a society passes from generation to generation. In precolonial Africa, it was the duty of education to sort out worthwhile traditions and to transmit these traditions from one generation to the next. It is often wondered how traditional education performed this feat without schools as we know them today. It is to be pointed out, however, that in traditional society skills, knowledge and attitudes were acquired and transmitted through nonformal institutions. These include parents, age-grades, secret societies, and so forth.[2] The aim of traditional education was to "produce an individual who is honest, respectable, skilled, cooperative and conforms to the social order of the day."[3] Chuka Eze Okonkwo, maintains that "traditional education in Africa . . . was a cultural action directed at creating attitudes and habits considered necessary for participation and intervention in one's historical process."[4] "Perhaps no educational system," Okonkwo adds, "even in contemporary times, articulated a clearer principle of unity, love and brotherliness between the land and the people and between the people themselves."[5] He goes on to say that unity, love and togetherness were highly functional in African society. Indeed, African children are taught from youth to recognize that they are members of an extended family system to which they owe loyalty, respect and affection.

In traditional society, while it was mandatory for the family, both immediate and extended, to educate its offspring in order to make them well adjusted members of society, education was the responsibility of the entire community.[6] Hence, the African proverb "It takes a whole village to raise a child." Thus, a child who was not well behaved was considered a disgrace to his/her family in the first instance and to his/her clan in the next, because even though a child bore the names of his/her immediate family he/she was *prima facie* a child of the clan.[7] In traditional African society, education was so highly prized that I consider Abdou Moumouni's observation insightful here: "In the social sphere, even in the feudal societies of pre-colonial Black Africa, education was considered far more valuable than even high birth or fortune, to the point where the title of 'man' was inseparable from a certain number of traits linked to education."[8]

African education was not compartmentalized and was not cut off from the daily experiences of the learner, for in Africa school and life were the same. A. Babs Fafunwa maintains that the main guiding principle of African education was functionalism. He states, "African society regarded education as a means to an end and not as an end in itself. Education was generally for an immediate induction into society and a preparation for adulthood."[9] Fafunwa summarizes the aims, methods and contents of African education as follows:

African education emphasized social responsibility, job orientation, political participation and spiritual and moral values. Children learned by doing, that is to say, children and adolescents were engaged in participatory education through ceremonies, rituals, imitation, recitation and demonstration. They were involved in practical farming, fishing, weaving, cooking, carving, knitting, and so on. Recreational subjects included wrestling, dancing, drumming, acrobatic display, racing, etc., while intellectual training included the study of . . . history, poetry, reasoning, riddles, proverbs, storytelling, story-relays. Education in Africa... combined physical training with character-building, and manual activity with intellectual training."[10]

One of the primary concerns of traditional education was its emphasis on social sensitivity, that is, the individual was inseparable from the group.[11] In his famous anthropological work on traditional African education, K. A. Busia wrote: "Though traditional Africa had many cultures, they all appear to have emphasized as a *summum bonum*, a social sensitivity which made one lose one's self in the group; the kinsfolk were, and lived as, members of one another. It was the goal of education to inculcate this sense of belonging, which was the highest value of the cultural system. The young were educated in and for the community's way of life."[12] In this way, an educated person in African society was required to conduct him- or herself in such a manner as to bring honor and not disgrace to the family, for honor or disgrace was shared by all the members of the family.

Traditional education emphasized endurance, courage and bravery as demonstrated during initiation into secret societies and during the traditional circumcision ceremonies. These rites were intended to "make the young adults into fully-developed persons, capable of discharging their duties in society."[13]

Among the Mende of Sierra Leone, K. L. Little notes: "The boys are expected to bear hardships without complaint and grow accustomed to it. They sleep at night on a bed of sticks under covering cloths, which have been soaked in water, and they remain out-of-doors if it rains. The singing and drumming lasts until one or two o'clock in the morning, and the boys are wakened again at dawn. They are expected to get up and sing anytime they are called."[14] Francis X. Sutton maintains that in traditional Africa, initiates were often circumcised and scorified, and through pain they acquired the marks of adulthood. Their common experience in practical, magical, religious and rigorous routines provided a bond among them.[15]

In traditional African society, honesty was considered the best policy. Indeed, A. Babs Fafunwa maintains; "In traditional [African] society all parents want their children to be upright, honest, kind and helpful to others, and will spare no pain to instill these qualities.... All [African] parents, irrespective of ethnic group, prefer to remain childless than to have children who will bring shame and dishonor to the family."[16]

Also, the development of the child's mind went together with the development of his or her character. Character building took the form of moral and religious values "imparted through parental advice, group pressure, taboos, moral tags, legends, myths, proverbs, and wise sayings of the tribe."[17] Indeed, in Africa even names have moral implications.

Therefore, children are often named after those ancestors who led particularly exemplary lives. Since names were believed to have significant influence on those who bore them, great care was taken in selecting a name for a newborn for the express purpose of character building, influence and inspiration to the child. Kofi A. Opoku maintains that in Africa "names have moral implications, . . . names are character molding and help to shape the character of the child."[18]

It is important to note that character building was an uncompromised virtue in traditional society and it formed an essential part of traditional education. Abdou Moumouni claims that:

Moulding character and providing moral qualities are primary objectives in traditional African education. Almost all the different aspects of education of the child and adolescent aim towards this goal, to a greater or lesser degree. In the family, parents concern themselves with the bearing, manners, honesty and integrity of the child. Outside the house, games, the society of his friends in the same age group, and the demands they make on each other, constitute a real source of character building. Sociability, integrity, honesty, courage, solidarity, endurance, ethics and above all the concept of honor are, among others, the moral qualities constantly demanded, examined, judged and sanctioned, in ways which depend on the intellectual level and capacities of the child and adolescent.[19]

How was character training developed in children in traditional society? This was done in three different ways. First, a child was taught directly by his/her parents and elders the moral requirements of the community because a child who was not well behaved was considered a disgrace to his/her family. Hence, children were severely reprimanded by their parents if they did not benefit from their moral training. Second, morality was learned by example, especially from those who had acquired experience in public life, native laws and customs and in self-discipline. Third, a child learned lessons of morality from the numerous folklores and proverbs often told by parents and other members of the extended family on moral and ethical behaviors and on the possible consequences of misconduct. Indeed, in traditional African society proverbs and storytelling were used as pedagogical tools.

Another important feature of traditional education was its emphasis on the development of the physical well-being of the child. This was to enable the child to meet the exigencies of his/her environment. However, it should be emphasized that unlike other aspects of traditional education, there was no deliberate effort made either by parents or members of the extended family to teach these skills. Given the open nature of the African topography, children often embarked on physical activities to satisfy their natural curiosity and inclinations and in the process exercised their nerves and muscles. African children often engaged themselves in various games and activities, for instance, wrestling, jumping, climbing, racing, balancing and swimming, which enabled them to develop their physical well-being. A vital factor in the development of the physique was children's involvement in acrobatic shows and displays—common features of traditional African dances, which a child learned as a matter of course from birth. Without being taught, the African child developed his/her physical self through imitation, intuition and curiosity.

Traditional education also encouraged intellectual training. In traditional society, a child was taught local geography and history right from youth. Indeed, being able to recite one's family tree and genealogy was a must for every child. Oral history was a matter of prestige for those endowed with the intellectual gift. In African society, parents taught their children plant and animal behaviors for protective, cultivation and rearing purposes. Knowledge of the various seasons of the year was a requirement for survival in a purely agrarian society so dependent on the clemency of the weather. Children learned through the process of observation, imitation and participation most of their intellectual skills. Thus, by early adolescence, children were already conversant with the topography of their community and could distinguish between fishing and hunting seasons and knew when to plant crops and when to harvest them. Through precepts from proverbs, folk-tales, riddles, poetic verses, recitations, games, incantations and praises, a child developed most of his/her reasoning, judgment and mathematical skills. Those who grew into adults graduated into advanced levels of intellectual training by learning the art of maintaining and retaining their secret cults, which, to a large extent and to a surprising degree, incorporated some elements of social psychology and philosophy. As V. L. Crosson and J. C. Stailey have argued, "Storytelling is one of the oldest art forms. Through the telling of stories the wisdom, strength and values of a people are expressed."[20]

Within its limitations, traditional education combined manual activity with intellectual training. This is most noticeable in poetic chants of the Yoruba hunters called "Ijala." A. Babalola describes Ijala as,

The oral poetry of Yoruba hunters and it is one of the various genres of the spoken art of the Yoruba people. It is a type of speech utterance with rudimentary musical characteristics, rather than a species of song. It is a border-line type of spoken art. . . . It is uttered from memory in chanting style but it is essentially a type of verbal art.[21]

Other professional groups like priests, diviners, herbalists, native doctors, chiefs and cult leaders used poetic chants and incantations in the performance of their duties. Poetic chants require considerable intellectual ability indeed since a "recitation can go on for hours with little or no repetition except for the chorus."[22] Poetic chants were learned for long periods of time by professionals in order to attain perfection. As integral parts of their professions, the more one perfected in them, the more it was taught he/she could perform his/her duties successfully. Hence, admission to the professions in traditional society was restricted to the intellectually able.

An important aspect of intellectual training was in the area of mathematics. Most ethnic groups in Africa had developed their own ways of counting and numbering long before the advent of the Europeans. Most African children, for instance, were introduced to counting quite early in life by concrete means, that is, by objects, counting rhymes, folklores, plays and games either at home or in the farms. Also, special attention was given to vocational education in traditional society. Farming, fishing, trading, hunting and weaving were introduced to children quite early. But most of the occupations, however, were run on an apprenticeship basis. This was a system in which children were trained, not by their parents, but by master craftswomen and master craftsmen, relatives or friends in their chosen professions in order to maintain discipline and concentration. Serious attention was given to agriculture, which was and still is the mainstay of African economy. Agricultural education involved training children to discriminate between fertile and infertile lands. This was a very painstaking exercise indeed since a soil declared suitable for one type of crop could be found unsuitable for another. One way of distinguishing between suitable and unsuitable soil was by dipping a cutlass into the soil. A stony encounter was indicative of a poor soil unsuitable for deep-rooted crops. Agricultural education also involved teaching children when and how to set a fire into the bush, how to plant crops, what time to plant crops and in what direction. With respect to yam cultivation, Matthew Ogundijo has this to say:

There were as many methods [of planting the seeds] as there were crops. Yam was usually cut into sets. Before the father who was also the teacher began to cut the yam, he instructed the children to observe very keenly. Some sets were small while others were big. In each case the teacher explained why certain types were small while others were big. Like a good teacher, he let the children practice with the cutting knives. Anyone who did it very well was praised and those who did not were reprimanded for their failure.... Before real planting of the yam sets began, knowledge of arithmetic was again brought into play. The children were made to count the yam sets, usually in groups of two hundred.... The yam sets were distributed on the heaps and the children buried them.[23]

Boys who had the flair for fishing apprenticed in fishing boats of family friends or relatives. They were taught navigational techniques including seafaring, the effects of certain stars on tide and ebb, favorable fishing grounds, and fish migrational patterns and habits. Whether it was fishing, farming, trading or weaving, the method was teaching by example and learning by doing. In an interview with an older man on the techniques of fishing in traditional society, my informant observed: "In those days we had no navigational instruments. We followed the sun by day and the moon by night. The position of a certain star could be indicative of a storm or good weather. You only needed to have the eyes to see it and the ability to recognize it."[24]

Apart from farming and fishing, children learned trades and crafts. Most important among them were blacksmithing, weaving, wood carving and bronze work. Since these trades needed a high degree of specialization and internship, children were apprenticed outside their homes for the express purpose of discipline. Those who took to the professions—priests, village heads, kings, medicine-men and women, diviners, rainmakers and rulers—underwent long periods of painstaking training and rituals. John S. Mbiti describes the making of medicine-men among the Azande, which I find interesting enough to reproduce here in its entirety:

In every case, medicine-men must undergo formal or informal training. Among the Azande, for example, their training is long and expensive, even starting the preliminary preparations at the age of five years in some cases. When a young person has made his wishes known that he intends to become a medicine-man he is carefully scrutinized by his would-be teacher, to ascertain that he really "means business." Then he is given medicine to eat, which is believed "to strengthen his soul and give him powers of prophecy; he is initiated into the corporation by public burial; he is given witchcraft phlegm to swallow; and he is taken to a stream-source and shown the various herbs and shrubs and trees from which the medicines are derived." That is the procedure to becoming a medicine-man among the Azande, but in reality it takes a long time to reach the goal, and it is a complicated affair.[25]

However, while boys were being trained in the farms, rivers and workshops, girls were trained in homemaking. They were taught how to prepare food, make clothes, care for children, take care of the dwellings and wash utensils. These tasks they did most often under the strict supervision of their mothers. Girls were sometimes apprenticed to housewives for certain trades such as dying, weaving and plaiting. Above all, girls were drilled in their future roles as housewives and brides.

Traditional education also concerned itself with community participation and promotion of cultural heritage. In summary, Chuka Eze Okonkwo maintains that:

traditional education left nothing to chance. It was very well organized, and its curriculum was geared toward achieving the spirit of love and an ordered, rich, and beautiful life.... Its curriculum emphasized all those virtues and values, ideas and ideals that encouraged healthy growth.... The traditional curriculum prepared men against the dangers and challenges of the time and offered them the confidence and the strength to confront those dangers instead of surrendering their sense of self through submission to the decisions of others.[26]

African education was comprehensive and was designed to produce an individual who would fulfill his or her social roles as well as individuals who could be entrusted with the day to day functioning of his or her society. Children in Africa learned by doing because education emphasized the total involvement of the learner. Michael Gelfand gives one example of the comprehensive and practical nature of African education that he witnessed as a British medical officer in Zimbabwe and states:

The son watches his father make a circular hole in the ground and places in it some charcoal. Air is forced through a tunnel into the hole. The charcoal is lit with lighted sticks and embers to a high temperature. When the iron in the fire turns red, the father uses a source-shaped implement to grip the top. His son holds it firmly while he hits it with a hammer to fashion the molten iron into a desired object.[27]

Traditional African education provided equal educational opportunity for all as recalled by an elderly African: "Before the coming of Europeans to our country, no aspect of our life, no boy or girl was ever neglected by our educational system because it was constantly being innovated to make it relevant to the needs of all students. Every person had an opportunity for education. Today, we are told that only so many can go to school. Why so many only and not all?"[28] Also, Dominic T. Ashley argues that education in Africa was "not just learning for the sake of learning, it was a deliberate effort to perpetuate and reinforce social solidarity and homogeneity."[29]

In Africa, however, the responsibility for the education of the child fell on the entire family because it was the responsibility of the family to develop in the child a sense of social solidarity, ethical values, harmony and commitment to one's society. These commitments among others, were deemed to be more important than the individual. In other words, the family was charged with the responsibility of passing on knowledge, skills, modes of behavior and beliefs from generation to generation.[30] On their part, African children were required to conduct themselves in a manner that would bring honor to the family because the family was required to provide a bedrock for the child's education.[31]

African family here does not refer to the nuclear family in a narrow sense, but instead, it connotes a consortium of all persons with a common ancestry because African tradition calls for close cooperation among family members. Indeed, K. A. Busia maintains: "There is everywhere, the heavy accent on family—the blood relatives, the group of kinsfolk held together by a common origin and a common obligation to its members, to those who are living and those who are dead. For the family is conceived of as consisting of a large number of people, many of whom are dead, a few of whom are living and countless numbers of whom are yet to be born."[32] Busia continues by arguing that "the individual is brought up to think of himself always in relation to this group and to behave always in such a way as to bring honor and not disgrace to its members. The ideal set before him is that of mutual helpfulness and cooperation within the group of kinsfolk. Each member should help the other, in health or sickness, in success or in failure, in poverty or plenty."[33] African education emphasized social responsibility, which required the individual to surrender to the group. Kinsmen lived as members of a group and education was to inculcate a sense of belonging to the group. African education was also designed to foster good relationships between groups and their environments.

In traditional Africa, an educated person was one who was capable of finding practical solutions to problems. He or she was required to have the capacity of judging rightly on matters relating to behavior. He or she was required to show sound common sense in all practical matters. He or she was to be a thinking person desirous of enhancing and advancing the moral peace of society. Michael Gelfand maintains that "there were no professional schools or teachers in the traditional society in Africa. But the child learned from various members of the family and community as he grew. He learned from his grandparents, parents, and members of the community. Yet, his entire education was as complete as it is in Western culture, whether it was agricultural pursuit or taking part in games."[34] African education covered all ramifications including religion, law, medicine, music, language, trade and commerce.[35] Indeed, F. G. Loveridge, a colonial senior education officer in Zimbabwe once noted: "In his traditional society the African was given all the education which he needed to function in his culture. Today, he has fallen away because Western education does not prepare him to function in Western culture. At the same time it does not prepare him to function in his own culture. Therefore, the African who goes to school in a Western cultural setting is placed in a socioeconomic limbo."[36]

Morality was a cherished virtue in African education and K. A. Busia states:

Moral peace is the ideal man's main concern. If he is blessed with wealth, nonattachment to his wealth, demonstrated in the liberal exercise of hospitality, it is a feature of his relationship with other people ... and whenever the moral peace of society is threatened he is ready to bind himself with an oath, and to take risks to restore it, for wounds received in the interest of the eyes are the only wounds worth receiving.[37]

Traditional African education was complete and was relevant to the needs of the individual and his or her society. In traditional African society education was an integral part of the social, economic and cultural fabric of society. Education connected the individual to the group and to the social environment in a kind of symbiotic relationship. K. A. Busia tells us that:

the essential goal of traditional education was admirable, and remains challenging. Traditional education sought to produce men and women who were not self-centered; who put interest of the group above their personal interest: whose hearts were warm towards the members of their family and kinsfolk; who dutifully fulfilled obligations hallowed and approved by tradition, out of reverence for the ancestors and gods, and the unknown universe of spirits and forces, and a sense of dependence that human life was the greatest value, and increase in the number of the members of the community the greatest blessing the gods and spirits and supernatural powers could confer on the living.[38]

Kofi A. Opoku argues that the ideal person in African society was one who reached beyond him or herself, moved from individual self to a state of selflessness because in Africa the quality of one's life was measured by his or her obligations to others.[39] Indeed, Dickson A. Mungazi and L. Kay Walker conclude that education in Africa emphasized, in no unmistakable manner, values that were essential to the well-being of its society and the individuals in it.[40] In conclusion, African education was relevant to the needs of African society. It provided access for all students. The purpose of African education was functionalism because Africans regarded education as a means to an end rather than an end in itself. Indeed, Canaan Banana of Zimbabwe maintains that "in traditional society in Africa, education was an integral part of the entire social, economic and cultural system. It was related to the individual, the human group and the environment. Each part was essential to the coherent operation and sustenance, of the whole system."[41] A. Babs Fafunwa concludes that "in Old Africa, the warrior, the hunter, the medicine man, the priest, the farmer, the nobleman, the man of character who combined and embraced features of knowledge in its comprehensive form with specific skills on a variety of whom society benefitted was a properly educated person."[42]

Dominic T. Ashley has characterized traditional African education in the following words:

(a) [Traditional African education] was community-oriented. There were no formal buildings or a specialized cadre of teachers who were removed from the productive activities of the society. Everyone was a producer and consumer, and the goal of the system was the full development of the individual into a useful and considerate member of his society.

(b) The educational system was concrete and pragmatic. It was acquired through total involvement and active participation. A child learned about fishing... while fishing with his elders; and in the evenings he learned about the elements of geography, history, cultural science, morality, linguistics, and other subjects while listening to the folk stories and experiences of the elders.

(c) It was a comprehensive system of education that transmitted relevant skills, knowledge, values and attitudes for the development of the individual and his or her society.

(d) It was a democratic system of education oriented towards an egalitarian society.[43]

3

Christian Missionary/Colonial Education in Africa

In most parts of Africa, the establishment of schools and, indeed, Western education itself was virtually a monopoly of the Christian missions during colonial rule. The colonial governments paid very little attention to formal education in Africa. James Coleman makes this point very succinctly:

Until 1898 all education was under the direct control of missionaries. As late as 1942 they controlled 99 percent of the schools, and more than 97 percent of the students in [Africa] were enrolled in mission schools. By 1945 there were comparatively few literate [Africans] who had not received all or part of their education in mission schools.[1]

Indeed, in the 1920s the Church Missionary Society (CMS) general secretary stated that the demand for education and Christianity were inextricably interwoven in Africa. Throughout the period covered by this chapter, the terms missionary and colonial education will be used interchangeably to mean the type of education provided by missions in Africa.

ORIGINS OF NINETEENTH-CENTURY MISSIONS IN AFRICA

Following the evangelical revival movements in Europe during the late eighteenth century, missionary fervor, dormant since the fifteenth century, was rekindled regarding the largely unrewarding endeavor of evangelizing the African interior. The European evangelical movement was due largely to the work of John Wesley. Wesley's challenge to the established Anglican church led to the anticlerical and evangelical movements, and consequently, to the "Protestant Awakening" that swept across Europe and America in the nineteenth century. This awakening demanded renewed zeal and commitment on the part of individual Christians as well as deep concern for personal acts of conversion. It was Wesley's message that strengthened the desire for missionary work.[2]

The work of a group of influential Victorian Englishmen known as the Clapham Sect was responsible for the formation of one of the first Protestant missionary societies to venture into Africa. Prominent members of the Clapham Sect included William Wilberforce, Granville Sharp and Zachary Macaulay.[3] In 1799 these men and others formed the Church Missionary Society as an evangelical arm of the Church of England. Other missionary groups represented in Africa were the Wesleyan Methodist Missionary Society (WMMS), the Presbyterian Church of Scotland, the Baptists, the Baptists from the (American) Southern Baptist Convention, the Society of African Missions (the Catholic Mission) from France, the Jesuits, the Basel Missionaries, and the Lutherans.[4]

THE CHURCH MISSIONARY SOCIETY AND THE AFRICAN MISSIONARY FIELD

The CMS entered the African missionary field as a result of the advocacy of one of its members, Thomas Fowell Buxton, a prominent member of the British Parliament and a vice president of the society. It was Buxton who, in his book *The African Slave Trade and its Remedy*, advocated the regeneration of Africa by "calling forth her own resources."[5] Buxton urged the abolition of the nefarious slave trade at its roots by advocating the exploration of the Niger River into its hinterlands, the negotiation of treaties with the inhabitants, and the establishment of peaceful trade. Buxton argued that if Christianity, commerce and civilization (by "civilization," the Victorians meant British culture and control) were pursued, the slave trade would be destroyed and civilization would be achieved naturally through cause-and-effect. In return, he maintained, England would acquire cheaper raw materials, new markets and increased productivity, employment and profits.[6] Consequently, Buxton urged the cooperation of government and the missionary societies in the "deliverance" of Africa. He declared:

Let missionaries and schoolmasters, the plough and the spade, go together and agriculture will flourish; the avenues to legitimate commerce will be opened; confidence between man and man will be inspired; whilst civilization will advance as the natural effect, and Christianity operate as the proximate cause, of this happy change.⁷

Education of Africans was indeed on the agenda of the missionary societies. As one of the outstanding members of the CMS (and its later general secretary), Henry Venn declared in 1857 that by restructuring the economy of Africa in favor of legitimate trade, a new generation of enlightened, educated, African middle-class elites would emerge in the church, commerce, industry and politics of the emerging African nations. According to Venn these elites might "form an intelligent and influential class of society and become the founders of a Kingdom which shall render incalculable benefits to Africa and hold a position among the states of Europe."⁸

THE BEGINNING OF INTENSE MISSIONARY SCRAMBLE IN AFRICA

The year 1885 marks the beginning of intense missionary scramble for the souls of Africans because, after the Berlin Conference of 1884–1885, European nations were required to show evidence of effective occupation for any territory to which they laid claims. Accordingly, soldiers, traders, merchants and particularly missionaries were sent afield and used by the various imperial governments to satisfy this clause of the treaty. The result of this scramble was the establishment of unprecedented numbers of schools by the various religious organizations in Africa because schools, unfortunately, became important avenues for proselytization.

MISSIONARY RIVALRIES IN AFRICA

Evidence abounds in the research literature to show that wherever the Protestant and Catholic missionaries met in Africa, opposition, antagonism and rivalry flared between them. For instance, the Lutherans were expelled from Abyssinia (now Ethiopia) in 1832 because of Jesuit intrigues. The Jesuits also frustrated the efforts of Johann Krapf (a Lutheran missionary in Abyssinia) and his work among the Gallas in the Kingdom of Shoa in 1844. A. M. Mackay's attempt to spread the gospel among the Ugandans was similarly foiled by Roman Catholic missionaries.⁹ In Buganda, a French Catholic missionary order called the White Fathers effectively challenged the Anglicans and spread their own brand of evangelical and educational work throughout east and central Africa.¹⁰ Intense rivalry between the Catholics and the Church Missionary Society in the Sudan warranted the intervention of the governor-general, Sir Stewart Symes in 1935. In the Belgian Congo (now Zaire), Catholic missionaries stalked and tailgated the Protestants to ensure that they were not outplayed by the Protestants.[11]

In southern Nigeria, however, missionary rivalry was even more intense. Apart from theological differences, nationality factors came into play. While most of the Protestant missionaries in southern Nigeria came from England and Scotland, most of the Catholic missionaries came from either France or Ireland.[12] Indeed, France was Britain's greatest rival for colonies in Africa in the nineteenth century, and Ireland was (and remains to this day) Britain's unruly colony. In eastern Nigeria, the Protestant and Catholic missionaries bypassed each other's sphere of influence thereby creating conditions of perpetual rivalry between villages.[13] According to David B. Abernethy, "Intense rivalry began [in southern Nigeria] during the early years of this century. As both Catholics and Anglicans spread out from their common headquarters, ... they quickly became engaged in leap-frogging operations."[14]

COLONIAL EDUCATIONAL POLICIES IN AFRICA

The French

In theory, the French considered their colonies in Africa as "territoires d'outre-mer," that is, as overseas provinces of the mother country. French educators were charged with the responsibility of turning Africans into "black Frenchmen." However, this practice was terribly flawed in Africa because the French had very limited resources from the start. The responsibility for education in their African possessions therefore revolved around Africans themselves particularly Senegalese ex-soldiers who had received some rudiments of education in the army. A large segment of the French population opposed education for Africans because they thought that the purpose of colonialism was to satisfy the need for new markets for French industrial production and to be the source for cheap labor and cheap raw materials. Proponents of this point of view argued in favor of limiting schooling for Africans because "the more you educate individuals in this situation, the more they hate you."[15] Other leaders in France argued that education in its colonies should be restricted to the children of chiefs and the elites.

However, people on both sides of the political divide were unanimous in their pronouncement that educational programs for Africans should be qualitatively limited and elitist.[16] Given the tempo in French thought toward the education of Africans, in the period following World War II, the French decreed that "school enrollments should be determined by the pace of economic and social development of each colony and in all cases would remain less than that of metropolitan France itself."[17] Such a policy was responsible for the big gaps that existed in student enrollment in the various French African colonies. For example, because the economy of the Ivory Coast rested primarily on agriculture, enrollment in schools in Ivory Coast was kept decidedly low because it was reasoned that Ivory Coast needed only unskilled labor. Besides, for the Africans in Ivory Coast, advantages accruing from education were neither apparent nor obvious. This gave them little or no incentive to pursue education. The French curriculum imposed additional limitations because it was designed to educate very few Africans for the very few vacancies that existed at the lower public service cadres and in the industries. Also because of its overemphasis on agriculture, the French curriculum placed no premium on professions such as engineering, teaching, sales and allied subjects. Because the French initially wanted to turn Africans into Frenchmen, they decreed in 1917 that education in the French Congo must be in French and ordered that all instructional materials must be printed in French as well. And in addition, all school officials had to be French subjects.

The British

The British, unlike the French, considered their colonies as separate entities. However, British educational enterprise in Africa was dominated by missionaries whose curriculum was modeled after the curriculum "serving the poorest segments of European societies."[18] Like its neighbor, France, the British believed that the quality of education in Africa should vary according to the social characteristics of the student population. The Education Committee of the Privy Council enunciated British educational policy for Africa in its report of 1867. In that report, the British Committee advised that the educational curriculum in Africa should vary according to the social characteristics of the student population. Following this report, the British government recommended four types of educational institutions for Africans. First was the elementary school, which provided children with the core curriculum of reading, writing and arithmetic. After learning to read and write, some students attended boys' or girls' schools where boys were taught trades, agriculture and gardening, while the girls were taught housewifery. Some of the students then went into normal schools where they were trained to be teachers.

The committee report of 1867 criticized what it called a "bookish type of education" and instead advocated "a strong vocational orientation which would lead to a settled and thriving peasantry."[19] The report recommended that there should be a correlation between education and economic development and criticized the lackadaisical educational developments in Africa. Indeed, earlier in 1842, the Royal Commission to West Africa report had enjoined missionaries to teach Africans to work and to outlaw literary subjects in schools. In South Africa, British policy on education was dictated almost exclusively by Cecil John Rhodes, a man who arrived in South Africa in 1870 in search of fortune. As the Prime Minister for the Cape Province, Rhodes enunciated an educational policy in South Africa that later became the hallmark of apartheid policy in South Africa. In 1896, Rhodes openly declared: "I say that the Natives are like children. They are just emerging from barbarism. If I may venture a comparison, I should compare the Natives with regard to European civilization to the tribes of the Druids. I think that we have been extremely liberal in granting barbarism forty or fifty years of training what we ourselves obtained only after many hundreds of civilization."[20] Rhodes' policy toward Africans was derived from his ardent belief that Africans were barbarians who should be lorded over by the civilized people of Europe. He emphasized that Africans should be given only the type of education that would enable them to become laborers and assistants. In a speech he delivered in 1887, Rhodes stated:

I will lay down my own policy on the Native question. Either you receive them on equal footing as citizens, or you call them a subject race. I have made up my mind that there must be a class legislation, and that we have got to treat the Natives where they are, in a state of barbarism. We are to be lords over them. We will continue to treat them as a subject race as long as they remain in a state of barbarism. What is civilized man? It is a person with sufficient education to enable him to write his name. The Natives should be a source of assistance to the white man as laborers. This must be the main purpose of his education.[21]

Indeed, Paul Kruger echoed the thinking of Cecil Rhodes about Africans when, as president of the Transvaal Province in South Africa, he stated that "Africans [should] be trained so that they would fulfill tasks appropriate to their presumed intellectual and social inferiority."[22] Like Rhodes, Kruger argued that the "black man must be taught to understand that he belongs to an inferior class and that his function in society is to serve as a laborer."[23] When the National Party came into power in South Africa in 1948, they enthusiastically pursued a policy geared toward sustaining the principles of white superiority through the Bantu Education Act of 1953. Hendrik Verwoerd, then minister of Bantu affairs and education, stated: "Native education must be controlled in such a way that it should be in accord with the policy of the state. If the Native is being taught to expect that he will live his adult life under a policy of equal rights, he is making a big mistake. The Native who attends school must know that he must be the laborer in the country."[24] Nothing explicates apartheid educational policy better than the statements above.

The British educational policy in Zimbabwe was modeled after that of South Africa. And like Cecil Rhodes, Earl Grey, the colonial administrator in Zimbabwe, argued forcefully in 1898 that the "purpose of education for Africans was to train them as laborers."[25] Similarly, the chief native commissioner in Zimbabwe maintained in 1905: "It is cheap labor which we need in this country, and it has yet to be proved that the Native who can read and write turns out to be a good laborer. As far as we can determine, the Native who can read and write will not work on farms and in mines."[26] The commissioner went on to conclude that the natives will not want to work on farms and in the mines if they acquire good education. Indeed, Ethel Tawse Jollie spoke for all the European administrations when she stated in 1927 that "Africans must be educated differently to prepare them to function as laborers," stating, "We do not intend to hand over this country to the Natives, or to admit them to the same political and social position as we ourselves enjoy. Let us therefore make no pretense of educating them in the same way we educate whites."[27] And Hugh Williams concurred, "If we close every school and stop all this talk of fostering education and development of Natives, we would much sooner become an asset to the British Empire."[28] It was for these and similar reasons that the British government promulgated Ordinance Number 133 in 1907 to train Africans for manual labor. Dickson A. Mungazi and L. Kay Walker argue that "there is no question that the strategy that the colonial government in Zimbabwe designed to reduce the education of Africans to a level where it helped serve the labor needs of the colonial society was synonymous with its desire to have education prepare Africans to serve its own political, social, and economic purposes."[29] Indeed, the colonial education policy in Zimbabwe was so pleasing to whites in that country that one of them wrote to the editor of the *Rhodesia Herald* in 1912 saying: "I do not consider it right that we should educate the Native in any way that will unfit him for service. The Native is and should always be the hewer of wood and the drawer of water for his white master."[30]

The Portuguese

The Portuguese regarded their territories in Africa (Angola and Mozambique) as their overseas territories in which childlike Africans must be educated and civilized gradually to attain Portuguese status. In theory, any African who managed to attain the moral, cultural and educational status of a Portuguese was to be given the title *assimilado* or a black Portuguese, but in practice such a status was very elusive to attain because in order to achieve assimilado status one had to be a Catholic, speak fluent Portuguese, be at least eighteen years old and well educated. And, according to Anedeto Gaspar, "After application for this status is made and the non-refundable application fee rendered, officials check the security rating of the applicant, discuss his religious commitment with the local priest, make surprise visits to his home to ascertain, among other things, if he eats with the appropriate cutlery and wears shoes."[31] The Portuguese Colonial Act of 1930 recognized the Catholic Church as the sole authority to "Christianize and educate, to nationalize and civilize" Africans. Hence, as noted by the minister for Overseas Territories: "All this work has been done in harmony and cooperation between the state and the church which, according to the missionary national tradition, must continue making Christians and Portuguese."[32] However, the educational philosophy of the Catholic Church merely complemented the "sociopolitical ideologies of Portugal." Based on the concordat of 1940, the Catholics fashioned out two different educational systems in Angola and Mozambique that were different and for all intents and purposes unequal. While the one, *ensino de adaptacão* was designed for Africans, the other *ensino oficial* was designed for Europeans, mulattoes and the assimilados. The purpose of education for Africans was to "prepare the students for their future roles as peasants and artisans. The *ensino oficial*, on the other hand, [was] a state-maintained system virtually duplicating the academic model of metropolitan Portugal."[33] Indeed, the Catholic Church Congress for Overseas territories in 1909 stipulated that "the negro must learn to work for work, indeed, is an indispensable factor in all civilization."[34] Indeed, the official Portuguese policy contained in the Regulation of 1899 stated the following: "The state, not only as a sovereign of semi-barbaric populations, but also as a depository of social authority, should have no scruples in obliging and, if necessary, forcing the rude Negroes in Africa ... to work, that is, to better themselves by work, to acquire through work the happiest means of existence, to civilize themselves through work."[35]

Accordingly, the Portuguese designed a three-tier system of education for Africans. The first tier was designed to teach Africans the rudiments of Portuguese culture, while the next two layers were designed to teach the "3Rs" and political history.[36] However, the Portuguese educational policy in Africa was a dismal failure because the high fees charged by the schools kept most students out. Hence, the success rate of Africans in the *ensino de adaptacão* was minimal. In 1954, for example, even though there were 35,361 students in Angola, only 959 of them were successful in the third-year examinations. Similarly, by 1960, there were only about 100 Africans enrolled in academic and technical high schools. The Portuguese established inferior education for Angola and Mozambique because they wanted different levels of development for the natives and the Portuguese nationals. Education for Africans, the Portuguese colonial authorities reasoned, "would have the same effect on the Africans" as it had on the Brazilians who declared their independence from Portugal in 1822. The Portuguese thought that education would raise the consciousness of Africans. On the contrary, the Portuguese hoped to use the schools to spread the Portuguese language and culture and to create a civilization that essentially would be completely non-African in character.[37] In conclusion, it is therefore fair to say that the Portuguese educational system was designed to keep the elite status in the hands of the Portuguese.

The Belgians

The Belgians, like the French, linked educational development to economic growth and, like the British, surrendered educational matters to the missionaries. The Belgians emphasized primary and vocational education to the complete neglect of postprimary and university education. Hence, they built no bridges between postprimary schools and the universities. As a consequence, by 1951, even though there were about 30,000 students enrolled in schools in the Belgian Congo, none of them qualified for university admission. Thomas Hodgkin describes the Belgian educational policy toward Africans as platonic. He maintains that:

Platonism is implicit in the sharp distinction, social and legal, between Belgian philosopher-kings and the mass of African producers; in the conception of education as primarily concerned with the transmission of certain unquestioned and unquestionable moral values, and intimately related to status and function; in the belief and thought that behaviour of the mass is plastic, and can be refashioned by a benevolent, wise and highly trained elite; that the prime interest of the mass is in welfare and consumer goods . . . not liberty; and in the conviction that it is possible, by expert administration, to arrest social and political change.[38]

The Germans

General von Trotha was the principal architect of German educational policy in Namibia. Trotha wanted Africans to be trained as laborers without political and economic skills. When in 1894 the German colonial administration permitted missionaries to open schools in Namibia, such schools were to follow a general education curriculum. The only education that Africans were allowed to have was practical training as laborers to ensure the supply of workers to the Germans. Indeed, Victor Uchendu argued that the main objective of colonial education in Africa was to "allocate Africans to subordinate roles in the colonial system."[39] Education for Africans was to prepare them for the inferior positions they were designed to fill vis-à-vis the Europeans. Lord Lugard perhaps expressed the views of most when he wrote:

The object which education in Africa must have in view must be to fit the ordinary individual to fill a useful part in his environment ... and to ensure that the exceptional individual shall use his abilities for the advancement of the community and not to its detriment or to the subversion of constituted authority.... The education of the sons of native rulers is particularly desirable in order to avoid the present danger of a separate educated class in rivalry with the accepted rulers of the people. I have placed the formation of character in the foreground of African education ... [because] among the primitive tribes ethical standards must be created—among few are they a vital, potent force.[40]

Paulo Freire argues that the colonialists were involved in the business of education for the purpose of deculturating Africans or in acculturating them into a predefined colonial model. Colonial schools, according to Freire and Macedo, "functioned as part of an ideological state apparatus designed to secure the ideological and social reproduction of capital and its institutions, whose interests are rooted in the dynamics of capital accumulation and the reproduction of the labor force."[41] However, this educated labor force in Africa consisted of only low-level functionaries whose assigned tasks were to promote and maintain the status quo. These harbingers of Western education were used as intermediaries to further colonial interests in Africa. Western education created what Paulo Freire and Donaldo Macedo call a petit-bourgeois class who had internalized the notion that they were superior to the peasants, although their education was doctored to place them at a political, social and economic disadvantage to the Europeans. In Angola, Anedeto Gaspar tells us a familiar story:

In order to obtain *assimilado* status ... an African has to be Catholic, speak fluent Portuguese, be educated, and be at least eighteen years of age. After application for this status is made and the non-refundable application fee tendered, officials check the security rating of the applicant, discuss his religious commitment with the local priest, make surprise visits to his home to ascertain, among other things, if he eats with the appropriate cutlery and wears shoes. In short, they attempt to ascertain if the applicant lives a "civilized" [by Portuguese standards] life.[42]

Gaspar goes on to say that because his father had a good education, upbringing and vocation, he enjoyed all the rights and privileges of Portuguese citizenship. However, he admits that his grandfather worked as a force-labor agent for the Portuguese in Northern Angola.

In conclusion, colonial education did not meet the needs of Africans, and as Bishop James Crane Hartzell worte in 1918: "Africa has suffered many evils. Slave trade and exploitation by the white man have, through many years, preyed upon the life of the people and have left them uncertain about the future. To their dismay, the Natives of Africa have realized that the white man has offered them his form of education only to enable them to function as laborers."[43] And Albert Schweitzer stated: "Who can describe the misery, the injustice, and the cruelties that the Africans have suffered at the hands of Europeans? If a record could be compiled, it would make a book containing pages which the reader would have to turn unread because their contents would be too horrible."[44] Colonial educational planners in Africa favored a selective approach to education, and therefore concentrated education in particular areas and among certain interest groups to the utter neglect and detriment of others—a practice that Victor Uchendu argues created disparity in educational opportunity "between the rural areas and the urban centers, between the areas of missionary activities and those that lacked them, and between geographic and ethnic groups in . . . Africa."[45] These disparities today pose serious political problems in the continent.

The colonial education philosophies were indeed based on the principles of domination. Hence, while the French policy was paternalistic, the British pursued a policy of opportunism, pragmatism and imperialism. The Belgians, on the other hand, pursued a policy that is characterized as Platonic, and the Portuguese favored an assimilationist policy that "bordered on benign neglect."[46]

The colonialists, whenever they encouraged the education of Africans, did so for pragmatic reasons in anticipation of a quid pro quo. For example, in 1842 a Royal Commission was sent from London to Freetown in Sierra Leone to investigate the effectiveness of missionary education in Gambia, Sierra Leone and the Gold Coast (now Ghana). The commissioners were very unequivocal in their conclusion that "missionaries were wasting their time with the current educational fare because the underdeveloped African intellectual faculties precluded retention of abstractions."[47] The commissioners recommended instead that "the curriculum should be scrapped and the children taught to work" because work "would be beneficial both to Africans, by providing paid employment, and to the representatives of commerce and government, who would have available a supply of semi-literate and semi-skilled labor."[48] Indeed, most colonial administrators criticized some of the Christian missionaries who devoted serious attention to the education of Africans because they believed that these missionaries were involved with efforts in futility.

T. J. Hutchinson perhaps spoke for many like himself when he stated that "ages must elapse before any educational principle in its simplest form can produce an amendment on temperaments such as [the African] possess."[49] But James S. Coleman argues that "education is a correlate, if not a requisite, of a democratic order." In examining the relationship between education and politics, Coleman attributes the underdevelopment of most of the Third World to colonialism, for not only did the colonial authorities neglect education for their dependencies qualitatively, they did so quantitatively as well. The attitude of the colonial governments, Coleman explains, was based purely on imperial self-interest.⁵⁰ Western education proved to be dysfunctional to African social structure because it constructed a completely different dimension of the social order. Indeed, Philip Foster argues that "the most significant latent function of Western formal education was to foster nascent conceptions of social status . . . based on education and occupation."⁵¹ Francis X. Sutton concludes that there is a correlation between Western education and social status in African society because both secondary and higher education have traditionally been confined to the economically well to do in Africa.

Regarding inequality of educational opportunity, Dickson A. Mungazi and L. Kay Walker state: "(D)ifferences in educational facilities and economic opportunity form the basis of social and economic conditions that translate into differences between rural and urban areas." They go on to argue that "neglecting the development of rural areas is tantamount to neglecting the development of 80 percent of the population."⁵²

THE IMPACT OF MISSIONARY/COLONIAL EDUCATION ON AFRICANS

In his book *Things Fall Apart*, Chinua Achebe describes the impact of Mr. Brown's school (a missionary school) on the people of Umuofia in eastern Nigeria in the following words:

Mr. Brown's school produced quick results. A few months in it was enough to make one a court messenger or even a court clerk. Those who stayed longer became teachers; and from Umuofia laborers went forth into the Lord's vineyard. New churches were established in the surrounding villages and a few schools with them. From the beginning religion and education went hand in hand. Mr. Brown's mission grew from strength to strength, and because of its link with the new administration it earned a new social prestige.⁵³

As one of the early missionaries in Africa put it, the intense missionary rivalry in Africa produced an atmosphere of war, and Edward H. Berman affirms that "the most important outcome of denominational rivalry was the rapid expansion of mission schools in all parts of Africa."⁵⁴ In Nigeria for example, the Church Missionary Society, which started out with 6 schools in 1849, increased its number of schools to 150 by 1909. The Wesleyan Mission went from 3 schools, 255 pupils and 9 teachers in 1861 to 138 schools, 5,361 pupils and 285 teachers in 1921. The Roman Catholic Mission increased its number of schools from 2 in 1893 to about 127 in 1922.⁵⁵ In Uganda, the CMS had 72 schools with 7,683 students in 1900, but by 1913 they had 331 schools with 32,458 students. In Nyasaland, the Dutch Reformed Church reported 111 schools and 10,000 students in 1903, but in 1910 the figures went up to 865 schools and 25,796 students. Similarly, the Basel Mission Society in the Cameroons counted 100 students in 1904, but 2,520 in 1910 and 6,600 in 1914. The Moravian Mission in Tanganyika (now Tanzania) reported 329 students in their schools in 1900, but 7,931 in 1913. Similarly, the Lutheran Berlin Mission, also in Tanganyika, reported 63 students in their school in 1900, but 11,101 in 1913.[56]

CONSEQUENCES OF EDUCATIONAL PROLIFERATION IN AFRICA

The educational propaganda of the missions eventually fell upon the receptive ears of Africans who came to associate European technological achievement with Western education and who were willing to pay the price to learn the secrets of white power. Apart from being the source of this power, formal education conferred several definite advantages to the colonized Africans. The consolidation of European control, for instance, created opportunities for European-trained Africans because literate indigenous men were needed to fill minor administrative positions. The churches needed teachers and catechists, and business concerns needed clerks, accountants, buyers and sales representatives. Consequently, a European education soon came to be viewed by Africans themselves as an investment and an exciting opportunity. Writing in 1923, Talbot maintained the following: "An extraordinary longing for book-learning, and the power to speak and write ... has invaded the native mind in the last few years; this appears to arise partly from a genuine wish for European culture and partly from a desire to raise themselves in the social scale and get away from manual work.[57]

Not surprisingly, therefore, as early as 1896 a CMS superintendent, P. A. Bennett, reported from Obosi in Nigeria as follows: "People are burning with the desire to learn; they give us little or no rest. We are obliged to be keeping school three times a day; the big men show interest and are trying to learn with all their might.... Our house is generally crowded to suffocation."[58]

Little wonder, then, that in 1905 the CMS mission secretary wrote to complain about the pathetic nature of his work arising from the competition of Ibo villages in Nigeria for schools and learning. He states his case as follows: "My work is pathetic in the extreme now, in one aspect: almost every week I have to turn away deputations from towns both near and distant begging us to come and teach them."[59]

CONTEMPORARY AFRICAN VIEW OF MISSIONARY/ COLONIAL EDUCATION

Contemporary African responses have characterized missionary/colonial education as negative and sometimes destructive to Africans.

Karim Hirji of Tanzania maintained, "It was missionary education which facilitated the separation of the African from his traditional society for absorption into the socioeconomic system."[60] Another Tanzanian, Jerome Kiwia, wrote:

The principal role of the missionaries was to prepare Africans spiritually and mentally for physical domination.... Missionaries did not introduce education in Africa, they introduced a new set of formal education institutions which partly supplemented and partly replaced those which were there before.[61]

Similarly, a radio commentator in Tanzania said:

Mission schooling supported imperialism. We should remember not what they gave us but what they took away from us. Educating children is, in principle, fine and worthwhile. But there is a question to be asked: what were they being educated for? They were being educated for subservience, they were being educated to turn their backs on their own past and their own peoples.[62]

Denis Herbstein and John Evenson of Namibia once stated that Christian missionaries were "to a large extent, the advance guard of empire."[63] Nghidi Ndilula of Namibia argued that missionary education was "merely religious indoctrination"[64] that paved the way for German colonizers. Indeed, Ernest Emenyonu of Nigeria argued that European missionaries did not come to Africa to prop up native institutions but to justify their downfall.[65]

A. Babs Fafunwa has argued that the earliest Christian missionary schools in Africa were without doubt "adjuncts of the church."[66] A. F. Leach explains missionary interest in education in a forthright manner:

The missionaries had to come with the Latin servicebook in one hand and the Latin grammar in the other. Not only had the native priests to be taught the tongue in which their services were performed, but their converts ... had to be taught the elements of grammar before they could grasp the elements of religion. So the grammar school became in theory, as it often was in fact, the necessary ante-room, the vestibule of the Church.[67]

William Boyd points out that the church went into the business of education not for its concern for education as good but because the church wanted to give the adherents some formal learning to enable them to read the Bible. This being the case, A. Babs Fafunwa argues that Christian-oriented education slowed down the progress of secular education in most Muslim parts of Africa because, as missionary schools were established mostly to convert children to the Christian religion, Muslims in Africa saw this as a threat to their religion, and accordingly refused to send their children to Christian schools. D. Westermann once wrote, "No missionary... goes to Africa to study languages, nor is his chief purpose to educate natives. His aim is to evangelize the African and make him Christian."[68]

In the late 1950s the advent of nationalist governments in Africa ushered in intense debate concerning church participation in schools in Africa partly because Africans were unhappy with the literary curriculum of the Christian mission schools, which did not place much emphasis on science, technology and agriculture—the last of which was and remains the mainstay of Africa's economy. Indeed, participants at the conference on the Review of the Educational System of Eastern Nigeria were unanimous in their misgivings of mission education and stated "The colonial type of education... did not adequately meet the needs of the country. ... The result is that manual, agricultural and technical education have come to be associated with inferior status and to be accorded low instead of high regard in the scheme of things."[69] Africans were also very concerned about the unnecessary duplication of schools, programs and facilities in certain areas resulting from rivalries between missions. These rivalries were sometimes replicated in African communities. David B. Abernethy reports such unhealthy rivalries in Igboland in Eastern Nigeria and states:

Traditional rivalries... were reinforced by denominational rivalries, and the reinforcement often had the effect of weakening or even destroying the village's sense of identity. The rivalry in Owerri Province, where in many areas Catholics had arrived first, followed a somewhat different pattern. A village with a Roman Catholic Mission (R.C.M.) school or church would be "presumed lost" by the Church Mission Society.... The Catholics in their turn would bypass the C.M.S. village and open a station in some neighboring area. Thus Orlu and Emekuku soon became known as Catholic towns whereas Nkwerre was generally considered an Anglican stronghold. When an influential chief was converted to one faith or the other, he sometimes discouraged other Christian groups from entering his territory.[70]

Also attracting criticisms of Africans was the utter disrespect shown to African culture by Christian mission education in preference for Western cultural values. Again, the participants in the Report on the Review of Education in Eastern Nigeria had this to say: "(T)he present political and social status of [Africa] demands a reorganization of the existing educational system which would better reflect our spiritual, moral and cultural values and at the same time meet the challenge of the growing needs of [Africa]."[71] Indeed, even before the rise of African nationalism, some African rulers were skeptical of the corrupting effects that Christianity would have on African traditions. King Jaja of Opobo of Nigeria, for example, believed that African traditional religion held the society together, that the introduction of Christianity would tear the society apart. Not too long, King Jaja's worse fears appear to have been realized when the Interdenominational International Missionary Council affirmed in 1938 that "the missionary is a revolutionary and he has to be so, for to preach and plant Christianity means to make a frontal attack on the beliefs, customs, apprehensions of life and the work and by implication ... on the social structures and bases of primitive society."[72]

Christianity's encroachment on African traditional beliefs was so severe that J. E. Casely-Hayford, the pioneer Ghanaian nationalist wrote to say, "A great blunder ... [was] committed by the meddlesome missionaries."[73] Casely-Hayford went on to state that continued meddling in African traditions by missionaries would force African customs underground. Indeed, in 1931, Nana Annor Adjaye, of Nzimaland stated that he did "not believe in a Christianity which spells denationalization" but rather on "Christianity which preserves the best in the social institutions of the people."[74] Educated Africans were further denationalized because they as converts were segregated from the people as were the missionaries. Such segregations painted in the minds of Africans a sense of European superiority. Hence, Oginga Odinga opined that the missionary was preaching unity and love while he "lived aloof from the people to whom he preached," and J. E. Casely-Hayford noted that "the European quarter of Akrokeri occupied the finest site."[75] Indeed, in his study of East African churches, F. B. Welbourn pointed out that "while the African clergy lived in primitive housing and depended on bicycles for transportation, European missionaries lived in large well-equipped houses and drove cars."[76]

The practice of segregating Christians was "naturally very resented by [African] chiefs who claim their hereditary rights ... to make the converts in common with their fellow tribesmen obey such laws and orders as are in accordance with native custom."[77] Missionaries often drove wedges between children and their parents by teaching children, "Blessed is he who forsakes his father and mother for my sake." By such pronouncements missionaries were able to pitch children against their parents thereby causing a splinter in African families. As Oginga Odinga argued, missionaries "were not satisfied to concentrate on the word of the Bible; they tried to use the word of God to judge African traditions: An African who followed his people's customs was condemned as heathen and anti-Christian."[78] And as Mbonu Ojike of Nigeria later recalled, missionaries induced Africans to imitate Western culture in every aspect because, according to the missionaries, every good Christian must take a Western name at Baptism. As he later confessed, he "mocked his father's religion as 'heathen,' thinking his inferior to white man's."[79] Indeed, Edward W. Blyden accused missionaries in Sierra Leone and Liberia of showing disrespect to Africans. In 1876 he wrote that European missionaries regarded the "African mind . . . as blank or worse than blank, filled with everything dark and horrible and repulsive."[80] This comment was particularly borne out by missionaries' attempt to turn Africans into Christian Europeans. Blyden's sentiments were predicated on the European racist and condescending attitude toward Africans and their culture and out of his concern that Europeans, including missionaries, were arrogantly denationalizing Africans and their culture. Berman argues that "implicit in European behavior towards Africans was the replacement of traditional culture with something 'higher,' something new, something European."[81] Similarly, Henry Johnson of Nigeria was quite appalled by the contempt shown for African culture and by Europeans' refusal to allow Africans to manage their own affairs.

It should also be pointed out that missionaries were collaborators who, through the kind of education they offered to Africans, had helped in promoting the stability of the colonial regimes. Besides, Africans believed that colonialism had grips not only on the body politic but also on the economy and the educational system as well. The state control of education, most Africans reasoned, would not produce the type of citizens needed in the new nation states. The African position will be appreciated if we understand that missionaries and colonial administrators were birds of the same feather who flocked together on many occasions. Indeed, Emmanuel Ayandele maintains that "missionary propaganda from its inception was inextricably bound up with political consideration." "From the start," he adds, "missionary propaganda in Africa was not just a religious invasion. In effect it was associated with a political invasion as well."[82] David B. Abernethy corroborates Ayandele's assertion when he states: "Although it would be an oversimplification to describe them as advance agents of British (or French) imperialism, the missionaries were linked in many ways to the traders and officials who came in increasing numbers to [Africa]."[83] Both contentions are confirmed by Professor Du Plessis who, in 1929, wrote: "Missionary enterprise is so intimately related to the political movement on the one hand and to the commercial undertaking on the other, that its history cannot be accurately traced without continued reference to both."[84]

It is therefore not an overstatement or bigotry when Ayandele describes missionaries as pathfinders to European rule in Africa, for according to him, not only did missionaries prepare the way for the colonialist, but they facilitated peaceful occupation by the colonial forces. Indeed, James S. Coleman maintains that missionaries were "the front troops of the Government to open the hearts of the people and while people look at the Cross white men father the riches of the land."[85]

Abernethy maintains that rather than bridge the gap or integrate, missionary education has bred inequality in Africa because of the uneven distribution of facilities. He argues that:

The uneven spread of mission schools, by creating objective differences between various ethnic groups, stimulated rivalry between them.

Insofar as mission patterns of advance gave certain ethnic groups an educational head start over others, the missionaries unintentionally contributed to the ethnic rivalries [in Africa].[86]

Consequently, he concludes that the optimism with which African nationalists welcomed education as a source of national integration has not been justified. Okwudiba Nnoli, like Abernethy, believes that the role of missionary education as a means of social, political and economic reward makes it a hot commodity in Africa. This status of education, he maintains, has unfortunately led to ethnic competition and hostility between groups in search of the scarce commodity.

Victor Uchendu argues that education is more than an instrument of national development, for in postcolonial African societies, it is one of the few institutions that allocates and regulates privileges. It is because of its significance, he points out, that interest both public and private is so great in education. But regrettably, the disparity in educational opportunity between rural and urban areas of Africa, between Christian and Muslim areas and between geographic and ethnic groups has turned education into a political bomb capable of blowing up the whole social, political and economic fabric of African society.[87] I agree.

Emmanuel Ayandele holds African educated elites, products of the Christian mission schools, responsible for the sociopolitical instability in Africa. Another feature of missionary education is the uneven acquisition of education between ethnic groups or regions within a particular country due either to a policy of protecting or favoring one group over another or by the "differential adaptive capacity or receptivity to education on the part of indigenous cultural groups."[88]

These imbalances have led to underrepresentation of certain groups in the party leadership, the bureaucracy, the army, the police force, and so forth, which indeed often called for immediate redress at the time of independence.

My worry about missionary/colonial education in Africa is of a different sort. In the first place, colonial schools in Africa reflected the power and the needs of the colonizers because schools were designed to serve the needs of the colonizers. The aspirations of the Africans were ignored.[89] Colonial administrators, for example, were interested in training people who would fill the ranks of their lower civil service. On their own part, the missionaries were interested in producing catechists, clergies and assistants to missionaries. The natives were not consulted in the development of the scope and contents of schooling. Schools, therefore, were detached from the social fabric of society including indigenous cultures, social values and languages. Schools were alternatives rather than complements to traditional African education. Most colonial schools were boarding schools that were physically separated from indigenous communities. Even the "adapted" schools in East Africa shared this trait because, while teachers emphasized Bantu culture, the schools were located away from Bantu society. Neither parents nor students had any role in the running of these schools nor in determining their educational contents or curriculum.

While most of what was taught in colonial schools had nothing to do with indigenous culture, schools in Europe at this time reinforced the cultural and social context of European society. In other words, while schools in Europe reinforced European cultural heritage, those in Africa deculturized their students. Indeed, the process of deculturization of Africans was so efficient and thorough that Khedive Ismail of Egypt once remarked that "Egypt is part of Europe now."[90] Also in Egypt, Muhammad Abdu concentrated his whole efforts on spreading Western-style education and on religious reforms. Western influence on Egypt was so strong that Ahmad Lutfi-al-Sayyid, the great nationalist pioneer in the nineteenth century Egypt, is said to have drawn his inspirations from Voltaire, Locke and Rousseau.[91]

On the other hand, colonial schools did not provide the best of European type education for Africans because colonial administrators objected to such an education. For example, missionary schools did not provide Africans with vocational or industrial skills as many schools in Europe did at this time. Instead, many taught spear-throwing, herding, basket making or taught African culture as Europeans saw it.[92] On the other end of the spectrum, some colonial authorities established schools in the "bush" that emphasized moral training with little practical skills in agriculture, animal husbandry and manual trades but failed to provide education "deemed necessary and desirable for the youth they served."[93]

Colonial schools neglected the teaching of indigenous languages. Indeed, in most colonial schools the indigenous history that was taught devalued indigenous culture by emphasizing civil wars, tribal conflicts, famines and barbarism. Colonial schools taught very little science, and when they did, they restricted instruction primarily to domestic science and personal hygiene. Gail P. Kelly and Philip G. Altbach conclude that "the schools omitted the child's past, as in history instruction . . . and at the same time denied him skills for anything other than what he had traditionally done—farming and engaging in crafts—except in the area of hygiene."[94] They went on to say:

The implications of this are enormous, for what occurred in colonial education was a simultaneous obliteration of roots and the denial of the wherewithal to change, except on limited terms. With this education, one might become a secretary or interpreter; one could not become a doctor or a scientist or develop indigenous cultures on their own terms.[95]

Although colonial education provided opportunity for social mobility for those who had little status in society, Emmanuel A. Ayandele maintains that colonial education was an endorser of a revised indigenous culture.

The rapid economic development, the establishment of "Native" Courts and Councils, Posts and Telegraphs, the introduction of the bicycle and commercial lorries, construction of motor roads and the "iron horse"—all these introduced a new wealth, opened up countless opportunities, excited immeasurable hopes and created fresh values. To the masses education was the only key that could unlock the mysteries and prosperity of the new world being created. In Yorubaland the prestige of the chiefs fell sharply and passed on to the white man's scribblers, the clerks who could appropriate other people's wives with impunity or to the converts who could elope with ladies of their own choice without paying dowry. So high did the prestige of learning become that, as it was recorded, it was *infra dig* for a man who knew how to read or write to carry any load of any kind, including Bibles and hymn-books which had to be carried for the Christians.[96]

Finally, some have argued that missionary/colonial education had unintended political consequences because it prepared the minds of African political elites who were able to demand and eventually obtain independence from the colonialists. James Coleman, for instance, maintains the following:

The introduction of modern educational system in colonial areas had significant political consequences. It was the single most important factor in the rise and spread of nationalist sentiment and activity. From the modern educational system emerged an indigenous elite which demanded the transfer of political power to itself on the basis of the political values of the Western liberal tradition or the ethical imperatives of Christianity, both of which had been learned in the schools. ... Designed essentially to serve only evangelizing or imperial purposes, Western education became a prime contributor to the emergence of new independent nations.[97]

But these unintended consequences of missionary/colonial education cannot be celebrated because another feature of the colonial legacy was the uneven acquisition of education between ethnic groups or regions within particular countries in Africa. Colonial education created what Gail P. Kelly and Philip G. Altbach call "marginality" of those educated in colonial institutions.[98] The consequences of this marginality are that Africans are today unable to build viable economic and political systems because it is only through the right type of education that people can build a better order of society. Indeed, as Carter G. Woodson once put it, we must approach people through their environment in order to deal with conditions as they are rather than as they should be.[99] Woodson argued against education designed from without.

> When you control a man's thinking you do not have to worry about his actions. You do not have to tell him not to stand here or go yonder. He will find his "proper place" and will stay in it. You do not need to send him to the back door. He will go without being told. In fact, if there is no back door, he will cut one for his special benefit. His education makes it necessary.... [Educational] opportunity ... should not be determined from without ... but should be determined by the make-up of the [individual] himself and by what his environment requires of him.[100]

If we can learn anything from the words of Carter G. Woodson, it is that education should not be cut off from the daily life of the learner or from his or her work as a citizen. Indeed, I. Kandel maintains that education is a living thing that can only be spontaneous if it is inspired by the cultural foundations of the people it serves.[101] A good education therefore, must be based on the environment, experiences and particular circumstances of the learner. Such an education must fit the learner for the type of work he/she is bound to perform in that society. Vernon Mallinson argued that every educational system should embody the cultural patterns and ways of life of its society because it is through the written record that a nation comes to grips with the consciousness of its real being.[102]

POSTCOLONIAL EDUCATION IN AFRICA

The period beginning from the 1960s to the present can be described as the era of postcolonial education in Africa because it was in the 1960s that most black African nations gained their independence. However, apart from minor structural and organizational changes, very little has changed in the philosophy, curriculum, context and contents of education in Africa. Education in Africa is still designed after Western models and paradigms that are not connected to life as it is in Africa. African institutions, particularly African universities, still teach economics, political science, sociology, philosophy, geography, science, and so forth, as they are taught in Europe and America and with books imported from Europe and America. Very little is taught about Africa based on research done in Africa. Therefore, what is taught in Africa has no direct relevance to the needs and circumstances of the people of Africa. But as Carter G. Woodson warned in 1933: "History shows that it does not matter who is in power . . . those who have not learned to do for themselves and have to depend solely on others never obtain any more rights or privileges in the end than they had in the beginning."[103]

Abdou Moumouni argues that postcolonial education in Black Africa is essentially a colonial legacy. After the overthrow of colonial regimes, he maintains, colonial educational systems in Africa were merely replaced by those that, although satisfying the aspirations of many for educational reforms, conformed, to a large extent, to the system in the colonial country. He explains that it was the avowed policy of the colonial governments to make education in their dependencies similar to those at home as a means of depersonalizing the African and for paternalistic and assimilationist reasons. It was also an attempt to limit the number of intermediate and top-level African cadres. In most of French Africa, for example, secondary school education was meant for the most gifted and was almost a preserve for the children of the bourgeois. Under the system, the more brilliant students studied for the baccalaureate while the exceptional ones went on to higher education. This concept is a replica of the system utilized for over a century in France itself before secondary education was liberalized in 1945.[104]

Although some independent black African countries have attempted reforms in principle, in practice education has remained a colonial legacy in all the former colonial dependencies of Africa, except Mali and Guinea. Colonial education, it must be said, is unsuitable for Africa because it is closely allied to the histories of their respective countries. In the case of France, for example, there is a definite separation between the different levels of education as there is a real difference between primary and secondary school enrollments. Although primary education is universal, only a small percentage of primary school graduates proceed to secondary schools. This, according to Moumouni, is reminiscent of the social injustice perpetuated against the children of working-class parents, particularly in higher and advanced technical education. And indeed, only 2 percent of the children in these institutions come from working-class families in France.

The justification for this state of affairs is that the ensemble of children who will become salaried workers, peasants, workmen and intermediate-level cadres, are given only the absolutely necessary basic education, which is primary education. Secondary education, which will train the cadres of the country, and particularly higher education, is reserved mainly for bourgeois and petit-bourgeois children, the middle classes.[105]

In Africa, just as in France, he maintains, the duration of studies in primary, secondary and higher education has been designed to keep children of working-class parents out of school. Consequently, "Secondary school curriculum designed originally only for bourgeois children had an intellectual orientation... which was removed from the people's lives."[106] But the reality of the situation is that colonial education cannot be adapted to conditions in Black Africa because of the near absence of a clear-cut social class structure. Besides, African

> "neo-bourgeoisie" or at least its representatives, has a national character as a whole and espouses popular aspirations up to a certain point; more precisely, it considers them as synonymous with its own or even employs real praiseworthy ideological efforts to put itself in the position of the popular masses. When this occurs, the political, economic and cultural orientation this class gives to the nation cannot be adapted to the educational system inherited from colonialism, or to the underlying conception of this system.[107]

Hence the urge to reevaluate the educational system inherited from colonialism is often greatly felt though not necessarily achieved. The point needs to be made that, in some instances, African neobourgeoisie have prolonged the life of colonialism inadvertently by talking so much of educational changes and achieving very little in this direction and by sustaining imperialism through neocolonialism. Where this is the case, only the narrow interests of upper-class children are taken care of. This attitude is derived from the notion that "peasant children should remain 'attached to the land' and therefore only receive brief training which will not qualify them for a more complete education. Middle-class children will have schools of the present type, primary and secondary, and (bourgeois) children have special schools designed to give them accelerated education."[108]

These types of neobourgeois, Moumouni maintains, are discriminatory in their educational policy, and they see no need for changes in the curriculum despite their overt pronouncements of Africanizing the syllabuses. They are content with maintaining the educational status quo and except for minor

> "adaptations" in subjects like history, geography, and natural sciences (botany and zoology), where the discrepancy between the actual content of the courses in the history and geography of France and Europe, or the study of the plants and animals of France or Europe, is so blatant that it cannot be ignored.[109]

This blind adherence to the French or British system derives from the nostalgia of having a diploma that is comparable in tone and content to that of France or Britain. What the proponents of this doctrine have failed to understand is that the systems of education in France and Britain were designed for conditions in France and Britain. It must be pointed out, though, that any condition that restricts educational opportunity for children of the lower classes cannot but do great disservice to the entire African continent, for a policy in which the majority of the children are given an education adequate only for agricultural production and urban employment can only heighten political tensions and worsen the unemployment and economic problems except in a situation where there is sufficient foreign capital to utilize the excess manpower—and this is hardly the case in Africa. Moumouni concludes that:

[T]he general concept of the educational system inherited from the period of colonial domination cannot be applicable [in Africa] if one is to respond to the new political conditions and to the economic and social objectives which have resulted from the accession to political independence.[110]

He recommends the reorganization of the entire formal education to reflect the economic, political and social realities of Africa. And like Paul Langerin, he maintains, "I plead for the unity of school and life, of reality and thought, of matter and ideas, of academic learning and professional training."[111]

4

Western Education and the Rise of Educated Elites in Africa

In precolonial times, traditional African societies were governed by traditional elites. These included chiefs, priests, influential men in society and people of wealth. At this time, chiefs had the power to wage war, administer punishment and adjudicate cases.[1] During the early colonial period in Africa, traditional elites were used by the European administrators to manage the affairs of individual states. Hence, they (traditional elites) still retained some elements of their power. But with the advent of independence, authority passed into the hands of the Western educated elites in Africa, and the vestiges of power and prestige passed into their hands as well. These elites began to broker power between Europeans and the African populace. By definition, members of the Western educated elite include those Africans with a high level of education and wealth. Their number varies from country to country. They represent all those commonly characterized as political, business, religious and artistic elites in the West. African educated elites have the following characteristics: They are the intelligentsia, they have occupations that pay them living wages; some of them have acquired family wealth; they have adopted European styles of dress; they maintain nuclear families though they still owe allegiance to the extended family system; and a large majority of them are Christians.[2]

THE RISE OF WESTERN EDUCATED ELITES IN AFRICA

As stated elsewhere in this book, until the 1970s the establishment of schools and, indeed, Western education in many parts of Africa was virtually a monopoly of the Christian missions. The missions' interest in education evolved from the missionaries' perceptions of schools as important avenues for conversion. According to Bishop Shanahan, one of the pioneer Catholic missionaries in Nigeria, "Those who hold the school, hold the country, hold its religion, hold its future."[3]

However, the work of the missionaries in Africa was not easy sailing, for while a few Africans and their rulers patronized missionary enterprise, others rejected missionary intrusion in any form. On the whole, support or lack of support for missionary work was greatly influenced by internal developments in Africa. In Yorubaland, for instance, the Egbas, under their ruler Sodeke, accepted missionaries because they expected military help from the British government against their enemies. King Manuwa of Ijebuland patronized missionaries because he wanted his town to become a trading entrepot for the Ijesha, Ondo and Ekiti districts. Kurumi, the ruler of Ijaye, patronized missionaries because he thought that the settlement of missionaries in his midst would enhance his prestige and attract traders to his territory. The Efik people of Calabar patronized missionaries because they wanted agricultural development and instruction in methods of making sugar. When the chiefs of Bonny wrote asking for missionaries in 1848 they insisted on those who would be capable of teaching their young people the English language.[4]

Indeed, in other parts of Africa similar stories were told. For example, King Moshesh of the Basuto placated the Paris Evangelical Missionary Society in the 1830s in order to increase his influence and to ward off Boer threats. King Mutesa of Buganda befriended the CMS in order to thwart Egyptian and Muslim threats to his kingdom in the 1870s. Similarly, the Lozi rulers of Barotseland and the people of Buganda courted the friendship of missionaries. But many others, such as King Jaja of Opobo, did not want missionary intrusion in any form because, as he saw it, traditional religion was the fabric that held African societies together. The Masai wanted nothing to do with missionary schools or with their churches. Indeed, J. W. Tyler argues that "the achievement opportunities offered by schooling could only be accepted by contracting out of Masai society. Few Masai were prepared to do this.... The opportunities offered by the missionaries were attractive, possibly, to social misfits, but on the whole, Masai society did not produce them."[5] The Ashanti and the Ijebu strongly resisted missionary advances. In Kenya, the African Inland Mission opened a school for sons of the chiefs in 1909, but they were forced to close it down in 1914. Indeed, Felix Ekechi maintains that even when the Ibos of Nigeria accepted Western education, they did so because they wanted to use education as a weapon against European exploitation. He explains: "The Ibos demanded the best of Western education not merely for its utilization purposes, but also to use . . . as a weapon against colonial exploitation."[6] The people of Uzuakoli in Nigeria were very hostile to Reverend F. W. Dodds of the Primitive Methodist Mission because the Uzuakoli elders thought that missionaries would interfere with their customs, trading patterns, methods of justice and ways of doing business. In most parts of Africa, missionaries were seen as pathfinders to European rule. Indeed, Cetewayo, a Zulu leader, said this concerning the advancement of Europeans toward his territory: "First a missionary, then a consul, and then come army."[7] Emmanuel A. Ayandele concludes that "allied with, and in many cases inseparable from the [European] secular arm, . . . missionary enterprise resulted, politically, in the suppression of [African] chiefs by Christian white officials."[8]

Except for pockets of acceptance, missionaries were neither accepted nor tolerated in most parts of Africa. Consequently, missionaries turned their attention to youths and schools as sources of conversion because they soon realized, to their utter dismay and puzzlement, the futility of trying to convert men of good standing in African society. As one Roman Catholic missionary lamented, "For a man of social status to accept Christianity in this country . . . is to expose himself to poverty for the rest of his life; it is to renounce, as the Lord asks of the Religious only, his fortune, his future and even his family."[9]

As Ekechi claims, "Formal education became the bait with which the young generation was enticed to Christianity."[10] Good education, it was believed, would enable young African men to earn a good living as well as exert their own influence and that of their adopted religious denomination upon the society at large.

RESULTS OF CHURCH AND MISSIONARY RIVALRY

The intense rivalry between the missions produced what one Holy Ghost Father called an "atmosphere of war."[11] Otonti Nduka states:

The opening of Dennis Memorial Grammar School . . . [was] not unconnected with the vicissitudes of the rivalry. . . . The origins of D.M.G.S. are traceable at least in part, to the attempt of the C.M.S. authorities of the Niger Mission to escape from the dilemma into which their previous policies had landed them. They thought that the establishment of a grammar school would give them an upper hand over their arch rivals—the Roman Catholic Holy Ghost Fathers.[12]

The fallout from the intense missionary rivalry in Africa ushered forth a school revolution, and a good number of mission schools were established in Africa during the 1890s. David B. Abernethy attests that "the activity of the most education-minded denominations usually spurred the others to follow suit. For this reason school enrollment grew at a faster rate ... with several missions operating than it might have with only one."[13]

The educational propaganda of the missions fell upon the receptive ears of the people of Africa who came to associate European technological advancement with Western education and who were willing to pay the price to learn the secrets of white power. Apart from being the source of this power, formal education conferred several definite advantages to the colonized Africans. The consolidation of European control, for instance, created opportunities for European-trained Africans because literate indigenous men were needed to fill minor administrative positions. Moreover, the churches needed teachers and catechists, and business concerns needed clerks, accountants, buyers and sales representatives. Consequently, a European education soon came to be viewed by Africans themselves as an investment and an exciting opportunity. In Buganda, for example, missionary schooling became an integral part of the social fabric of society. As Philip Foster points out, "The schools, by increasingly functioning as a gateway to new occupations, represented one of the few alternate avenues of social mobility operating independently of traditional modes of status acquisition."[14]

With the growth of colonial government services the demand for educated Africans increased but without a corresponding increase in the number of students from poor families attending secondary schools. This is because children of the poor most often were unable to pay the exorbitant fees charged by mission schools. Also, in Africa, family differences and home environments affect poor children disproportionately. For example, in secondary school entrance examinations, the children of the rich have all the advantages because they have grown up literate in the language of the school. These children also have books and other facilities to help them succeed in school. On the contrary, poor children in Africa spend enormous amounts of time doing domestic chores and running errands for their parents. Indeed, most poor children live in homes without even electricity. Although competition for entry into secondary schools in Africa is often very intense, the odds are in favor of the children of the rich. In his study, Peter Lloyd found that in Africa, children of professionals and higher technical and administrative staff have a higher rate of entering secondary schools than children of the poor. He notes that the child of a "Ghanaian University graduate has over eight times as good a chance of entering secondary school as has the son of a man with only primary education."[15] It is no wonder that top professional schools in Africa have a higher representation of students from professional families and well educated parents than children from poor families. Remi Clignet and Philip Foster conclude from their study of education in the Ivory Coast that "the relation between occupational aspirations and social or cultural background is anywhere overwhelmingly strong."

In a recent study by John B. Knight and Richard H. Sabot, it was found that in Kenya and Tanzania workers with elementary education earned more money than those without, and those with university degrees earned more money than those with only secondary school education even though the "returns to cognitive achievement are not significantly lower for manual than for nonmanual workers."[16] The same study found that, in Africa, the returns to employment experience varied positivity with educational level. The researchers concluded that the determinant of occupational attainment is education. However, because of the academic advantages conferred by family background, children of the poor are almost excluded from the educational process. Hence, the long held adage that education "is the great equalizer" might not hold true in Africa. Peter Lloyd sums up this point: "In Africa . . . schooling gives the elite parent a very good chance of ensuring that his children will enjoy the same status as himself." He goes on to add that the "well-educated and wealthy elite is tending to become a predominantly hereditary group."[17] James Coleman concludes that "upward mobility into the more prestigious and renumerative roles available to the indigenous inhabitants in the modern sector . . . was usually determined by educational achievement alone"[18] even though education was not made available to all on an equal basis. In their landmark study in Kenya and Tanzania, Knight and Sabot found that differences in reasoning ability account for little of the large gap in mean wages between primary and secondary school completers.[19]

It should be pointed out here that the European colonialists adopted a selective approach to education in Africa, which means that they concentrated education in particular regions, areas and among certain interest groups. As Victor Uchendu puts it, "The selective approach is not only evolutionary in tone and practice but tends to be exclusive in terms of its target groups." He goes on to say:

Whatever stratification model one may apply to traditional Africa, the fact is that modern Africa is dominated by men and women who benefitted most from Western-type education. The men and women of power and influence are the educated Africans. Education, because of its effects in the stratification system, makes African society one of the most unequal in the world. The disparity in income levels tells the story, for there are few areas in the world where the wages of the laborer and the top government officer or university professor are as incomparable as they are in modern Africa. Few countries protect the inherited colonial privileges of the educated elite as African countries do. This is the basis of the private interest in education—an important factor in the politics of education.[20]

Indeed, Uchendu argues pointedly that education is more than an instrument of national development because in postcolonial African society, it is the most important institution that allocates societal privileges. He goes on to add that Africa is dominated by men and women of power and influence who had benefitted from Western education. He adds that because of its stratifications, education makes African society the most unequal in the world. He laments that "the disparity in income levels tells us the story, for there are few areas in the world where the wages of the laborer and the top government officers or university professor are incomparable as they are in modern Africa."[21] Uchendu concludes that "few countries protect the inherited colonial privileges of educated elites as African countries do."[22]

Studies have shown that in Africa there is a direct correlation between economic achievements of individuals, social groups and schooling. G. S. Becker makes the point in an interesting way:

Few, if any, countries have achieved a sustained period of economic development without having invested substantial amounts in labor force. Inequality in the distribution of earnings and income is generally positively related to inequality in education and other training. Unemployment tends to be strongly related, usually inversely, to education.[23]

Uchendu argues convincingly that since labor productivity depends on labor skills and labor skills are determined by education, then education in Africa determines one's place in society. But as he sees it, education is not only an important mechanism of social control, but educational opportunities in Africa are far from balance. For example, he tells us that the educational infrastructure is better developed in Western Africa than in East and Central Africa. There is "disparity in educational opportunities between the rural areas and the urban centers, between the areas of missionary activities and those that lacked them."[24] In Africa individual and group inequality are attributable to the pattern of educational facilities. David B. Abernethy maintains that education had created serious inequality in Africa because of the uneven distribution of facilities. Uchendu argues convincingly that "the qualitative indicators of educational opportunity tend to be paralleled by sharp regional differences in the quality of existing schools. Schools with better facilities and teachers are not randomly distributed and tend by and large to be concentrated in or close to town."[25] James Coleman, in his characteristic honesty, maintains that an important feature of the colonial legacy in Africa was the uneven acquisition of education between ethnic groups or regions within a particular country caused by protecting or favoring one group over another or by "the differential adaptive capacity, or receptivity to education on the part of indigenous cultural groups."[26] In 1974, J. W. Hanson and D.J.S. Crozier drew attention to the "disruptive effects of gross inequalities in the distribution of educational opportunities in the new African States." They went on to conclude that "education cannot serve as an instrument of national unity when the opportunities for education are grossly unbalanced."[27]

It is also argued that apart from the policy of selective approach to educational planning adopted by the various European powers in Africa that resulted in inequality of opportunity for most Africans, Islam presented an impenetrable obstacle to the spread of Christianity and, by implication, Western education in many parts of Africa. As we know, Christianity came as a distant second to Islam in Africa. Indeed, Islam predated Christianity in Africa by many centuries. Islam and the Islamic system of education, which were introduced into Africa in the ninth century, had been heavily entrenched before the coming of the Europeans. By 1900, a well-orchestrated system of Islamic education was already in place in some parts of Africa with a large number of Islamic schools and students. A literary class known as Mallamai had emerged. This group formed the administrative corps of native authority administration throughout parts of Africa. The colonial government report on Northern Nigeria of 1919, for example, recorded that the Mallamai were a "very influential class, some of them very well read in Arabic literature and law and deeply imbued with the love of learning."[28]

By 1960, there were about 50,000 Islamic scholars with about 27,000 Islamic schools in Northern Nigeria alone. In addition, there were about 2,777 Islamic secondary schools (*ilm*) with about 36,000 students throughout Northern Nigeria where Islamic law, Arabic grammar, mysticism, moral ethos, ethics, and customs and traditions of Islamic society were studied. Through the years, there had developed in most of Africa an educational system that was not only acceptable but that was considered by most Africans superior to Western education.[29] According to A.R.I. Doi, "Islam provided believers with a Universalist religion, an Islamic social and religious pattern, and an attitude of cultural and religious superiority over Pagans (and Christians)."[30]

The introduction of Western education into Africa was vehemently challenged because Western education was considered not only as counterculture and counter-Islam, but missionaries were perceived as pathfinders of European imperialism. Muslims were unwilling to forego a well-organized system of Islamic education for an ill-organized and a very uncertain system. Also, Western education, it was feared, would affect the whole social, religious, political, cultural, ethical and psychological fabric of African society. In addition, the roles and means of livelihood of the Mallamai were threatened. Muslims, therefore, did not want to adopt a system of education for which they had great contempt.

From 1906, even the British administration in northern Nigeria was antimissionary. (It is instructive to point out that Christian missionaries were the forbearers of Western education in Nigeria before 1970. Resentment of missionaries meant resentment of Western education as well.) According to Emmanuel Ayandele, "Education along Western lines was frowned upon as a disintegrating and demoralizing agency."[31] Indeed, a Kano poet wrote to say that Christian schools "are not beneficial at all and there is nothing in them but lies, evil and paganism.... They have also established churches so that they might lead the people astray."[32] Consequently, Muslims did not allow missionaries to build schools in their territories. Indeed, antimissionary sentiment reached a fever pitch in northern Nigeria, for example, during the period covered by this book, and fear of a Mahdist uprising gripped most British officials. In the words of one Kano trader, the coming of the British and Christian missionaries was a sign of the "last days."[33] As another Kano Muslim trader wrote, "There is evidence indicating imminent appearance of the Mahdi. Among the proofs are the coming of the Europeans to Hausaland.... Emirs have no power but they go to Kaduna ... legal cases will not be dealt with by the Qu'ran ... sons of Ulama go about like Pagans from one end of the country to the other without any guidance ... they cut their hair like Christians. Many women go about with their heads uncovered ... a boy will not be obedient to his parents and one who is learned will not tell the truth. The Christians prevent all things."[34]

It is important to note that the Muslim leaders in Africa were uncompromising adherents of the tenets of Islam (Ayandele, 1967, 1980). Indeed, as the political and religious leaders of their people, Muslim leaders were required by Muslim law to protect the religion, for not to do so would be apostasy—a great sin. A. Babs Fafunwa captures this sentiment well when he says this of Muslims in Northern Nigeria: "All the northern Emirs were political and spiritual leaders of their people and would not tolerate any local or foreign interference." He went on to add that "the advent of Christianity in Nigeria in 1842 caused a head-on collision with Islam, especially in the north where it was more firmly established."[35]

It is important to note that the rate of expansion of Western education in southern Nigeria contrasted drastically with that of northern Nigeria. By 1921 there were only 103 Christian-run primary schools, with 2,964 pupils and 162 teachers in northern Nigeria despite its larger land mass. In 1937, northern Nigeria had 549 primary schools with a total enrollment of 20,296 pupils and only one secondary school serving 65 students.[36] In the north of Nigeria, however, church and missionary rivalries were almost nonexistent due to the British colonial government's official policy of restricting Christian missionaries to non-Muslim areas. For this and other reasons that are irrelevant to the present discussion, the development of Western education was painfully slow in the Nigerian north, while intense missionary and church rivalry in the south led to its rapid expansion.[37]

In Ghana, Philip Foster tells us that education was completely concentrated in the southern regions because of Ashanti hostility to the missions in the north. Indeed, by 1950 while the southern section of the country had 2,916 schools, 275,901 students representing 17.7 percent of the school age population, the northern section of the country could only boast of 83 schools, 5,059 students representing only .5 percent of the school age population.[38] Similarly, in Kenya and Tanzania, at the time of their independence, formal schooling was a preserve of a very minute number of people in both countries. Hence, at their independence both countries had very visible signs of inequality. For example, by 1961, there were only three secondary schools offering the higher school certificate spread mostly among the urban dwellers in Tanzania. And quite shockingly, while Asians constituted only 3 percent of the population in Kenya, they occupied 30 percent of the secondary school population in that country by 1963. In Buganda, status in society was very clearly associated with schooling. Indeed, D. E. Apter notes that "an educated elite embracing modern values was in the making through the mission-sponsored school system."[39] He goes on to add that "to remain aloof from mission schools was to become powerless because schooling had become one important point of entry into positions of power and prestige."[40]

This chapter concludes that, although education was and still is the main institution for the allocation of privileges and power in Africa, it was and still is not made available to all on equal terms.

5

Western Education and Political Socialization in Africa

For the most part, Western education in most of Africa was provided by European missionaries up to and until the 1970s in many instances. Missionaries envisioned the creation of larger, more powerful African states because Christianity could not flourish in chaotic social, political and economic conditions. They also realized that they would not succeed in their work in Africa without an indigenous corps of educated Africans. Having come to this painful realization, the various missionary bodies began to build schools and to train local staff. Also important in the education of Africans was the high mortality rate among Europeans in Africa as well as the uncertain relationship between Africans and the Europeans. Given these circumstances, the missionaries reasoned that the best way to go about the evangelization of Africans was to train local parishioners as their own "recruiters." Indeed, as early as the nineteenth century, an American evangelist, T. J. Bowen stated that Africans should not only be taught to read the Bible, but they should also be taught to make Bibles themselves.

We desire to establish the Gospel in the hearts and minds and social life of the people, so that truth and righteousness may remain and flourish among them, without the instrumentality of foreign missionaries. This cannot be done without civilization. To establish the Gospel among any people they must have Bibles, and therefore must have the art to make them, or the money to buy them. They must read the Bible and this implies instruction.... To diffuse a good degree of mental culture among the people, though a secondary object, is really and necessarily one part of missionary work in Africa; and he that expects to evangelize the country without civilization will find, like Xavier in the East and the Jesuits in South America, and the priests in Congo, that his labors will end in disappointment.[1]

Of all the foreign missionaries in Africa, Bowen's zeal for the education of Africans was most visibly demonstrated. Like Buxton before him, Bowen believed that the whole social existence of the African would be changed with the emergence of eminent scientists, technocrats, intellectuals and intelligent rulers. Consequently, he believed that Christianity will only be implanted in Africa when these categories of people were produced through civilization or education.[2]

Similarly, the Church Missionary Society entered the African missionary field as a result of the advocacy of one of its members, Thomas Fowell Buxton, a prominent member of the British Parliament and a vice president of the society. It was Buxton (1839) who, in his book *The African Slave Trade and its Remedy,* advocated the regeneration of Africa by "calling forth her own resources."[3] Buxton urged the abolition of the nefarious slave trade at its roots by advocating the exploration of the Niger River into its hinterlands, the negotiation of treaties with the inhabitants and the establishment of peaceful trade. Buxton argued that if Christianity, commerce and civilization (by "civilization," the Victorians meant British culture and control) were pursued, the slave trade would be destroyed and civilization would be achieved naturally through cause-and-effect. In return, he maintained, England would acquire cheaper raw materials, new markets and increased productivity, employment and profits. Consequently, Buxton urged the cooperation of government and the missionary societies in the "deliverance" of Africa: "Let missionaries and schoolmasters, the plough and the spade, go together and agriculture will flourish; the avenues to legitimate commerce will be opened; confidence between man and man will be inspired; whilst civilization will advance as the natural effect, and Christianity operate as the proximate cause, of this happy change."[4]

Education of Africans was indeed on the agenda of the missionary societies. As one of the outstanding members of the CMS (and its later general secretary), Henry Venn, maintained in 1857, by restructuring the economy of Africa in favor of legitimate trade, a new generation of enlightened, educated, African middle-class elites would emerge in the church, commerce, industry and politics of the emerging African nations. According to Venn, these elites might "form an intelligent and influential class of society and become the founders of a Kingdom which shall render incalculable benefits to Africa and hold a position among the states of Europe."[5]

In order to produce native growers of cotton and traders who would form an intellectual and influential class of society, the various missionary bodies began to put in place educational schemes to prove to the world that Africans were as competent as other races. Different training schemes were initiated in Africa by the various missions while the abler African students were sent abroad for their education in fields ranging from business management to navigation, tile making, botany, the humanities and medicine. Qualified Africans were given employment on the basis of equality with Europeans both outside and inside the church, culminating in the elevation of Reverend Samuel Ajayi Crowther to the rank of Bishop of the Anglican Church in 1864. Bishop Crowther headed an all-African staff on the Niger.

Teaching Africans to read meant introducing printing presses and Euopean technology. Hence, "from the practical need of providing African missionaries and auxiliaries, the European missionary societies began to think in terms of raising up an African middle class on the lines of Europe and America."[6] As J. F. Ade Ajayi puts it, "These would be men to carry through the revolution initiated by the missionaries."[7] Edward H. Berman concurs that "missionaries not only helped fan the flames of nationalism through their teachings and their actions, they also played crucial roles in forging alliances which cut across ethnic lines, creating the basis for plural societies."[8] He goes on to state that "Christianity provided the common element that had been lacking before the advent of the missionaries among Africans of diverse ethnic backgrounds."[9] He concludes that "(e)ducation in a mission school—Anglican, Baptist, or Catholic—afforded African students similar experiences and was more often a unifying factor than a divisive one, despite denominational differences."[10]

With the establishment of firm colonial rule in Africa, education began to acquire very high visibility because it served as a major avenue for elite status recruitment. During colonialism, the African economy became increasingly dominated by innovations with the result that educational institutions came to occupy very strategic roles. Education therefore became almost the sole determinant of the economic, political and cultural elite status, and by implication the determinant of elite status in Africa. With time, educated Africans became clearly aware that education was the kingpin of their continued political development and participation as Africa joined the committee of nations. The historical transformation that took place in Africa was largely the byproduct of the educated minority. Whether as "activists, organization builders, ideologists, or members of literary class, the nationalists were those who had received one type of formal education or the other."[11] Numerous studies have shown that there is a fit between education, upward mobility, occupational mobility and political elite status in Africa.[12] Indeed, Robert

D. Grey argues that education, under certain conditions, has a major impact on political attitudes.[13] In other words, those who were educated in formal schools have a higher propensity to participate in politics in Africa than those who were not. How did schools perform the tasks of political socializations? Education trained Africans for citizenship by emphasizing that they belonged to one nation that crosses the boundaries of family, tribe and village. History was taught as a means of stirring interest in national affairs. Interest in government grew out of the study of civics. Schools created self-awareness. Through the teaching of courses like political science, government and citizenship, schools became venues for agitation for self-government. Indeed, in some instances, schools were organized on democratic models that gave students a taste of democratic arrangements as practiced in the West. Ayo Ogunsheye describes the inner workings of some of the colonial schools in Africa and states, "Every class in the primary school had its monitor and every teacher training college and every secondary school had its prefects." "By giving monitors and prefects varying degrees of responsibility in the class or school," Ogunsheye continues, "a crude attempt was made to inculcate the virtues of self-government." Ogunsheye goes on to state that "some schools even had their fag systems, thereby moving closer to the tradition of the English public schools."[14] He concludes that "no primary school was complete without its school uniform, not just caps and badges, but shorts and shirts, jumpers or girls' frocks made of the same material and cut in the same style. To complete the symbol of school solidarity, there was invariably a school band with possibly a flag."[15] Moral and character training were enhanced in the schools by membership in the Boy Scouts. And according to Ogunsheye, the Boy Scouts emphasized character-building, organization, cleanliness, truthfulness, readiness to help others and above all hardiness.[16] Games, sports and athletics promoted team work, team spirit, esprit de corps, moral training, intergroup competition and cooperation among students from the same school and from competing schools. Similarly, schools like William Ponty in Dakar, Senegal; King's College in Lagos, Nigeria; St. Andrew's College Oyo, Nigeria; the Protestant King's College at Budo, Uganda; the Catholic Colleges at Kisubi and Namilyango also in Uganda and Achimota College in the Gold Coast (now Ghana) attracted students from far and wide. This provided a forum for youths to mix freely and exchange ideas. Indeed, David B. Abernethy maintains that the Hope Waddell Training Institute enrolled students from as far away as Ghana, the Cameroons, Sierra Leone, Togo and Liberia. Students came from the Niger Delta to attend St. Andrew's College, Oyo. By bringing together students from various parts of the country and Africa, schools helped to broaden students' horizons and perspectives in political organization. Students sometimes also learned the art of political organization firsthand in school through participation. In Methodist High School, Uzuakoli, Nigeria, Reverend H.L.O. Williams, for example:

> developed a student government that combined traditional and English patterns of government. The pupils lived in a large rectangular compound divided into four houses, each headed by a "Captain", and the equivalent of the Senior Prefect was known as "Chief". The Chief, the Captains, and a few boys elected by the students themselves formed a "Cabinet", which held court fortnightly to try those charged with offenses. Trustworthy students called "Police Constables" served as prosecutors in these cases.[17]

It is therefore no wonder that during the Eastern House of Assembly elections held during 1951–1961 period, Uzuakoli produced ten members of the House of Assembly including, a premier, a minister of education and four members of the Federal House of Assembly.[18] Similar arrangements as reported at Uzuakoli were also implemented elsewhere by Mr. E. L. Mort, the principal of Toro College in northern Nigeria. Mr. Mort described the organizational workings of his school:

> Students lived in the style of a village with self-contained compounds according to tribes. They built their own houses, which were better spaced and plastered than the ordinary local village ones. They worked on the farm—twenty-five acres in area—pooling their experience and knowledge of farming. In the dry season they worked on building and carried out repairs to tools at the smithy. There was classroom work for four hours till 2 p.m. followed by games and dancing, in the evening. The women did the marketing and cooking, and the children formed the beginning of a kindergarten class. Each tribal group elected its own head, and these heads formed the 'village elders' who ran the village.[19]

Also significant in the political socialization of Africans were the extramural departments attached to the early universities in Africa. In Nigeria, for example, the extra-mural department attached to the University of Ibandan ran development courses in cooperative extension, local government, business management and others. The extra-mural departments provided a link between the universities and the wider African communities. Those who could not enter universities as full-time students were given access to university education through extra-mural courses. These courses helped to create a new breed of political activists. Courses were run for teachers, agricultural extension officers, civil servants, trade unionists and legislators, and in so doing a new kind of political consciousness was created among African educated elites.[20]

THE AFRICAN INDEPENDENT CHURCHES AND SCHOOLS

The African independent church movements deserve mention here because they served as catalysts in the education and political socialization of Africans. These movements were the handiwork of mistrust between European missionaries and Africans. Before colonialism took a firm grip on Africa, Africans played important roles in the early missionary efforts: They were interpreters, teachers, itinerary evangelists, missionaries, language workers, translators, instructors and grammar school principals. Some educated Africans joined missionaries in the fight against the slave trade. They supported legitimate trade in ivory, cotton, palm-oil and kernel, shea-butter and indigo. Some of these Africans began to advance trade in new areas and were involved in import and export trades.

However, later in the nineteenth century, competition began to develop between Africans and Europeans for positions of power. As J. F. Ade Ajayi says it, "There was often competition for office, and on such occasions, the missionaries on the spot cautioned the officials at home not to go too fast about promoting Africans to positions of responsibility on the grounds that there were limitations to their capabilities, weaknesses to their character, and defects to their Christianity."[21] However, since real power was in the hands of the Europeans, they were able to use it to undermine and retard African progress in the church, government and business.

Consequently, a small group of Africans began to question the relationship between educated Africans and European missionaries. In West Africa, this group was led by Edward Wilmot Blyden who began by "denouncing the mental slavery which, . . . the missionaries were substituting for the old physical slavery in Africa,"[22] and urged a mental emancipation. Blyden pressed for reform in education and called for the establishment of an Independent West African University. In Abeokuta, Nigeria, George William Johnson led a revolt against "the petticoat policy of the missionaries in keeping Christian converts and educated Africans away from the society and the politics of the old community."[23] Archdeacon James Johnson incited and led a revolt against the Church Missionary Society. Bishop Samuel Ajayi Crowther supported a proposal for the creation of an independent African controlled Niger Delta Pastorate in 1891. Similar schisms among the Baptists in Nigeria caused some Africans to break away to form the African Baptist Church.

These churches began to institutionalize African forms in the church. In Nyasaland, John Chilembwe established the Providence Industrial Mission (PIM). In Kenya, the Kikuyu deserted mission schools to form the Kikuyu Independent School Association, which was to become a major political force in the history of Kenya. In Nigeria, members of the independent church and school movements included J. K. Coker, F. E. Williams, A. A. Obadina, Reverend J. A. Lakeru, T. B. Dawodu and S. S. Jibowu.[24] These men and others helped to introduce vocational education in Nigeria. In the period following World War I, many more Africans broke away from European churches and founded self-governing native churches and schools.

Indeed, in Nigeria, in 1891, when a religious group seceded from the Anglican church, its members "resolved that a purely Native African Church be founded, for the evangelization and amelioration of our race to be governed by Africans."[25] Another independent church to come into being in the period after World War I was the United Native Church in the French Cameroons. There was also the National Church of Nigeria and the Cameroons, which came into being during the 1940s. In 1921, Simon Kimbangu founded the movement Kimbanguism in the Belgian Congo. Similarly, William Wade Harris founded his own religious movement and he is said to have baptized about 120,000 people in the Ivory coast in 1915.[26] The Ethiopian churches, as Thomas Hodgkin argued, served "as a kind of ecclesiastical instrument of radical nationalism."[27] It is to be pointed out, however, that leaders of the African Ethiopian churches particularly emphasized and patronized education and even financed the education of some academically able African students abroad. It should also be pointed out that some of the leading African political elites played very prominent roles in the Ethiopian and Independent schools movement. For example, the Lagos Baptists produced M. L. Stone and Mojola Agbebi who were leading figures in the nationalist struggle in Nigeria. The proprietor of the Accra Baptist School, Reverend Mark Hayford, was very active in the nationalist movement in Ghana. The spectacular South African nationalist John L. Dube opened the Ohlange Institute in Natal. Barrister Eyo Ita opened the West African People's Institute in Calabar, Nigeria. In Uganda, Ernest Kalibala founded the Aggrey Memorial School in 1934. It should be said also that the African church and school movements nurtured African political leadership to maturity in limited but significant ways. It is therefore safe to say that missionaries both European and African prepared the groundwork for African nationalism because, through their education, African political elites were produced. These were the men and women who crystallized the formation of political parties in Africa.

In some instances, missionaries contributed in very direct ways to the political socialization of Africans. For one thing, some missionaries often protested the economic exploitations of Africans by Europeans. For example, in Kenya the attempt by the government to coerce Africans into a form of slave labor was met with increasing missionary opposition and condemnation. This policy was severely challenged by the Alliance of Protestant Missionary Societies founded in 1918. In addition, opposition and protestations were made by the Alliance when the Kenya Legislative Council decided to raise the poll tax by about 60 percent. Indeed, the document declaring in 1923 that " 'primarily Kenya is an African territory . . . (and) the interests of the African native must be paramount' was largely the product of missionary lobbying in Britain."[28]

Notable among the missionaries who opposed British policies were J. H. Oldham, secretary of the International Missionary Council and some representatives of the Church of Scotland Mission. Edward Berman argues that "just as Africans became increasingly cognizant of the role of the mission schools in creating a new status hierarchy, so occasionally did missionaries attempt to establish elite institutions in the hope of gaining more converts."[29] "The Buganda-based representative of the CMS during the 1880s, the Reverend Alexander Mackay," Berman went on to say, "wanted an institution to train an elite which he hoped would have Anglican proclivities."[30] Berman observes that Alexander Mackay "felt that trying to win as many converts as quickly as possible was not necessarily the best policy."[31] Hence, he persuaded his mission that instead of working many feeble stations, the CMS should "select a few particularly healthy sites, on which we shall raise an institution imparting a thorough education, even only to a few."[32]

Mackay's proposal led to the establishment of the prestigious King's College at Budo in Uganda. The Catholics followed suit by establishing their own prestigious colleges at Kisubi and Namilyango. As Berman maintains, "Most of the leaders of Buganda society after 1900 and the leaders of the post-1945 nationalist struggles attended one of these institutions." In the 1870s, the United Free Church of Scotland founded the Livingstonia Institute, which was at the forefront in the training of Nyasaland's political leaders. For example, Levi Mumba who was the first president of the Nyasaland African Congress; Charles Domingo, a leader in the Ethiopian Church movement and Hastings Kamuzu Banda, who was the first president of the Republic of Malawi, were products of these prestigious institutions.[33] In Nyasaland, indeed, students from Livingstonia Institute "dominated the civil service, the private sector of the economy, and nascent political parties throughout the country."[34] Similarly, in Sierra Leone, the Creoles dominated the political scene because they had easy access to Fourah Bay College, the only university college in West Africa at this time. The Mende, because of the great concentration of prestigious schools in their midst, dominated the professional services in the Protectorate as did the Creoles in Freetown, Sierra Leone. In Ghana, the Wesleyan Methodist Missionary Society concentrated its educational efforts among the Fanti, and as would be expected, the Fanti's played dominant roles in the intellectual, political, economic and civil society in Ghana. John Mensah Sarbah, J. E. Casely-Hayford, J. W. de Graft Johnson, Attoh Ahuma and Mark Hayford were all products of the finest institutions in Ghana and, as I stated earlier, they were all great political players in their own rights.[35]

TRADE UNIONS AND YOUTH MOVEMENTS

The period following the end of World War II saw the emergence of several unions in Africa, namely youth clubs, students clubs, old boys clubs, ethnic mutual benefit groups, craft groups and trade unions. These groups served as "vehicles of new ideas and a proving ground for political leaders."[36] After World War II, trade unions and youth movements in Africa were transformed into mass organizations that were linked to emergent nationalist movements. Indeed, as I. Wallerstein has noted, voluntary associations were largely responsible for African nationalist movements. In Guinea, Sékou Touré, the president of Parti Démocratique de Guinée (PDG) came from a trade union. Also, the Union Générale des Travailleurs d'Afrique Noire (UGTAN) was a byproduct of several trade unions, and it played an important part in the independence of Guinea. In Kenya, trade unions had strong ties with the Kenya African National Union (KANU). Indeed, the Kenya Federation of Labor (KFL) under Tom Mboya "conducted a holding operation for KANU."[37] In the Cameroons, the Union Camerounaise, led by Ahmadou Ahidjo, led the people of the French Cameroons to independence in 1960. Trade union movements played important roles in the political crystallization of Africans because the trade union leaders had come to believe that the "economy was geared to foreign commercial and industrial interests; they believed that the standard of living of the workers could not be significantly improved until political independence was achieved."[38] In Tanganyika (now Tanzania), unionists were allowed to join the Tanganyika African National Union (TANU) and union leadership was recruited mainly from party ranks. The 1930s, according to William Tordoff, "saw the emergence in . . . Africa of territorially based youth movements, congresses and leagues" that later were turned into full-fledge political parties. Some examples of the congresses and youth movements that were turned into political parties include "the National Council of Nigeria and the Cameroons [NCNC], formed in August 1944; the Rassemblement Démocratique Africain [RDA], an interterritorial party established in French Africa in 1946; the United Gold Coast Convention [UGCC] and the Northern Rhodesia African Congress, founded in 1947 and 1948 respectively."[39] Some political parties emerged through the instrumentality of cultural and/or voluntary organizations. Examples include the formation of the Parti Démocratique de Côte d'Ivoire (PDCI) in Ivory Coast in 1946, which started as an organization of African planters called "comité d'action politique" of the Syndicat Agricole Africain. In western Nigeria, the Egbe Omo Oduduwa formed the nucleus of the Action Group (AG). The Northern People's Congress (NPC) emerged from Jamiyyar Mutanen Arewa, which was an Hausa cultural organization. In Sierra Leone, the Sierra Leone People's Party was an offshoot of the Sierra Leone Organization Society, and TANU was the brain child of the Tanganyika African Association.[40] Without exception, all the leaders of the trade unions and youth movements in Africa were Western educated individuals.

J. F. Ade Ajayi maintains that Christian missions were responsible for the emergence of the new African educated elites in colonial times. Ajayi goes on to argue that "Christian missionaries introduced into [Africa] the ideas of nation-building of contemporary Europe. They also trained a group of [Africans] who accepted those ideas and hoped to see them carried out, and later began to use these ideas as a standard by which to judge the actions of the [European] administration. In doing this, the Christian movement sowed the seeds of [African] nationalism."[41] James S. Coleman argues that Western education is regarded as a determinant of political status in Africa and maintains, "the relationship between formal education and the formation of the new political elite in African countries is so clear-cut.... Indeed, because formal education has come to be viewed as presumptively determinative of political elite status, students now in school are uncritically regarded as preordained members of the second or third-generation successor elites."[42] Indeed, studies done in Africa have shown that those who are highly educated are "more aware of the impact of the government on the individual ... more likely to report that they follow politics and pay attention to election campaigns ... have more political information ... have opinions on a wide range of political subjects ... more likely to consider themselves capable of influencing the government."[43] This means that educated people in Africa have greater insights into their political potentials than the less educated. Those who are educated "feel that they have resources appropriate to influencing politics and can afford to spend these resources to maximize their well-being."[44] The educated elites have skills including those skills that are deemed necessary for intelligent political participation. Robert D. Grey argues that education develops one's wide interests, generally useful skills and a sense of one's competence to participate in politics and also increases not only one's tendency to participate in politics but one's tendency to be an active participant in various spheres of life.[45] Grey concludes, however, that "there are studies ... which suggest that the schools do convey attitudes such as a sense of civic obligation or a sense of high political efficacy."[46]

However, Western education had grave consequences for the colonial governments because it prepared the minds of the African political elites who were to demand and eventually obtain independence from the colonialists. Coleman again states the following:

The introduction of modern educational system in colonial areas had significant political consequences. It was the single most important factor in the rise and spread of nationalist sentiment and activity. From the modern educational system emerged an indigenous elite which demanded the transfer of political power to itself on the basis of the political values of the Western liberal tradition or the ethical imperatives of Christianity, both of which had been learned in the schools. ... Designed essentially to serve only evangelizing or imperial purposes, Western education became a prime contributor to the emergence of new independent nations. Intended not to be a structure for political recruitment, it in fact called forth and activated some of the most upwardly mobile and aggressively ambitious elements of the population—elements most determined to acquire political power, most confident in the rightness of their claim, and most convinced of their capacity to govern.[47]

Apart from the collapse of colonialism, Western education left no doubts in the minds of many as to its relevance in the new situation. After all, it was used as a raison d'être for the perpetuation of colonialism and for reward to high offices during the colonial era. Consequently, elite status in the newly independent nations became closely associated with the acquisition of Western education.

Also significant is the fact that external assistance from the United States and the USSR helped to break the circle of single-dependency among African nations. As students went abroad for further studies, they were enriched with diversified educational experiences that Coleman says emboldened them to challenge the status quo. He makes this point: "As new generations of persons return from abroad with more varied educational experiences, and with degrees from a variety of foreign educational systems... those derived from the colonial period (were) increasingly challenged."[48]

Western education enhanced the ability of African political elites to achieve their political objectives by giving them the tools to communicate with a wide audience, the production of a high caliber political and civil leaders, the efficacy and efficiency of its institutions and the ability of its institutions to solve societal problems. Through formal education, the political elites were able to communicate effectively with their populace through writing. Education was a process through which new members were inculcated with political beliefs and attitudes. In conclusion, it should be stated that Western education was not only the prime mover of political socialization in Africa but also its "Open, Sesame," for without any exceptions, political and military leaders in Africa are people who have gone through one form of formal education or the other. In short, African leaders are all Western educated elites who have used their education to wrestle power and perpetuate it either as political or military elites. The manner in which African political and military elites have manipulated and perpetuated their power is the topic of our discussion in the next chapter.

6

Educated Elites and Political Domination in Africa

Patrick Chabal said that politics is about power. Therefore, to understand politics is to understand relations of power.[1] Power, as H. Lasswell and A. Kaplan argue, is:

A form of influence in which the effect on policy is enforced or expected to be enforced by relatively severe sanctions. Power is participation in the making of decisions: G has power over H with respect to the values K if G participates in the making of decisions affecting the K-policies of H. . . . A decision is a policy involving severe sanctions (deprivations). . . . The definition of power in terms of decision making adds an important element to "the production of intended effects on other persons"—namely, the availability of sanctions when the intended effects are not forthcoming.[2]

Power, therefore, is the ability of an individual or group to cause an effect or, as Bertrand Russell put it, power is "the production of intended effects."[3] In other words, power is coercive and unlike influence; it may involve latent force. Robert Bierstadt argues that influence is inductive whereas power is coercive. He notes:

We submit voluntarily to influence but power requires our submission. . . . Power is not force and power is not authority, but it is intimately related to both. 1) Power is latent force; 2) force is manifest power, and 3) authority is institutionalized power. . . . Force means the production of an effect, an alteration in movement or action that overcomes resistance.... In the sociological sense, where it is synonymous with coercion, it compels a change in the course of action of an individual or a group against the wishes of the individual or the group. It means the application of sanctions when they are not willingly received. Only groups that have power can threaten to use force, and the threat itself is power.... Without power there is no organization and without power there is no order.[4]

Peter Blau defines power as the "ability of persons or groups to impose their will on others despite resistance through deterrence either in the form of withholding regularly supplied rewards or in the form of punishment in as much as the former, as well as the latter, constitutes in effect negative sanction."[5] Blau goes on to say that "physical coercion, or its threat, is the polar case of power, but other negative sanctions, or the threat of exercising them, are usually also effective means of imposing one's will on others."[6] Blau concludes that "differentiation of power arises in the course of competition for scarce goods."[7]

Thomas Hobbes, on his own part, saw power as the ability to fulfill one's desires by causing those effects that will enable and facilitate individual desires. As Seth Kreisberg puts it, "Hobbes argues that since individual desires inevitably conflict with the desires of others, power involves the ability to affect another, to cause another to act, think, or speak in a particular way."[8] "And because the power of one man," Hobbes explains, "resisteth and hindereth the effects of the power of another: power simply is no more, but the excess of the power of one above that of another."[9] He summarized the power-effect relationship and noted: "Correspondent to cause and effect are POWER and ACT; nay those and these are the simple things.... For whenever any agent has all those accidents which are necessarily requisite for the production of some effect in the patient, then we say the agent has power to produce that effect, if it be applied to a patient."[10] Seth Kreisberg argues that power connotes relationship of domination, power over others, imposition, control, force, coercion, manipulation, sanction, obedience, submission and getting others to do what you want.[11] Who are those who wield power? Michael Korda answers this question by stating that it is not only heads of nations who have power and use it, but others too. He explains:

In a world of global markets for virtually every commodity, including culture, it's possible to dominate territories and populations as much by controlling a corporate entity as by controlling a state.... The exercise of this new global power is more subtle and gradual than the political kind; a corporate chief, for example, usually cannot at a word have his enemies thrown into prison, though he may eventually be able to ruin them. But a company head can, with his decisions on production, pricing, and distribution of products, have as much impact on the lives of millions as any politician, short of one who declares war.

These men control the food we eat, the clothes we wear, the drugs we're allowed when ill, and even the news, information and entertainment we receive.[12]

Indeed, Korda notes that "all life is a game of power. The object of the game is simple enough: to know what you want and get it. The moves of the game, by contrast, are infinite and complex, although they usually involve the manipulation of people and situations to your advantage."[13] Korda goes on to conclude that power is accumulated and because it is scarce, it is coveted, hoarded and used to one's interest by those who have it. In the relationship of power, there are winners and loses as well as the powerful and the powerless.

Michel Foucault argues that "truth is linked in circular relation with systems of power which produce and sustain it, and to effects of power which it induces and which extend it."[14] He went on to add that "each society has its regime of truth, its 'general politics' of truth: that is, the types of discourse which it accepts and makes function as true; the mechanisms and instances which enable one to distinguish true and false statements, the means by which each is sanctioned; the techniques and procedures accorded value in the acquisition of truth; the status of those who are charged with saying what counts as true."[15] Foucault concludes by saying that modern forms of government have shifted from overt sovereign power to "disciplinary" power that is exercised through its invisibility by normalizing technologies of the self. He notes:

> Traditionally, power was what was seen, what was shown and what was manifested.... Disciplinary power, on the other hand, is exercised through its invisibility; at the same time it imposes on those whom it subjects a principle of compulsory visibility. In discipline it is the subjects who have to be seen. Their visibility assures the hold of power that is exercised over them. It is the fact of being constantly seen, of being always able to be seen, that maintains the disciplined individual in his subjection.[16]

In Africa, power means controlling the many by the few. It is epitomized by the powerful getting what they want by any means necessary. Power in Africa is a zero-sum game. David Nyberg defines power in the manner it is used in Africa:

> Power has been regarded as an end in itself, and as a means to other ends. As a means it is sometimes seen as a subcategory of influence, but influence is sometimes seen as a subcategory of power. Persuasion is regarded as the opposite of power, though it can also be an example of it, while manipulation is taken to be an aspect of both, of neither, or of power alone. Some claim that force is the root of all forms of power; others drastically limit its role. Violence has been regarded as the opposite of power and as its very essence. It can be argued that power and authority are inextricably related.[17]

Although the relationship of domination exists in most political systems, in Africa it is *ipso facto* because a few ruling elites manipulate the machinery of government to their own advantage. Relationship of domination also exists in the economic spheres. It is these conditions that often lead to violence and perpetuate powerlessness. Seth Kreisberg argues that domination takes "shape in hierarchial, alienating, and exploitative economic relationships, the core of which is differentiation between those who have access to and control over wealth and those who do not."[18] He concludes that "the drive to control others creates a spectrum of violent and unjust situations, ranging from war and political murder to torture, jailing of dissidents, terrorism, censorship, expropriation of property, and manipulation through propaganda and entrenched party politics."[19] Perhaps no where in the world is this more true than in Africa where any opposition to a particular regime is often construed as an affront to the nation itself requiring drastic clamp down.

AFRICAN POLITICAL EXPERIMENTS IN DOMINATION

True to the words of Michel Foucault, African leaders "ensemble rules according to which the true and the false are separated and specific effects of power attached to what [they deem] true."[20] And as Foucault noted, truth "is produced and transmitted under the control, dominant if not exclusive, of a few great political and economic apparatuses (university, army, writing, media)."[21] Indeed, Foucault maintains that power and knowledge are interconnected in a symbiotic manner. He notes: "(P)ower and knowledge directly imply one another.... There is no power relation without the correlative constitution of a field of knowledge, nor any knowledge that does not presuppose and constitute at the same time power relations."[22] Foucault explains the connection between power and knowledge by stating that "there is an administration of knowledge, a politics of knowledge, relations of power which pass via knowledge and which, if one tries to transcribe them, lead one to consider forms of domination."[23]

In Africa, such forms of power domination were exemplified by an obvious trend that surfaced in the political scenes in the 1960s, that is, the move away from pluralism to centralization of power in the hands of a single party. Indeed, by the 1970s, most countries in Africa (except a few like Botswana) had all abolished a multiparty system in favor of single party controls. This was true of Kenya, as well as Tanzania, Ghana, Mali, Senegal, Tunisia, Upper Volta, Zambia, the Cameroons, Mozambique and Guinea, to mention only a few. Single party control was followed by the personalization of power in the hands of the party leader as party leaders became state presidents in a sort of divine right of presidents' doctrine. William Tordoff argues that the divine right of president's model "carried obvious disadvantages." He goes on to add that: "sometimes, as in Ghana between 1960 and 1966 and in Malawi, it meant the heavy concentration of powers in the President's own office, to the detriment of other ministries; the virtual monopoly of policy-making by the President, without adequate consideration of alternative policies, and the erection of the President's own thought into the official ideology; . . . it carried the danger of succession crises."[24] The next political manipulation and machination by African political leaders was the adoption of socialism without professing or even accepting the basic tenets of Marxism such as the imperative of class struggle and also their refusal to espouse atheism. On the contrary, these leaders (Sékou Touré of Guinea; Nyerere of Tanzania and Félix Houphouet Boigny of Ivory Coast, for example) remained ardent followers of Christianity and Islam.

The late 1960s witnessed the "emergence of regimes in which governmental and administrative structures . . . were as salient as political parties in Africa."[25] This is to say, African states moved from single party states to administrative states where political parties were reduced to very peripheral roles. In 1966, Aristide Zolberg wrote that some states in Africa including "Ghana, Guinea, Mali, Senegal and Ivory Coast . . . were moving towards administrative . . . states while the political parties had been reduced to only symbolic roles."[26] The danger of overdependence on government bureaucracy, Zolberg warned, was great in view of incentive structures internal to bureaucracies such as exacerbation of the elite-mass-gap, lack of innovation and entrepreneurship, the perpetuation of neocolonial relationships, dwindling support for the political process, political instability and dissatisfaction of the masses. Other vices include nondevelopment orientation, risk-avoidance, careerism, embourgeoisement and indifference to rural development.[27]

Another shocking trend in African political development is the manner in which neocolonialism has been perpetuated in Africa. This is to say, neocolonialism has replaced colonialism as a political tour de force in Africa. What is neocolonialism? Neocolonialism is a process whereby colonial powers still extend their influence and dominance over political and economic matters in Africa. This means that what we had as independence in the 1960s was merely a change of guards.

Immanuel Wallerstein argues convincingly that African independence was merely a "compromise between the colonial powers and the middle-class leadership of the nationalist movements. The former turned over the political machinery to the latter, in return for which the latter implicitly promised to hold in check the radical tendencies of lower class protest, and to leave basically intact the overall economic links with the former."[28] Indeed, Tunde Adeleke argues that "neo-colonialism eroded the prospect for genuine independence by strengthening the dependency of African states on their former colonial rulers, to the mutual advantage and benefit of both the foreign powers and the domestic partners."[29] Because of such ties, African ruling elites have left unchecked the exploitative relationship that had existed during colonialism. This means African leaders are quite willing to subject their countries to European exploitation rather than work for the interest of their own citizens. Indeed, Adeleke makes the point that what African political leaders call nation building merely are "1) Political and administrative reforms aimed at experimenting with the political traditions of the Europeans; and 2) strengthening of the economic ties with the former colonial masters."[30] Strengthening economic ties with former colonial masters in this manner, Adeleke continues, involves the exploitation "of the domestic economy to the disregard of the interests and needs of the African people, and also the appropriation of public wealth, as the leaders [struggle] to amass as much personal fortune as possible."[31]

MILITARY AND POLITICAL DICTATORSHIPS IN AFRICA

Another cancer that has eaten deep into the fabric of African polity is the illegal usurpation of power by military dictators. This disturbing trend, which began in the early 1960s with the assassination of Sylvanus Olympio, president of the Republic of Togo, in January 1963, extended to the government of Congo-Brazzaville in August 1963 and Dahomey in October 1963. Between 1963 and 1990 the governments of Nigeria, Upper Volta, Dohomey, Niger, Ghana, Liberia, Sierra Leone, Mali, the Sudan, Libya, Algeria, the Congo, Togo, Chad and the Central African Republic had succumbed to the long arm of military dictatorship. In some cases, some disgruntled elements in one arm of the military have toppled another arm of the same military. This was the case in Nigeria in 1966 and 1975 and in Ghana in 1978 and in 1979. Since 1963, military dictators have taken over power in country after country in Africa. Several coup attempts or failed coup attempts have been reported in Africa, namely: Gabon in 1964; Angola, 1977; Kenya, 1982; Guinea, 1970 and Gambia, 1981. In all, nearly half of the nations in Africa have fallen under military dictatorships. Those countries that have survived the iron fist of military rule in Africa have done so not because the military has not tried to topple them, but because the military has tried and failed.

Once in power, these dictators have advanced dubious schemes aimed at promoting programs that advance their own interests and those of their allies. Besides, military and civilian dictators like "Jean Badel Bokassa, Samuel Doe, Siad Barre, Mengistu Haile Mariam, Idi Amin, Valentine Strasser of Sierra Leone, Ibrahim Babangida of Nigeria, Sani Abacha also of Nigeria, and Mobutu of Zaire, just to mention a few, have ravaged their countries and murdered hundreds of thousands of their citizens."[32] Indeed, between 1971 and 1979, Idi Amin murdered an estimated 300,000 people in Uganda, particularly among the Kakwa—an opposing ethnic group. The same could be said of Mengistu Haile Mariam of Ethiopia, Samuel Doe of Liberia, and Siad Barre of Somalia, though with less severity. Indeed, during his reign of terror in Liberia, thousands of opponents of Samuel Doe either disappeared or were murdered. A similar fate befell the Isaaqs and the Hawiye in Somalia under Siad Barre. According to a recent writer, Siad Barre "unleashed a reign of terror, destroying several villages and massacring thousands of Somalis."[33] Sani Abacha, the Nigerian dictator, imprisoned hundreds of opponents, two of whom died in jail. Adeleke argues that in Africa "individuals who assumed power with promises of a better life for the people, turned around and destroyed those ... same people."[34] Indeed, the whole continent of Africa is replete with totalitarian regimes—Zaire, the Central African Republic, Kenya, Angola, Rwanda, Malawi, Nigeria and the Sudan all fall under this category. Adeleke concludes, "In many parts of Africa, the leadership is at war against its people."[35] Max Weber's definition of power is most appropriate to the manner in which power is used in Africa. Weber defined power as "the chance of a man or of a number of men to realize their own will in a communal action even against the resistance of others who are participating in the action."[36] According to this definition, "power involves the confrontation of wills, where one will 'even against resistance' imposes itself on others."[37] Notice here that in Weber's definition, force and coercion are the *sine qua non* of power. He notes, "If no social institutions existed which knew the use of violence, then the 'state' would be eliminated."[38] According to this definition, force is an essential part of governance. However, although modern democracies do not rely on force and coercion as Max Weber conceived some sixty years ago, force is still a dominant tool of governance in most of Africa.

This is indeed one of the "tragic paradoxes of the post-colonial state because, no longer threatened from outside, the national sovereignties of African countries became victims of the policies of the very people entrusted with their defense." According to Adeleke, "There is hardly an African state that is not experiencing internal convulsions and disruptions [emanating] from ethnocentric and primordial disequilibrium."[39] African states that have turned to absolutism or have become tyrannical include Chad after the fall of Tombalbaye, the Sudan, Uganda under Idi Amin, Guinea under Sékou Touré, Equatorial Guinea under Macias Nguema, Nigeria under Sani Abacha, Liberia under Samuel Doe and Zaire over Mobutu's lifetime.[40]

CORRUPTION IN AFRICA

A lot has been written about corruption in Africa.[41] The latest is the comment credited to the regional director of Agence France-Presse in Dakar that "Cape Verde is the only African country where there is no corruption ... not because it (Cape Verde) is poor, but because the people there are honest."[42] To this Victor T. LeVine adds, "Assuming that Degioanni probably knows what he is talking about, the (relative) absence of official corruption in Cape Verde makes that country the solitary outlier to a well-defined generalized pattern of official corruption in Africa."[43] In 1983, Chief R.B.K. Okafor accused Nigerian intellectuals of being at the root of corruption in Nigeria:

> It was a matter for regret and tantamount to a national calamity that the intellectuals are the largest offenders in the nefarious, treasonable and corrupt acts of falsifying election results and declaring losers as winners and vice versa. The so called intellectuals who masterminded the rigging of the last elections were the same people on whom their parents and the nation at large had spent huge sums of money to enable them to acquire the highly coveted knowledge for utility and the over-all development and improvement of the Nigerian nation.
>
> But instead of working towards these ideals, "to our sorrow and detriment", the knowledge we had paid dearly to purchase is now being used by the possessors as a potent instrument for destroying the country we had all labored so hard to build.... He sees these intellectuals, who become cheap instruments of rigging and instability, as a defiance to, and a negation of all that the ideals of intellectualism are ever known to stand for.... The responsibility for the impending calamity in Nigeria, as a result of the "Kangaroo Elections" just concluded, should be squarely placed at the door-steps of those intellectual "cheats-turned-returning officers". This group of people are worse than armed robbers and should therefore be tied at stakes and shot publicly.[44]

Similarly, in his novel Chinua Achebe had argued that "corruption has passed the alarming and entered the fatal stage; and Nigeria will die if we keep pretending that she is only slightly indisposed."[45] Indeed, a contributor to the Nigerian *Weekly Star* once stated that "keeping an average Nigerian from being corrupt is like keeping a goat from eating a yam."[46]

Corruption is not limited to Nigeria alone, but rather it is an African phenomenon. The Nigerian example is used to illustrate the extent of corruption in Africa because it is the most well-documented in Africa. Chinua Achebe gives the following examples of corruption in Nigeria: "(A) Federal Government Department paying N50 million every month as salaries to nonexistent workers! ... Nigerian importers who, having applied for and obtained scarce foreign exchange from the Central Bank, ostensibly to pay for raw materials overseas, leave the money in their banks abroad and ship to Lagos, containers of mud and sand."[47] Achebe goes on to argue that "a Nigerian does not need corruption, neither is corruption necessary nourishment for Nigerians. It is totally false to suggest, as we are apt to do, that Nigerians are different fundamentally from any other people in the world. Nigerians are corrupt because the system under which they live today makes corruption easy and profitable; they will cease to be corrupt when corruption is made difficult and inconvenient."[48] These examples pass for other African nations as well, some of which are much worse than Nigeria.

Corruption and politics are also issues to be tackled in Africa. Corruption by politicians in Africa is caused by the close relationship between wealth and power in African politics. As is well known, Western democratic theory is based on the separation of power from wealth. Although in Western democracies wealth and ascribed privileges can make it easier for an individual to attain political power, they are not a *sine qua non* for political office. Because power and politics commingle in Africa, African politicians are left to assume that it is legitimate to use their power to acquire wealth.[49] Indeed, Patrick Chabal argues, and I agree, that "the legitimacy of power (in Africa) derives in some significant part from the acquisition, possession and display of wealth. Indeed, there is overwhelming evidence to suggest that, in the minds of rulers and ruled alike, wealth is a *sine qua non* to power, just as it is well understood that power brings wealth."[50] Chabal goes on to state that "political Africanization implies here that there is an inescapable dialectical relationship between power and wealth. The search for power goes hand in hand with the will to be rich,"[51] He concludes that "it is precisely because power and wealth are so intimately connected that the personal 'integrity' of [African] political leaders is revealed as different, exceptional, or even odd."[52] African leaders are remarkable if they do not enrich themselves as most have. In addition, African political leaders have continued to maintain or even strengthen their economic ties with the countries of Europe and America. These economic associations involve the exploitation of the domestic economy to the advantage of the metropolis at the expense of the needs of the African people.

Embezzlement of public funds by a few individuals has exacerbated internal tensions in Africa due to acute poverty, neglect and marginalization caused by such unpatriotic behavior on a large proportion of Africans. Indeed, Seth Kreisberg notes, "Relationships of domination exist in political institutions. They take the form of ruling elites who manipulate the apparatus of governance to their own advantage, whether the form of political power be totalitarian, authoritarian or ... democratic."[53] He further states that "the ability to control and manipulate others also derives from privileged access to and control of valued resources such as education, personal wealth, housing, food, health care and weapons of war."[54]

Corruption is rife in the entire African body politic. As a recent writer, Tunde Adeleke, has noted, "Mobutu Sese Seko of Zaire has, according to one estimate, well over $6 billion in foreign account, again, about the size of his country's external debt. Just before subjecting him to a violent death, the captors of Samuel Doe of Liberia pleaded in vain for information on the whereabouts of the funds that he had appropriated over the years. The record of the extravagance of Jean Badel Bokassa, Idi Amin, Kamuzu Banda and Ibrahim Babangida are very fresh in the memories of their compatriots."[55] Félix Houphouet Boigny is said to have boasted that his ill-acquired wealth was as a result of his hard work. In 1983, he gave a speech in which he bragged that his enormous wealth was a case of hard work. In the said speech, Boigny extolled the virtues of hard work and justified his foreign bank account on the grounds that interests on the account would be reinvested for the good of the people. He called on his people to be proud of him because of his wealth, which represents his substance. He concluded the speech by saying that because he was rich, he should be trusted.[56]

Corruption in Africa has created powerful forces leading Africans away from egalitarianism. Today, African societies have become more stratified than ever before, and the gap between the haves and the have-nots has widened. Also, a few enjoy living standards as high as those of the colonialists while the majority lives on mere subsistence. The new educated elites, according to David B. Abernethy, have enormous financial resources. For example, while an average farmer makes only about $1,000 a year, a young civil servant right from college may earn about $12,000 a year. The young civil servant lives in heavily subsidized government housing. University professors and bureaucrats in Africa enjoy enormous financial security because taxes are more regressive in Africa than in the advanced industrialized world. Abernethy concludes that the biblical saying "Unto him that hath it shall be given [comes] close to fulfillment for those who have benefitted most from the transition to independence."[57]

7

Schools in Africa as Sites of Cultural and Structural Inequalities, Disempowerment, Sexism, Domination and Hegemony

Schools in Africa today are colonial legacies, and as Paulo Freire had noted, colonial education imposed a culture of silence on African people and the peoples of the Third World.[1] This plot was hatched by the deliberate efforts made by the colonizers to use education to prevent the colonized from understanding themselves, their consciousness and their culture. Through manipulation of the curriculum, colonial schools only exposed the colonized to elements of the colonizer's culture in order to facilitate the perpetuation of the colonial exploitation of Africa.

Consequently, the colonized have experienced alienation both of themselves and of the foreign culture itself, because the practices, ideologies and philosophies of the colonizers were quite alien to the colonized. The first alienation for the colonized came from his/her "exposure to educational and cultural stimuli [which tended] to erase the significance of his/her own past."[2] The second alienation came from the "selective nature of the elements of the metropolitan culture with which [the colonized] were confronted."[3] For one thing, the machinery, the books, the language of instruction, the movies and the curricula reflected the needs of the metropolitan society and its labor needs. In other words, the colonial curricula in Africa were determined by immediate and long term needs of the metropolitan culture, and in nearly every case, the curriculum did not facilitate the transfer of students to metropolitan schools whereby they could reap similar rewards for their education. Indeed, even the method of recruitment of students into colonial schools was alien to the African. Paulo Freire and Donaldo Macedo argue that colonial schools in Africa "served the purpose of deculturating the natives; on the other hand, it acculturated them into a predefined colonial model." "Schools in this mold," they go on to say, "functioned as part of an ideological state apparatus designed to secure the ideological and social reproduction of capital and its institutions, whose interests are rooted in the dynamics of capital accumulation and the reproduction of the labor force."[4] They state very convincingly that "the educated labor force in [African] colonies was composed mainly of low-level functionaries whose major tasks were the promotion and maintenance of the status quo. [But] their role took on a new and important dimension when they were used as intermediaries to further colonize [colonial] possessions in Africa."[5] Freire and Macedo believe that the colonialists "were successful to the extent that they created a petit-bourgeois class of functionaries who had internalized the belief that they had become 'white' or 'black with white souls,' and were therefore superior to African peasants."[6] They see colonial schools as "political sites in which class, gender, and racial inequalities were both produced and reproduced."[7] Similarly, "the colonial educational structure served to inculcate.... [Africans] with myths and beliefs that denied and belittled their lived experiences, their history, their culture, and their language." "The schools," Freire and Macedo note, were "purifying fountains where Africans could be saved from their deep-rooted ignorance, their 'savage' culture, and their 'bastardized' language."[8] They conclude that colonial schools in Africa reinforced in children the thinking and ideology that the colonizers had intended, which is a class of people who believed that they were inferior in every respect.

Very surprisingly, after independence, most of the characteristics of colonial education were retained in Africa. For example, African educational systems are without exception controlled centrally by the Ministry of Education, which determines the appointment of teachers, curriculum, textbooks, teaching materials and philosophy. Such central control makes it possible for the promulgation of consistent political messages and for the curriculum to be designed to serve political ends. Textbooks are selected for the power of their political messages and the educational systems are not only bureaucratic and authoritarian, but they also tow official ideological lines. Indeed, John Cramer and George Brown argue that "educational systems in Africa generally reflect the social and political philosophies of their countries, whether or not those philosophies are clearly stated." Given these realities, teachers are oriented toward certain political messages and educational structure, and education decision-making often comes under political influence.

In Africa, education has become a means of social control by transmitting and preserving the beliefs of the educated ruling elites. The educational aims of schools and teachers in Africa today represent stability, authority, discipline and preordained values. It is therefore not an overstatement to say that, today in Africa, schools are sites of cultural and social inequalities, disempowerment, sexism, domination and hegemony. However, although schools in Africa perpetuate structural and cultural inequalities, teachers do not know that schools perpetuate such inequalities. It has also been argued that educators in Africa are authoritarian—that they limit the learner to a "passive role in the meaning-making process, and fail to produce a type of political knowledge that can expose and challenge the production and reproduction of oppressive relationships, especially those associated with class, gender, and [deskilling of teachers]."[9] In this chapter, I will highlight the problematic relationship between African society at large, teachers, students and schooling as exemplified by structural and cultural inequality, unequal power relations, domination, sexism, hegemony and deskilling of teachers. I argue that there is a close link between education and class, and education is glaringly biased in favor of the elites as against lower-class and rural children. Parents and students do not have any power in educational policies, and teachers are more often than not subordinated to the dictates of the Ministries of Education and governmental bureaucracies. The question is, what are the mechanisms through which schools in Africa disempower the poor and women and create inequalities, domination and hegemony?

It is important to note that in Africa, the main function of education is socialization into the status quo as well as obedience. Biases permeate school structure as well as the school curriculum, contents and teaching methods. Teachers play out relationships of domination in the classrooms in what Martin Buber calls I-It relationship as opposed to I-Thou relationship. Students are told to take their correct places in the learning process because they know nothing. In other words, teachers deposit knowledge in their students and make withdrawals through the process of testing, quizzes and Socratic questioning. Paulo Freire refers to this type of relationship between students and teachers as "banking" education. Anedeto Gaspar gives us some insights into the inner workings of "banking" education in African schools in this passage about the school he attended at Dilolo-Gare, a border town school between Angola and the Congo.

Each teacher received a schedule and syllabus from the vicarate educational offices. On any one day all students in grade three of the Franciscan system in the Congo were supposed to be studying the same things. Since the promotion of the teachers was linked to the results of the examinations administered to the students, teachers taught from the approved books almost exclusively. The examinations were not tricky in any way; they came from the assigned books. The teachers, many of whom were former seminary students, knew full well that promotion was contingent on good examination results.[10]

Gaspar also tells us that the population of the school consisted of Congolese, Angolans and some Zambians. He noticed official indoctrination by teachers and states: "If the history teacher was French, we could be certain that French history and institutions were stressed; if he were Belgian then the emphasis would be on Belgian history and institutions."[11]

Paulo Freire describes "banking" education as the relationship between students and teachers where:

(a) the teacher teaches and the students are taught;
(b) the teacher knows everything and the students know nothing;
(c) the teacher thinks and the students are thought about;
(d) the teacher talks and the students listen meekly;
(e) the teacher disciplines and the students are disciplined;
(f) the teacher chooses and enforces his choice, and the students comply;
(g) the teacher acts and the students have the illusion of acting through the action of the teacher;
(h) the teacher chooses the program content, and the students (who were not consulted) adapt to it;
(i) the teacher confuses the authority of knowledge with his or her own professional authority, which she and he set in opposition to the freedom of the students;
(j) the teacher is the subject of the learning process, while the pupils are mere objects.[12]

He also tells us that the "outstanding characteristic of ... narrative [banking] education ... is the sonority of words, not their transforming power."[13]

This type of teacher/student relationship exemplifies what Freire calls teacher/student contradiction, which is at the core of the pedagogical relationship of domination and submission. This is the type of pedagogical arrangement where the teacher has all the powers and the students have no power at all.

The curricula in African schools stress hegemonic social values and students are made to accept values, rules and attitudes of the ruling elites as though such values are gospel truths that are predetermined, neutral and unchangeable. There is also a problematic relationship between schools and society in Africa in that as a microcosm of the larger society, schools maintain the beliefs, values and the interest of the ruling elites through the type of knowledge produced, the pedagogy and the curriculum. As we know, knowledge is produced within historical and social contexts and knowledge is socially constructed. Truth, as Michel Foucault puts it, "is linked in circular relation with systems of power which produce and sustain it, and to effects of power which it induces and which extend it."[14] Teachers in Africa who are mostly of the traditional persuasion often impute to their students that the world is made of hierarchies and that students must learn their roles either as controllers or the controlled.

Indeed, in Africa, teachers' attitudes reflect the thinking of the broader society for studies done in the Cameroons, Sierra Leone, Malawi, Guinea and Rwanda indicate that male and female teachers believe that boys are superior to girls academically.[15] Teachers surveyed in these countries responded that they preferred to teach boys more than girls because boys are more intelligent than girls. This type of attitude follows from the thinking among some Africans that girls' education is a waste of money because girls will ultimately end up in the kitchen and that women are incompetent citizens. Indeed, Barry Kanpol makes the point that "sexism in schools is not only related to sexual harassment and/or sexual abuse but becomes a national pastime amplified in many areas of curriculum, teacher-student relationships, and home relationships with mothers, fathers, grandparents, brothers and sisters."[16] He continues by saying that "sexism varies for different cultures, depending on the culture."[17] I agree because attitude surveys conducted in Malawi, the Cameroons, Gambia, Sierra Leone and Kenya show that even female students have very low expectations of their achievement in school as well as low career prospects, just as it is the belief among the general population.

Teachers in Africa, through the process of "banking" education, "cultivate passivity, conformity, obedience, acquiescence, and unquestioning acceptance of authority." Banking "education makes objects out of students, it dehumanizes, it denies students experiences and voices, it stifles creativity, it disempowers."[18] On a similar note, Pepi Leistyna and Arlie Woodrum state that "teachers who work within the traditional paradigm, with its model of teacher as knower/lecturer and student as passive recipient of information, inevitably reproduce and maintain particular forms of identity, meaning, authority, and interaction." They go on to say that "teachers work and speak from within historically and socially determined relations of power and privilege that are based on their race, ethnicity, class and gender."[19] However, they maintain that "while the possession and wielding of the [elite] values and beliefs serve to legitimate the voices of some teachers and students, they [do] also work to silence others." They conclude that "in the same way, curricula can either affirm or exclude certain voices and ... it can demean, deny, or disfigure the lived experience of a great many people who are not part of the [elite] group."[20]

Let's hear what Seth Kreisberg says about banking education. Kreisberg tells us that banking education "reinforces, legitimizes, and replicates those social, political, and economic structures and relationships of domination that render people powerless."[21] Concerning the relationship between students and knowledge in the traditional educational setting Paulo Freire has this to say: "The teacher talks about reality as if it were motionless, static, compartmentalized, and predictable. Or else he expounds on a topic [that is] completely alien to the existential experience of the students. His task is to 'fill' the students with the contents of his narration, contents which are detached from reality."[22] In order words, these teachers do not take into consideration the world-views of their students in the acquisition of knowledge. Similarly, teachers sometimes inject their own opinions and preferences to be learned as objective facts by students. It should be said that banking education influences the way people see the world and act on it. Paulo Freire cautions that:

the banking concept of education regards men as adaptable, manageable beings. The more students work at storing the deposits entrusted to them, the less they develop the critical consciousness which would result from their intervention in the world as transformers of that world. The more completely they accept the passive role imposed on them, the more they tend simply to adapt to the world as it is and to the fragmented view of reality deposited in them.[23]

He argues convincingly that the banking method of education is closely related to other forms of oppression, domination and violence in society. He states:

The capability of banking education to minimize or annul the students' creative power and to stimulate their credulity serves the interests of the oppressors, who care neither to have the world revealed nor to see it transformed. The oppressors use their "humanitarianism" to preserve a profitable situation. Thus they react almost instinctively against any experiment in education which stimulates the critical faculties and is not content with a partial view of reality but always seeks out the ties which link one point to another and one problem to another.[24]

Freire concludes that "the interests of the oppressors lie in changing the consciousness of the oppressed, [through banking education] not the situation which oppresses them,"[25] because the more the oppressed adapt to their prevailing conditions, the more they can be dominated. To achieve these objectives, Freire opines, "the oppressors use the banking concept of education."[26] Henry Giroux draws our attention to the process in which traditional education reinforces and reproduces the status quo and notes:

First, schools provided different classes and social groups with the knowledge and skills they needed to occupy their respective places in a labor force stratified by class, race and gender. Second, schools were seen as reproductive in the cultural sense, functioning in part to distribute and legitimate forms of knowledge, values, language and modes of style that constitute the dominant culture and its interests. Third, schools were viewed as part of a state apparatus that produced and legitimated the economic and ideological imperatives that underlie the state's political power.[27]

DE-SKILLING OF TEACHERS

Teachers in Africa are exceedingly de-skilled. For one thing, all the primary and secondary schools come under the Ministry of Education, the State School Board or a central examination body. Teachers have no control over their lives and their curricula. The Ministry of Education or the State School Board is responsible for all matters concerning education including the appointment and recruitment of teachers, development of the curriculum and building of schools and school budgets. Directives are sent from the Ministry of Education or the State School Board, as the case may be, to the zonal school districts and to teachers. Teachers are treated as civil servants and are subject to civil service rules, but they are completely excluded from the decision-making process because, in most African countries, the curriculum is drawn by a central examination body that also recommends the textbooks. Schools in Africa do not include teachers' and students' voices in matters that affect their lives. Schools are also very hegemonic because competing views are not tolerated. Barry Kanpol argues that teachers who adhere to these policies without question are de-skilled even though they may be certified to teach in their particular subject area. He goes on to state that the epitome of deskilling is reached when teachers have no control over their teaching methods. However, reskilling occurs "when teachers are better able to intellectualize the role that the state plays in hegemonic constructions."[28]

LANGUAGE INEQUALITY

In Africa, poor children are disenfranchised because of the continued use of the language of the former colonial masters in schools. As we know, language serves as intermediary in knowledge distribution because accessibility of a certain knowledge base is determined by the medium of instruction. In Africa, most poor children fail to do well in school because they do not understand the language of the school and schools do not address their needs. The school system tacitly reinforces and rewards middle-class values, attitudes and behaviors, including the way of talking, acting, socializing, values and styles of dress.[29] Accordingly, social inequalities are transformed into academic inequalities by the educational system itself. In other words, poor children do not do as well in school as their richer peers in Africa because they lack the background of their higher-class school mates. Indeed, according to Paulo Freire, students who lack familiarity with written words may have difficulty with writing in school.[30] Besides, class-based differences are also expressed in the curriculum content as well as in the cultural and linguistic preferences hidden in the curriculum. As a recent scholar reminds us, language is "related to socioeconomic and to some extent political processes, and is associated with the distribution of knowledge resources, and therefore power in society, it determines access to these resources, job opportunities, power and prestige."[31] Nowhere is this more true than in Africa because in Africa, students who do not understand the language of the former colonial masters are punished through low grades. In an extensive study of language codes, Basil Bernstein found that people develop family role systems because the structure of society has its own corresponding communication mode. These modes evolve as individuals partake in the experiences, expectations and assumptions of their class and society. Bernstein points out that because poor children's lives are organized around a family structure that is limited to playing only the traditional roles determined by age, class and gender, they develop restricted or particularistic code of meaning making. On the other hand, the family structure of the middle-class or upper-class children use elaborated or universalistic language code. Universalistic or elaborated language code is the language of the school. Therefore, middle-class and upper-class children are better able to participate in schools because their language is similar to that of the school. However, since poor children are not as competent in the language of the school, they often do poorly because they do not always understand what is expected of them. This explains why poor children in Africa often perform poorly in schools and why they are often led into vocational and blue-collar jobs.

Pierre Bourdieu went further than Bernstein's linguistic code to propound the concept of culture capital, which includes not only linguistic and social codes but also cultural background, knowledge and skills passed on from one generation to the next. Bourdieu argues that cultural capital differs according to the social class of individuals. Indeed, middle-class and upper-class cultural capital form the basis of formal education and the entire school curriculum, and therefore puts middle-class and upper-class students on the advantage. On the other hand, poor children's cultural capital puts them at a disadvantage in schools because their strengths are undervalued by the school system. In an extraordinary study of elites in Africa, Peter C. Lloyd concurs that "in Africa . . . the nature of the educational system, together with the great disparity in home conditions and parental attitudes to schooling, gives the elite parent a very good chance of ensuring that his/her children will enjoy the same status as him/herself."[32] In an empirical study conducted in Kenya and Tanzania, John B. Knight and Richard H. Sabot found that educational levels of parents influence the educational attainment of their children for the following reasons: educated parents are likely to make larger investments in their children's education; educated parents may transfer skills to their children; most of the educated in Africa live in areas where the quality of education is above average; out-of-school investment has the advantage of improving the quality of education.[33]

Finally, since educated parents generally earn more money they are much more able to make the financial commitments necessary for their children's education; and above all, children of educated elites have the cultural capital—familiarity with the metropolitan language that is needed to succeed in school. This is perhaps why Paulo Freire and Donaldo Macedo argue that educators should use native language for literacy in order to help students to appreciate their own culture. They conclude that "literacy [should] not be viewed as simply the development of skills aimed at acquiring the dominant standard language,"[34] but rather as cultural politics, which is those values that challenge dominant, oppressive values in society, or as Henry Giroux tells us, "Educators need a language that makes (students) sensitive to the politics of their own location."[35] Timothy Lintner argues that language must identify its own truth. In Africa, such truths have been identified by the language of others, but "language will never liberate if it is spoken by others to others."[36]

SEXISM AND EDUCATION IN AFRICA

Girls' education is severely limited in most parts of Africa. As such, there is a very wide educational gender gap between boys and girls in most of Africa. Also, in Africa girls are more likely than boys, to drop out of school and girls' academic performances are lower than those of boys.[37] Girls' education in Africa is constrained by a number of factors, including government policies and academic, socioeconomic, political and institutional factors. Other factors include poor student participation, high drop-out rate, class repetition, low morale, attendance, school effectiveness, teacher motivation, education management, resource mobilization and allocation of resources (see Table 7.1).

We will examine some of these factors in the remaining half of this chapter. The first factor is primarily related to government policy—lack of schools for girls. During the colonial period in Africa, girls/women were almost completely excluded from the educational process, and before 1960 only about 20 percent of girls attended school in Africa. Although enormous gains have been made, the gender gap in education

Table 7.1
Gross Enrollment Ratios by Gender and Level, Sub-Saharan Africa, 1970–1990

	Year				Average Annual % Chng		
	1970	1980	1985	1990	70–80	80–85	85–90
Primary enrollment (000's)	24,776	52,592	58,295	64,032	7.9	1.9	2.0
Female as % of total	39	43	45	45			
Gross primary enrollment ratio	46	78	75	70			
Male	56	88	83	77			
Female	36	68	67	63			
Secondary enrollment (000's)	2,694	9,243	12,528	14,571	13.2	6.1	3.2
Female as % of total	29	35	39	40			
Gross primary enrollment ratio	6	16	22	21			
Male	8	21	26	25			
Female	4	11	18	19			
Tertiary enrollment (000's)	189	419	819	1,219	8.1	15.4	7.1
Female as % of total	16	21	30	31			
Gross tertiary enrollment ratio	0.5	1.3	2.2	2.6			
Male	0.9	2.1	3.1	3.7			
Female	0.2	0.5	1.2	1.7			

Source: Association for the Development of Education in Africa. *Statistical Profile of Education in Sub-Saharan Africa*, 1994. Cited in Adhiambo Odaga and Ward Heneveld, *Girls and Schools in Sub-Saharan Africa: From Analysis to Action* (Washington, DC: The World Bank, 1995), 9.

in Africa still persists and is still alarming. Indeed, Adhiambo Odaga and Ward Heneveld argue that "significant gender gaps persist despite the growth in female enrollment ratios, widening as one goes up the education ladder."[38]

This gap widens more particularly at the secondary school level. A recent study conducted in the Ivory Coast indicated that girls were 37 percent less likely to attend secondary schools than boys.[39] However, those girls/women who enroll in colleges and universities are more likely to be concentrated in the areas of education, the arts and the humanities. Girls are least represented in math and the sciences. On the other hand, boys dominate math and the sciences. For example, a recent census in school enrollment in the Ivory Coast found that in all colleges and universities in that country, girls/women constitute 23.2 percent in literature, 13.2 percent in business, 12.2 percent in science and only 7.1 percent in math.[40] Lack of adequate representation of women in the sciences and math has the definite effect of limiting girls' career chances in engineering, medicine and in technical fields. In the parts of Africa where girls/women are able to obtain higher education, most of them are limited to career choices such as health care, education and teaching. B. Larson tells us why girls' education is not prized in Africa:

- the threat to female chastity;
- control over women's productive and reproductive labour;
- women's economic value in bride wealth and productive and reproductive activities;
- apprehension that educated girls will not make "controllable," "obedient" and "subservient" wives;
- the widely held belief that it is a waste of money to educate a girl who will leave home on marriage and not contribute to the maintenance of her natal home;
- limited relevance of formal education for girls;
- limited labour market opportunities available to educated girls; and
- the prohibitive costs of formal education.[41]

These remain restrictive factors in girls'/women's education in Africa. Studies done in Africa show that girls have higher repetition and dropout rates than boys. Indeed, a large percentage of girls who enter school do not complete (see Table 7.2). Girls also quite often do not perform as well in school because they are sometimes made to work for the survival of the family. Studies in Mozambique, Ethiopia and Kenya have shown this to be the case, and one of the authors of the studies notes that "particularly worrisome are the disparities in mathematics and the sciences."[42] In Ivory Coast, enrollment of girls in secondary schools stands at 30 percent and has been so for the past ten years. Repetition at the college and university levels are equally alarming. In the Cameroons, it takes a girl/woman 7.7 years to complete college in the arts, 8.9 years in law and economics and 18.2 years in the sciences. The repetition rate of girls/women in universities and colleges in Madagascar stands at 50 percent, and the dropout rate is about 20 percent.[43] At Makerere University in Uganda, while the dropout rate for boys/men is only 3 percent, that of girls/women stands at 20 percent.[44]

Part of the reason for the lack of interest in education by some girls and women in Africa emanate from unavailability of employment op-

Table 7.2
Gross Primary Enrollment Data for Selected Countries in Sub-Saharan Africa, 1960, 1970, 1980 and 1990

	1960		1970		1980		1990	
Country	*Male*	*Female*	*Male*	*Female*	*Male*	*Female*	*Male*	*Female*
Angola	23	11	98	53	187	163	95	87
Benin	38	15	57	23	87	41	81	41
Botswana	36	41	63	67	84	100	114	119
Burkina Faso	13	5	15	9	23	14	45	28
Burundi	33	10	36	18	32	21	79	66
Cameroon	77	37	105	78	107	89	109	93
Central African-R.	50	11	19	41	92	51	89	55
Chad	29	4	52	17	52	19	90	39
Congo	108	55	138	104	149	134	148	125
Côte d'Ivoire	59	25	75	43	95	63	83	58
Ethiopia	11	4	47	9	45	25	36	26
Gabon	67	41	175	158	158	154	174	166
Gambia	20	9	35	15	67	35	72	53
Ghana	60	32	71	54	89	71	84	69
Guinea	30	11	42	20	48	25	50	24
Guinea-Bissau	35	14	42	24	94	42	74	41
Kenya	64	30	72	52	120	110	97	93
Liberia	52	21	50	22	62	34	35	24
Madagascar	63	49	94	79	145	139	93	91
Malawi	50	26	46	26	72	48	76	62
Mali	13	5	29	16	34	19	30	17
Mauritania	11	2	21	8	47	26	58	43
Mauritius	97	90	97	95	98	98	104	108
Mozambique	64	39	51	27	114	84	76	57
Niger	8	3	18	9	33	18	37	21
Nigeria	54	31	46	27	118	90	82	63
Rwanda	69	30	78	61	66	60	72	70
Senegal	37	18	48	30	56	37	68	50
Sierra Leone	27	14	42	28	61	43	56	39
Somalia	10	3	9	3	24	14	13	7
Sudan	29	11	53	29	59	41	56	43

Table 7.2 (continued)

Country	1960		1970		1980		1990	
	Male	*Female*	*Male*	*Female*	*Male*	*Female*	*Male*	*Female*
Swaziland	58	57	91	83	104	103	109	107
Tanzania	33	16	41	26	99	86	69	68
Togo	64	25	99	44	146	91	134	87
Uganda	64	30	46	29	56	43	85	70
Zaire	80	29	120	70	108	77	81	60
Zambia	61	40	99	80	98	82	96	89
Zimbabwe	83	66	78	63	92	79	117	116

Source: Association for the Development of Education in Africa. *Statistical Profile of Education in Sub-Saharan Africa,* 1994. Cited in Adhiambo Odaga and Ward Heneveld, *Girls and Schools in Sub-Saharan Africa: From Analysis to Action* (Washington, DC: The World Bank, 1995), 77–78.

portunity for women. Indeed, it has been shown that only 38 percent of women in Africa are gainfully employed and most of these are in the agricultural sector. In the industrial sectors, women represent only 6 percent and are mostly employed at the lower end of the occupational hierarchy. In the public services, women are mostly involved in community, social and personnel matters. In Ghana, Rwanda and Togo women represent only about 1 percent of the bureaucrats and in Kenya and Uganda only about 3.5 percent.[45]

Another factor in the nonactive participation of girls in education is illiteracy. Illiteracy rate among African women is the highest in the world. Other factors have been identified as obstacles to girls'/women's education in Africa as well. First, because of the high cost of schooling, most parents cannot afford to send their girls to school. For example, the introduction of fees into Nigerian primary schools between 1982 and 1986 witnessed a drop in student enrollment from 92 percent to 75 percent. Most of those who dropped out at this time were girls. In the Cameroons where secondary schools are fee paying, girls are more adversely affected than boys (see Table 7.3). Second, studies conducted in Africa show that education is very prohibitive for girls. Education costs include tuition fees, registration fees, admission fees, examination fees, boarding fees, parent-teacher association fee, books, uniforms, furniture, transportation and tutorial fees. Because of the high cost, when decisions have to be made because of financial constraints, girls are more likely than boys to be held back or withdrawn from school."[46] It has also been

Table 7.3
Field of Study, Females as a Percentage of Total Secondary Enrollment, Selected Sub-Saharan Countries, 1980 and 1990

	General Education		Teacher Training		Vocational/Technical	
Country	1980	1990	1980	1990	1980	1990
Benin	26.2	28.1	25.1	34.7	33.8	39.9
Botswana	56.1	53.3	82.9	71.6	25.1	27.2
Burkina Faso	32.6	33.2	23.0	11.4	39.7	49.4
Cameroon	33.9	41.5	36.3	55.0	39.1	41.5
Congo	40.1	43.0	25.2	37.2	54.0	55.5
Ethiopia	35.6	42.6	28.4	23.1	35.0	19.0
Ghana	38.5	38.8	40.5	45.5	24.8	22.8
Guinea	27.7	23.4	13.5	47.7	43.9	26.9
Kenya	41.0	43.7	40.2	43.8	30.0	24.0
Mali	29.1	33.4	23.7	19.4	31.3	26.5
Mauritania	21.2	30.8	19.3	30.0	7.3	20.5
Niger	29.5	29.4	28.7	41.9	8.4	8.8
Nigeria	35.5	42.6	35.9	43.9	17.0	44.9
Senegal	33.7	33.7	32.3	18.1	24.7	29.9
Sudan	37.5	44.3	42.9	54.0	21.2	22.0
Swaziland	49.0	50.0	77.0	80.0	32.6	33.1
Zaire	28.0	30.3	27.2	32.4	24.4	35.6
Zambia	34.8	37.3	46.8	44.9	26.3	22.5

Source: Association for the Development of Education in Africa. *Statistical Profile of Education in Sub-Saharan Africa*, 1994. Cited in Adhiambo Odaga and Ward Heneveld, *Girls and Schools in Sub-Saharan Africa: From Analysis to Action* (Washington, DC: The World Bank, 1995), 79.

shown that girls who live in urban areas do better academically and stay in school longer than those from the rural areas.

In many African homes, marriage for girls is a source of income for the family through bride price. Therefore the need for additional household income often takes precedence over girls' education in some homes in Africa. Some families believe that boys are more intelligent than girls and as such boys make better educational investments than girls. Boys are also favored when investment decisions are made because they are the primary inheritors of family assets. Indeed, some parents do not want to make any investments in their daughters because they will eventually get married and move to another family. As we know, formal education in Africa is linked directly to employment prospects, and given the perennial discrimination against girls/women in employment in Africa, it therefore stands to reason in some families that girls' education is not a profitable investment. Girls are often directed toward trades like sewing, trading and hairdressing where there are better prospects for employment. The perception of girls as future mothers and wives adds to the parents' disincentive to educate their daughters. Also, in most Islamic countries in Africa, Western education is still associated with Christianity. Parents prefer that their daughters receive Islamic education and avoid Western education because Western education is perceived as an endorser of a revised indigenous culture. In Guinea, religion has been cited as the main reason why some villagers have refused to send their daughters to school. They believe that girls only need to learn prayers. Indeed, according to orthodox Islamic doctrine, women can never become scholars.

Studies have also shown that sexual harassment is a serious matter in schools in Africa. This was epitomized by one very serious incident in Kenya in July 1991 where male schoolmates staged a mass rape on girls at the St. Kizito Mixed Secondary School—seventy-five students were injured and nineteen others died. In a recent study conducted about sexual harassment in schools and universities in Africa, the researcher concluded that "there is a pandemic of sexual violence and harassment in educational institutions in Africa."[47] Boys, teachers and even law enforcement officers sometimes prey on girls, and because of this, some girls face very uncomfortable and, at times, hostile learning environments. A study in Tanzania showed that sexual harassment was sometimes responsible for some girls' poor performances in schools, and a good number of girls have been known even to leave school because of sexual harassment.[48]

Finally, studies in Ethiopia, Gambia, Guinea, Kenya, Mali, Sierra Leone, Tanzania and Zimbabwe have revealed that some girls leave school because of the long distance covered to school and parents' apprehension about the sexual safety of their children in these long journeys to school. In Ethiopia, for example, students travel more than 20 kilometers to and from school.[49] In a survey of school children in Freetown, Sierra Leone, students voiced serious concerns about the long distances they have to travel to and from school.

TEACHERS' BEHAVIOR TOWARD GIRLS

Evidence in the research literature shows that both male and female teachers in the Cameroons, Sierra Leone, Malawi, Guinea and Rwanda admit that they prefer to teach boys more than girls and that they devote more attention to boys than girls.[50] There is also a strong bias in favor

Table 7.4
Field of Study, Females as a Percentage of Total Tertiary Enrollment, Selected Sub-Saharan Countries, 1990

Country	Arts	Sciences
Angola	9	34
Benin	14	11
Burkina Faso	28	11
Burundi	33	19
Cameroon	11	14
Congo	19	14
Ethiopia	23	10
Ghana	29	14
Madagascar	51	36
Mali	15	12
South Africa	68	45
Swaziland	52	27
Uganda	32	13
Zimbabwe	1	1

Source: Association for the Development of Education in Africa. *Statistical Profile of Education in Sub-Saharan Africa,* 1994. Cited in Adhiambo Odaga and Ward Heneveld, *Girls and Schools in Sub-Saharan Africa: From Analysis to Action* (Washington, DC: The World Bank, 1995).

of boys in teaching materials and the curricula in Africa. In addition to the limited number of options open to girls within the educational system, teachers and schools emphasize subjects leading to traditional gender roles for girls, that is, literature for girls and the sciences for boys. As some recent authors have stated, "Girls also tend to opt for subjects that steer them into education, health and administrative support employment (see Table 7.4). This further limits options open to women in the formal labor market as women continue to remain concentrated in non-competitive fields."[51] Indeed, research findings conducted in Gambia, Kenya, Ghana, Ivory Coast, Liberia, Uganda, Mozambique, Tanzania, Senegal, Benin, Zaire, Egypt and the Sudan all support the fact that women are still depicted in nurturing and passive roles while men are depicted in brave and active roles. These have caused Adhiambo Odaga and Ward Heneveld to conclude that "textbooks, teachers and learning materials perpetuate a stereotypical and erroneous view that women's contributions to the economy are marginal."[52]

8

Education in the Service of Apartheid in South Africa, 1802–1993

During the seventeenth century education was not provided for either the settlers' children or for the children of the indigenes by the Dutch who controlled the Cape region in South Africa at that time. Later, efforts by Dutch missionaries to provide a modicum of education were limited to teaching converts to read the Bible. However, the coming of the British to South Africa marked the first systematic effort at providing education for the populace. In 1812, the British began to establish free schools with English as the only medium of instruction. In an effort to anglicanize the Afrikaners, the British passed the Cape Education Act in 1866 in which the use of English was made compulsory for all the first- and second-class schools.

Beginning in 1853, the British government started to invest in education for the poor through the provision of resources to the mission societies for the "purpose of furthering education of the poorer classes, including Africans."[1] At this time, many of the schools were mixed and served blacks, whites and colored alike. These mission schools indeed had no color bar. But with the discovery of diamonds in Kimberley in 1867 and gold on the Witwatersrand in 1886, the social, economic and political landscape of South Africa was changed dramatically and remained so for many years. Competition for the vast economic resources in South Africa led to the institutionalization of color stratification in South Africa. The first instrument used here to conquer Africans was education. Whites began to advocate inferior education for Africans because they knew "an uneducated man ... can be exploited as an economic asset"[2] and for the purpose of protecting poor whites. When Cecil John Rhodes arrived in South Africa in 1870, he quickly began to formulate his philosophy aimed at disenfranchising Africans. As the prime minister of the Cape Province, Cecil Rhodes argued in 1896 that "the Natives are like children. They are just emerging from barbarism. If I may venture a comparison, I should compare Natives with regard to European civilization to the tribes of the Druids. I think that we have been extremely liberal in granting barbarism forty or fifty years of training what we ourselves obtained only after many hundreds of civilization."[3] Following the lead of Cecil Rhodes, whites began to advocate for separate schools. In 1892, a different set of public schools was started in the Cape Province for whites. This made it unnecessary for whites to patronize the mixed schools founded by missionaries. Starting from this point, "clear stratification emerged, based on ethnic competition and vested interest," and "education [became] a tool in institutionalizing the new order."[4] To further retard the progress of Africans and advance the cause of the white minority, the British government withdrew all support for black schools. Between 1910 and 1980 very little financial support was given by the government for the education of Africans. And as noted by Walton R. Johnson, "education was a tool in institutionalizing the new order."[5] For instance, while education was used to prepare whites for leadership in the new economy, it was used to limit African children's preparedness to compete in the marketplace. Indeed, educational expenditure for white children increased by 263 percent between 1910 and 1948, and by 1910 South Africa spent five times more for the education of a white child than a black child. The teacher-student ratio stood at 1:15 for whites and 1:42 among blacks.[6] While black children were and still are schooled in poorly constructed buildings that are very overcrowded, the white schools have very up-to-date facilities that are even underutilized. The preparation given to black teachers is at best mediocre.[7] This lends weight to the poor quality of instruction in black schools. It is therefore no surprise that the failure rate among black students stands at about 50 percent. Accordingly, a very small percentage of blacks graduate from high school and go on to college. The lack of serious attention paid to black education has resulted in very "high attrition rates; high failure rates; high illiteracy rates and a general alienation from the schooling process among blacks."[8] In 1936, the Interdepartmental Committee on Native Education reported that about 70 percent of black children of school age did not attend school at all, due largely to a shortage of facilities. The report noted that many of the black schools were as overcrowded as they were understaffed. The report ended with the pronouncement that "the education of the White child prepares him for life in a dominant society and the education of the black child for a subordinate society."⁹

When the National Party came to power in 1948 in South Africa, it legitimized apartheid and quickly legislated inferior schools for Africans in 1953, coloreds in 1963 and Indians in 1965. In its manifesto for Christian National Education (CNE) published by the National Party in February 1948, the party stated, "Native education should be based on the principles of trusteeship, non-equality and segregation; its aim should be to inculcate the white man's way of life, especially that of the Boer nation, which is the senior trustee."¹⁰ Almost immediately after the National Party came to power in South Africa, it restructured white education, but prescribed for Africans "the formulation of the principles and aims of education for Natives as an independent race, in which their past and present, their inherent racial qualities, their distinctive characteristics and aptitude, and their needs under ever changing social conditions are taken into consideration."¹¹ From this time on, South Africa was on a path of a "social order predicated on legally sanctioned racial privileges."¹² Education became a means of social control by transmitting myths, norms and ideology that enhanced the theory of apartheid, and for Africans, education was to produce the "hewers of woods and drawers of water."¹³

In 1953, South Africa enacted the Bantu Education Act. Hendrik Verwoerd, then minister of Bantu affairs, explained to parliament the purpose of Bantu education in the following words: "Native education must be controlled in such a way that it should be in accord with the policy of the state. If the Native is being taught to expect that he will live his adult life under a policy of equal rights, he is making a big mistake. The native who attends school must know that he must be the laborer in the country."¹⁴ Indeed, in a speech in 1953 to Parliament, Hendrik Verwoerd outlined the aims of Bantu Education and stated the following: "Bantu Education would restructure the conditions of social reproduction of the black working class and create conditions for stabilizing a black urban underclass of semiskilled laborers."¹⁵ A couple of months after his address to Parliament, Verwoerd opined: "There is no place for (the black South African) in the European Community above the level of certain forms of labor . . . it is of no avail for him to receive a training which has as its aim absorption in the European community."¹⁶ It was Verwoerd who also said, "Education must train and teach people in accordance with their opportunities in life, according to the spheres in which they live."¹⁷ In order to protect white privileges, whites in South Africa provided African children with a racially skewed type of education that reinforced tribal identity, political subservience and distorted ideological contents. The Bantu Education Act of 1953 centralized education for all African children. It made it illegal for anyone to establish schools for blacks, and it reduced funding to black schools to the 1922 level.

The guiding philosophy for apartheid education was fundamental pedagogics formulated as a Manifesto in February 1948 for CNE in South Africa. Fundamental pedagogics provided legitimacy for apartheid in South Africa by stating that "different ethnolinguistic, cultural, and racial groups have different 'philosophies of life' and 'world-views' . . . and therefore should not have equal education."[18] By this statement, fundamental pedagogics provided justification for racist and separate schools in South Africa, and therefore formed the ideological foundation for apartheid. It provided scientific justification for racism and separate educational practices in South Africa.

Education in South Africa did not only help to perpetuate apartheid, but its contents reflected, supported and legitimized ethnically based stratification system. Indeed, in a review of textbooks from South Africa, du Preez identified numerous master symbols such as:

1. legitimate authority is not to be questioned;
2. whites are superior, blacks are inferior;
3. the Afrikaner has a special relationship with God;
4. South Africa rightly belongs to the Afrikaner;
5. South Africa is an agricultural country;
6. South Africa is an afflicted country;
7. South Africa and the Afrikaner are isolated;
8. the Afrikaner is militarily ingenious and strong;
9. the Afrikaner is threatened;
10. world opinion is important to South Africa;
11. South Africa is the leader in Africa; and
12. the Afrikaner has a God-given task in Africa.[19]

According to Mokubung Nkomo the aims of apartheid education were:

1. To produce a semi-skilled black labor force to minister to the needs of the capitalist economy at the lowest possible cost, and earlier on, especially after the introduction of the Bantu Education Act, the Colored Peoples' Act, and the Indian Peoples' Act, it was intended to blunt competition with white workers.
2. To socialize black students so that they can accept the social relations of apartheid as natural. That is, to accept the supposed superiority of whites and their own "inferiority."

3. To forge a consciousness and identity accompanied by a sense of "superiority" among whites.
4. To promote the acceptance of racial or ethnic separation as the "natural order of things", or as an arrangement better suited for "South Africa's complex problems of national minorities that can only be solved through the separation of the races or ethnic groups."
5. To promote black intellectual underdevelopment by minimizing the allocation of educational resources for blacks while maximizing them for whites.[20]

In 1967, the National Education Policy Act was issued, and it reaffirmed the policy of providing poor schools for black children. This policy halted the expansion of secondary schools in urban areas; barred parents who had no urban rights from sending their children to urban schools; stagnated technical education in urban areas; provided inadequate and poor training for teachers in urban schools and decreed the total exclusion of private funds for urban schools. These policies affected blacks adversely because, without adequate education, most Africans were forced to accept only menial jobs in South Africa. Indeed, in 1979, the Rickert Commission reported that 40 percent of all the male adult labor force in the urban areas in South Africa were functionally illiterate. In the rural areas, the percentage rose to 65.[21] As a recent author has written, many years after "Bantu Education, it was clear that the majority of African children in White farming areas are not receiving any education worthy of the name. . . . Most of these children, when they grow up, will thus be unfit for anything but farm labour."[22] Education in South Africa was used not only to indoctrinate, but also for the purpose of socialization and social control. Indeed, it was used to indoctrinate South African children with myths in order to perpetuate the apartheid policy.

TEACHERS AND APARTHEID IN SOUTH AFRICA

There is a popular adage that states that if you want to change the world, indoctrinate the teachers. An important means of perpetuating the apartheid philosophical ideology was through the control of teacher education in South Africa. Indeed, as one author has noted, education was the backbone of apartheid in South Africa. First and foremost, teachers were made to affirm and reproduce apartheid doctrine of segregation, unequal schools and to educate African children in "accordance with their assigned opportunities in life." As schools increasingly became instruments of social control, teachers were at the center of it all. Penny Enslin makes this point:

Black teachers find themselves located at a conjuncture within South African society which makes them both individually vulnerable and, collectively, potentially vital agents in the process of transforming the country. Within the schooling system, they are required to execute the aims of segregated, unequal schooling, preparing their students to take up their places in apartheid society. They often find themselves caught between the demands of militant students on the one hand and an authoritarian, bureaucratic schooling apparatus on the other. Politically active teachers may be arbitrarily dismissed or transferred far from the communities they wish to serve. Their daily professional lives are conducted in conditions which they know to be inferior to, and most stressful than, those in which their white counterparts work. White teachers in their turn, working under more comfortable but undemocratic conditions, have tended to play a pivotal role in the apparatus which reproduces apartheid society and its attendant inequalities.[23]

Mark Mathabane, a black South African, gives us an eye witness account of schooling under the apartheid regime in South Africa and states:

Segregation in South African society was so complete that the quality of education a child received depended strictly upon his race. Whites had the best schools, where, as part of the curriculum, they were indoctrinated about the necessity for racial purity; the divine mission of the white race in South Africa; the need to keep blacks subservient; and the Afrikaners' version of Christianity, which maintained, among other absurdities, that integration and equality were communist ideas which could be combated effectively only by a complete obedience to authority, a deep religious faith, and a literal interpretation of the Bible.[24]

From the above quotation we can see that schools in South Africa, instead of helping students to think critically, became a means of social control. This exemplifies and also reminds us of "power knowledge" relations enunciated by Michel Foucault, which according to him, can cause us to become subjects.

9

Education of Most Worth for Africa in the Twenty-First Century

A NEED TO RECONCEPTUALIZE THE PHILOSOPHY AND PURPOSE OF EDUCATION

As I have stated elsewhere in this book, Western education in Africa was a colonial legacy. As a colonial legacy, the colonial masters were interested in producing semiskilled workers who would minister to their capitalist economic interests. Education was designed to socialize Africans into accepting the supposed superiority of whites and the inferiority of blacks, and to advance the exploitation of Africans. With time, the colonial schools began to produce those that Paulo Freire and Donaldo Macedo call a "petit-bourgeois class of functionaries who had internalized the belief that they had become 'white' or 'black with white souls,' and were therefore superior to African peasants."[1]

During the later periods of colonialism, Africans began to hanker after a European-type education to enable them to fill the exploitative shoes of the departing Europeans, for, as Philip Foster has argued, "subordinate castes will normally attempt to emulate the social characteristics of the dominant caste." "In the case of Western education," Foster continues, "this emulation would appear to have been based on eminently realistic perceptions of the power structure of the colonial period."[2] He concludes, "Where Africans were involved with the European elite in an admittedly unequal competition for the highest rungs of the occupational ladder, access to these posts was determined by their ability to hold equivalent or often superior qualifications."[3] As a consequence, Africans demanded mostly the type of education that would qualify them for and enhance their entry into the government bureaucracies. As one author has stated, African educated elites are very much entrenched in the bureaucracy. African bureaucracies, however, are also very much characterized by corruption, nepotism, selfseeking and inefficiency.[4] Studies by eminent scholars have confirmed that corruption in public services in Africa has been institutionalized and is universal.[5] It seems to be the thinking that Africans obtain an education in order to enter the government bureaucracy so as to be able to share the wealth of the nation rather than create wealth for the nation. In other words, Western education is perceived by many as the quickest route to fame and wealth in Africa. Indeed, as one Nigerian wrote, "Those who had savings spent them to send their children to schools and colleges, because they saw that only salaried people were secure even in spite of salary cuts and stabilization. ... It was then that I began to look at education as a commodity that does not fall in price."[6]

Although some African governments had begun to perceive the shortcomings of the type of education bequeathed to them, in every case, they made the wrong diagnosis and therefore provided the wrong remedies. In the first place, most of the commissions on this matter reported that the problem was with the literary content of colonial education. Hence, these commissions conceived the development of technical education as the panacea that would usher in the much-longed-for divine event leading to a millennium of economic and technological development. For instance, the government of Eastern Nigeria in its policy paper on education since 1954 noted: "The colonial type of education ... did not adequately meet the needs of the country.... The result is that manual, agricultural and technical education have come to be associated with inferior status and to be accorded low instead of high regard in the scheme of things."[7] The report went on to state that "we must now evolve a policy, a system of education which will produce men and women who will not be out of place in a technological age ... a system which will feed our industries with personnel."[8]

During the 1970s and 1980s numerous innovations were introduced into the educational systems of various African countries including, (1) the introduction of work experience into primary and secondary school curricula, (2) integration of adults and children into a more flexible system of education, (3) vocationalization of the curriculum at the secondary school level, (4) introduction of a mandatory period of labor market experience between secondary and higher education, and (5) recruitment of dropouts from the educational system into a national youth employment service. The fact is that even with the introduction of these innovations and with the introduction of vocational and technical education, things have not drastically changed in Africa because the purpose of education for most Africans has not fundamentally changed since the colonial days—it is still considered by many as footpaths into the civil service and as avenues for plundering the wealth of the nation. This is to say, Western education remains a form of credentializing for the civil service. Indeed, Victor Uchendu argues, "Education [in Africa] is more than an instrument of national development. In post-colonial [African] societies it is the single most important national institution that allocates present and future societal privileges because of its critical role in the social structure."[9] Uchendu goes on to state that "the disparity in educational opportunities between the rural areas and the urban centers, between the areas of missionary activities and those that lacked them, and between geographic and ethnic groups in any African country is great enough and, not surprisingly, poses political problems."[10] The question is, why should the acquisition of Western education or lack of it pose political problems in Africa? The answer is very simple: Education is a means through which the national treasury is plundered. In an in-depth study of Tanzania and Kenya, David Court reports that:

At Independence ... the immediate perceived need was that of producing the technologists and administrators to replace departing expatriates. Given this perception it is likely that the new elite would take over not only existing positions but also their underpinning normative structure, defining relationships between education, wages and occupations as well as their associated rewards and lifestyle. Equally inevitable was the consequence that access to these rewards would become the measure of popular aspiration in defiance of economic realities.[11]

Similarly, Michael Omolewa points out that "many Nigerians from poor homes ... began to study for the London University Examinations to provide for themselves an opportunity to advance in political and social stature and material wealth."[12] The reason Western education is at the heart of almost all internal political crises in Africa today is because it poses the divide between the haves and the have-nots. Indeed, David B. Abernethy maintains that "the uneven spread of mission schools, by creating objective differences between various ethnic groups, stimulated rivalry between them." He goes on to argue that "insofar as mission patterns of advance gave certain ethnic groups an educational head start over others, the missionaries unintentionally contributed to the ethnic rivalries in Africa."[13] This means that, in Africa, education is not only a means of social, political and economic reward, but also a powder keg or megaton bomb. Victor P. Diejomaoh explains the Nigerian civil crises of 1966 in this way: "The communal riots in the North in September and October of 1966, in which numerous Ibos as well as other Southerners such as Yorubas, Edos, and Efiks were killed and forced to flee the North, were a reaction of Northerners against economic domination by Southerners. These Southerners were able to entrench themselves in a dominating position in the North largely by dint of their relatively higher levels of educational attainment."[14] Diejomaoh states very categorically that:

an examination of partial economic indices, such as per capita levels of human resource development, government expenditures and revenues, provision of health and transport facilities, and export levels, show quite clearly the differential in per capita income levels between the North and the South. While per capita income differentials are traceable to a large number of factors, differentials in the level of modern educational attainments between the North and South are largely responsible for the differentials in per capita incomes of Northern and Southern Nigeria.[15]

People in Africa perceive education as a preparation for the civil service. Indeed, as extensive studies in Africa have shown, the overwhelming majority of educated elites in Africa are in bureaucratic employment. Commerce, industry and private enterprise have almost no attraction for the educated African. This being the case, it should be made clear to students in Africa that education is not just a preparation for a career in the civil service or the bureaucracy, but a preparation for life. Education attempts to develop the talents in each and everyone of us. Such talents should be used to create, invent, invest and venture into the unknown. Our larger goal here is to produce citizens who will invest in the nation by creating wealth for the nation, rather than plunder the people's treasury. If this objective is accepted and pursued, then conflicts that often occur because of the underrepresentation of certain groups in the bureaucracy would be a thing of the past, for we would have defined the purpose of our education differently. In other words, education will no more be a means of credentialization that offers great rewards for a few at the people's expense, but poverty and failure for the many. Education would be seen as self-enhancement for the benefit of all. This means education will become a preparation for service to and for the upliftment of the community, not through handouts, but through investment in the economic, social and intellectual needs of the people. It is only then that education will become a true investment in human capital in Africa. Western education is the megaton bomb it is today in Africa because of the uneven acquisition of education between ethnic groups and regions. "These imbalances often translate into underrepresentation of certain groups in the state bureaucracies," and by implication, unequal distribution of national resources in favor of those who have academic qualifications because education in Africa is defined mainly as a preparation for government bureaucracy.

Education is viewed as a preparation for sharing national wealth rather than a preparation for creating national wealth. In Nigeria, for example, the Northern politicians were reticent about attaining independence because they feared that "administrative power would be monopolized by Southerners because of their long-standing educational lead." Sir Alhaji Ahmadu Bello, the Sardauna of Sokoto, made this point even better when he wrote:

As things were at that time [the early 1950's], if the gates to the departments were to be opened, the Southern Regions had a huge pool from which they could find suitable people, while we had hardly anyone. In the resulting scramble it would, we were convinced, be inevitable that the Southern applicants would get almost all the posts available. Once you get a Government post you are hard indeed to shift.... [This] was a matter of life and death to us.... If the British Administration had failed to give us the even development that we deserved and for which we craved so much—and they were on the whole a very fair administration—what had we to hope from an African Administration, probably in the hands of a hostile party. The answer to our minds was, quite simply, just nothing, beyond a little window dressing.[16]

Similarly, at the budget session of the Nigerian Legislative Council in 1948, Mallam Abubakar Tafawa Balewa, who led the Northern delegation, argued that "under self-government in a United Nigeria the North would furnish only the (menial) labor." Balewa's sentiments were shared by many in the north. For example, the editor of the paper *Gaskiya Ta Fi Kwabo* once editorized that if self-government is given:

Southerners will take the places of the Europeans in the North. What is there to stop them? They look and see it is thus at the present time. There are Europeans but, undoubtedly, it is the Southerner who has the power in the North. They have control of the railway stations; of the Post Offices; of Government Hospitals, of the canteens; the majority employed in the Kaduna Secretariat and in the Public Works Department are all Southerners; in all the different departments of Government it is the Southerner who has the power.[17]

In saying this, I do not want to minimize the importance of formal education and I am by no means suggesting, nor do I wish to be understood as saying that Western education is bad in and of itself. However, I want to argue that schooling in and of itself will not lead Africa to the economic promised land because schools are only good at confirming, reinforcing and extending attitudes that already exit in society. This means that schools simply canonize beliefs and tendencies which are strongly held by individuals in a given society. For example, in most of Africa, opposition to colonial rule provided the driving force for schools to act as catalysts and as think tanks for liberation movements. A. R. Thompson makes the point very clearly when he notes: "The school is a potent influence for national unity where the general trend is in favor of unity, but where it is not and where factors for disunity are strong and active, common schooling may not be strong to counter them."[18] Thompson goes on to explain that the purpose of education is to broaden horizons and heighten motivations that already exist in society.

Education provides individuals familiarity with modern concepts and institutions to enable them to carry out their grand designs. For example:

When an educated farmer settles down to farming, when he develops some commitment, and abandons the off-farm preoccupation . . . he is likely to be a more aggressively innovative farmer. There is evidence that such a farmer is somewhat more likely to seek out useful knowledge more aggressively from other agencies and institutions where it is available. There is also evidence that he is likely to use modern farming inputs more intensively and, in general, be more commercially oriented.[19]

Similarly, it is important to point out that in order for an individual to participate usefully in the development process, he or she should not only receive a just share of the national wealth but he or she should earn that share and most importantly must contribute to the creation of that wealth. It is only then that an individual can participate in the development process and only through such participation that effective development can be achieved. Indeed, in the late nineteenth century William Harris, United States Commissioner of Education, 1889–1906, had stated that it was important that "each person pursues his separate calling, assured that what he produces shall go to the market place and be added to the aggregate wealth of the community, and from thence be redistributed to all so that he shall receive his share of his own labor of humanity."[20] The Director of UNESCO once made a similar point as follows:

development can only come from within. It must be endogenous, thought out by people for themselves, springing from the soil on which they live and attuned to their aspirations, the conditions of their natural environment, the resources at their disposal and the particular genius of their culture. . . . Education should accordingly contribute to the promotion of such endogenous development.[21]

This type of thinking must permeate the psyche of Africans. However, due to unfortunate circumstances of acculturation occasioned by many years of colonialism, most African-educated elites do not think in terms of using their education to create national wealths (human and material), but rather they think mostly of sharing or presiding over the sharing of such wealth following after colonial models in Africa. In contemporary Nigerian politics, for example, the slogan is power shift, which is another way of saying, we want a shift of paradigm rather than a shift in the way things are perceived and done. What, we may ask, can we do to solve this problem of colonial mind-set in Africa? My answer is that we must use our schools for psychic conversion of Africans in favor of economic investment, wealth creation, entrepreneurial spirit, self-help and for creating wealth for the nation. As President Julius Nyerere once stated:

[P]eople cannot be developed. They can only develop themselves. For while it is possible for an outsider to build a man's house, an outsider cannot give a man pride and self confidence in himself as a human being. Those things a man has to create in himself by his own actions. He develops himself by what he does; he develops himself by making his own decisions, by increasing his understanding of what he is doing and why; by increasing his own knowledge and ability, and by his own full participation—as an equal—in the life of the community he lives in. Thus for example, a man is developing himself when he grows or earns enough to provide decent conditions for himself and his family; he is not being developed if someone gives him these things.[22]

What I am arguing here is that the purpose of formal education in Africa must be reconceptualized to shake off its colonial groove. I venture to reconceptualize the purpose and philosophy of such an education in Africa by saying that education should emphasize the following objectives: democracy and "critical consciousness with a vision of creating wealth for a nation." If only to elaborate on the last objective first, education for "critical consciousness with a vision of creating wealth for a nation" is the type of education that prepares the individual for self sufficiency, risk taking, adventure and for creating opportunities for others where none existed. The slogan here should be creating something or opportunities out of nothing, for as John Dewey once said, "Never in the life of farmer, sailor, merchant, physician, or laboratory experimenter does knowledge mean primarily a store of information aloof from doing."[23]

In the type of education I envision, Richard Kearney suggests that teachers should develop a "pedagogical language that emphasizes the importance of being able to identify with others, to empathize with their thoughts and feelings and to develop the capacity for ethical respect."[24] As a starting point, Henry Giroux recommends that educators should develop an emancipatory theory of leadership that should begin with the task of "creating a public language that is not only theoretically rigorous, publicly accessible and ethically grounded, but also speaks to a sense of utopian purpose."[25] In other words, Giroux argues that public education should provide the "principles and practices of democracy, but not in a version of democracy cleansed of vision, possibility or struggle."[26] Education in this context must be emancipatory, that is, provide the type of pedagogy that challenges oppression, kleptocracy and exploitation in any form in Africa. This means we need educational and national leaders who would defend "schools as democratic public spheres responsible for providing an indispensable public service to the nation; a language, in this case, that is capable of awakening the moral, [economic], political and civic responsibilities of our youth."[27] What I am advocating here is a change in behavior and consciousness from kleptomania to constructive engagement in the destiny of the nation by creating social and economic opportunities for the less fortunate. This means we must inculcate in students in Africa that those who study agriculture, for example, should do so in the hope of opening their own farms, engineers should desire their own small industries, business students should hope to open their own mercantile houses, artists and painters their own studios and so on, where the less fortunate could be employed. The civil service should be only a point of last resort. Education should empower the individual to create new ideas as well as new economic opportunities. The modifications in African educational purpose that I have proposed here are attributable to the present economic crises in Africa. Economic stresses and strains, as we know, have always played a part in education, and as H. F. Makulu has pointed out, "education should be an instrument for change, preparing people for any necessary adjustment to new social, political and economic forms." Henry Giroux states that "schools . . . need to inspire their students, by example, to find ways to get involved, to make a difference."[28]

Critics may wonder what a discourse based on Western Marxist philosophy has to do with "consciousness with a vision of creating wealth for a nation." My response is that critical theory has always emphasized consciousness of the society in relation to the economy. Today, in advanced industrial societies, this consciousness is focused on exploitation, oppression, racism, sexism and hegemony. In Africa, the focus is on raising people's consciousness to the dangers of totalitarianism, oppression, exploitation, sexism and, of course, enhancement of economic empowerment. Indeed, as Paulo Freire had stated, in order to transform the world, there must be reflection and action because the mere perception of reality not followed by critical intervention cannot lead to transformation of objective reality. Freire reminds us that thoughts have meaning only if generated by action. In this instance, African children should not only dream dreams, they must explore and act on those dreams for the betterment of society, for as William Harris, the United States Secretary of Education (1889–1906) once asserted, an individual should serve the state or social whole—giving up his strength at all events in plying a vocation whose products shall be for the social good. In other words, schools should be cultural, social, economic and political transformation sites because education, according to Ernest N. Emenyonu, is a powerful instrument for social reconstruction. But education can also mar a nation if it is poorly construed. As an investment in human capital, "its end products determine the nature and quality of life in the society,"[29] but if it is poorly construed the system will "produce 'weaklings' and individuals without solid roots." Emenyonu goes on to argue that "if education at the top is purposeless, so will the learner, at the end of the educational process, become a nuisance to the society and a liability even to himself. An educational system must be purposeful so that its products can be functional members of society."[30] He goes on to state, "When an educational process is misconceived, the consequences are socio-economic chaos, political instability, cultural indecorum and moral indiscipline and laxity."[31] He concludes, "When the goals of education are unclear or misguided, the learners become unmotivated and schooling becomes boring and mere drudgery."[32] Indeed, Dr. M. I. Okpara, the premier of Eastern Nigeria once said: "Education is . . . the main-spring of all national action. Unless it is right and purposeful the people either crawl or limp along."[33]

In Africa, our purpose should be harnessing the language of critique with the language of economic empowerment. Africans must move away from education for the civil service and self to education for the nation and all. This is the type of education in which its beneficiaries are willing to invent, take risks and invest for the economic betterment of the nation, and where the government would only be required to provide the infrastructure and defend and educate its citizens. This type of education can only thrive in a democracy. This means our educational system must prepare individuals to participate in a democracy.

What is democracy? Democracy is a system of government that operates under the following principles: liberty, equality and fraternity. Liberty refers to individual rights and responsibilities. The concept of equality includes fairness to all on the basis that all people are created equal; and fraternity deals with cooperation. The question is, what has education to do with democracy? Education has everything to do with democracy because, in the words of Thomas Jefferson, "education is a sine qua non of a truly viable democracy." In a letter to George Washington in 1786, Thomas Jefferson wrote: "It is an axiom of my mind that our liberty can never be safe but in the hands of the people themselves, and that too of the people with a certain degree of instruction."[34] In a bill he submitted to the Virginia legislature that Jefferson titled "Bill for the More General Diffusion of Knowledge," he stated, "Experience has shown that even under the best forms [of government], those entrusted with power have, in time, and by slow operations, perverted it into tyranny and it is believed that the most effective means of preventing this would be to illuminate, as far as practicable, the minds of the people at large."[35] By the middle of the nineteenth century, faith in American schools was already yielding fruitful results. In 1886, Andrew Carnegie, in his book *Triumphant Democracy*, bragged that America surpassed the countries of Europe in agriculture, commerce and industry. Carnegie attributed America's greatness to its schools. He wrote: "The free common school system of the land is, probably after all, the greatest single power in the unifying powers which produce the American race."[36] Schools should promote the ideals of democracy and effective teachers should emphasize democratic ideals in their classrooms. In such classrooms students should:

- enjoy and exercise freedom of speech, and accept the obligation to show respect for the rights of others.
- know and be committed to the steps of due process prior to the deprivation of life, liberty, property, and/or the pursuit of happiness.
- be knowledgeable and conversant about societal issues (i.e., environmental, ethical, social, economic, cultural, political) at the local, state/provincial, and federal levels.
- practice and communicate the acceptance of the equality of all humans.
- know how to reason well, consider various perspectives, test ideas, and develop informed opinions.
- demonstrate cooperative responsibilities by working with others.[37]

THEORY AND PRACTICE OF WESTERN EDUCATION: PAST AND PRESENT

In Africa, schools are characterized by domination and hegemony. This is to say, African schools display relationships of domination that are extensively played out between students and teachers. In schools in Africa, "students are confined to places where they are told, and too often accept that someone else knows what is good for them, where someone else controls their lives and daily choices, and where their voices are patronized or ignored."[38] Domination in schools in Africa is very clearly displayed in the relationship between students and teachers in the teaching-learning process. For example, students are compelled to sit in rows and columns in classrooms listening to teachers recite notes for endless hours. Students are compelled to accept these arrangements no matter how unpalatable they may be to them because students are often told that it is for their own good. Furthermore, education in Africa is authoritarian and domesticating; it focuses on obedience, socialization, and on silencing students' voices. Paulo Freire calls this type of education "banking education." He defines banking education as one in which "the teacher teaches and the students are taught; the teacher knows everything and the students know nothing; the teacher thinks and the students are thought about; the teacher talks and the students listen meekly."[39] According to Freire, banking education mythologizes reality so as to conceal certain facts that would explain the way people exist in the world. Banking educators regard students as adaptable and manageable beings who should not be encouraged to develop critical consciousness. Banking education mystifies canonical knowledge and celebrates relations of domination marked by gender, ethnic and class differences. Freire describes banking education as "teacher/student contradiction" which is at the core of pedagogical relationships of domination and submission. That is, "the teacher chooses the program content, and the students who were not consulted adapt to it; the teacher is the subject of the learning process, while the pupils are mere objects."[40] On the contrary, Freire argues that "authentic education is not carried on by 'A' for 'B' or by 'A' about 'B', but rather by 'A' with 'B', mediated by the world."[41] Education in Africa is also characterized by sexism, control and male dominance.

Given the above scenario, Henry Giroux argues that the fundamental public services generally associated with schooling, such as empowerment of all individuals regardless of race, class, gender or faith, are undermined by the very contradictions of schooling itself.[42] Nowhere is this more true than in Africa.

EDUCATION IN AFRICA: A NEW PARADIGM

Education of most worth for Africans in the twenty-first century would be the type of education that produces informed citizens who are capable of making intelligent decisions about everyday problems. This type of education must make a person think for him/herself. This is the type of education Paulo Freire calls education for critical consciousness.[43] This type of education should enable people to work by themselves; learn how to gather, analyze, synthesize and assess information; learn how to analyze questions and problems; learn how to enter sympathetically into the thinking of others; be able to make effective economic, political and social contributions to their own society and learn how to deal rationally with conflicting points of view.[44] Such an education should be grounded in a broad liberal education because liberal education provides the best breadth of understanding of human conditions and problems.[45] As John McPeck points out: "The disciplines which make up a liberal education (e.g., those in the arts, the sciences, and humanities) are not separate from, nor alien to, the everyday problems requiring critical thought, but rather they are the fundamental constituents of such problems."[46] Most liberal arts disciplines have their origins in human conditions and are decidedly about human conditions. They provide insights and understandings about human problems and enable rational discourse about problems that confront society.[47] However, it should be emphasized here that the subjects that make up these liberal education disciplines must be grounded in research done in Africa. Additionally, it must be pointed out that liberal education is not enough in and of itself. Such an education must be accompanied by the development of critical thinking skills. A critical thinker by this definition is a person who can adjust to different questions and different domains of thought. This is an individual who is fair-minded about not only his or her viewpoints, but about the viewpoints of others. A critical thinker is one who is able to explore and appreciate the adequacy of other people's position. A critical thinker is one who is willing and desirous to explore alien and even threatening viewpoints including those that contradict his/her deeply held assumptions and beliefs. A critical thinker is one who is willing to explore, take risks, invent, invest and create opportunities for others who are less fortunate.[48] This type of thinking should be an activity par excellence for Africa's children because, until our schools are able to produce these kinds of inquirers, the answers and solutions to Africa's problems will elude us.

EDUCATIONAL GOALS

How can students develop critical thinking skills and how can teachers develop in their students critical thinking ability? Critical theorists argue for dialogical pedagogy because they believe that dialogue enhances the development of critical thinking skills.[49] Paulo Freire points out, "Dialogue, as the encounter among people to 'name' the world, is a fundamental precondition for their humanization." He goes on to say that "problem-posing education sets itself the task of demythologizing. Banking education resists dialogue; problem-posing education regards dialogue as indispensable to the act of cognition which unveils reality." Dialogue is defined as "an active process of serious continuing discussion which allows people's voices to develop and be heard."[50] The use of dialogue is advantageous because it is free, social, inclusive, participatory, normative, propositional, ongoing, transformative and best of all anticipatory.[51] That is, "it implies taking responsibility for one's ability to influence and in some cases, determine the future."[52]

Dialogue is transformative because it enables students to construct knowledge by themselves, transform social relations in the classroom, and raise awareness. Indeed, dialogue creates the potential for human beings to reclaim and shape their world. Most important, dialogue promotes self-awareness, self-reflection and self-criticism. Dialogue generates reflection. When people engage in dialogue, they reflect, concentrate, consider alternatives, listen closely, give careful attention to definitions and meanings, recognize options and perform serious mental activities more than they would have engaged in otherwise, because true dialogue cannot exist unless the "dialoguers engage in critical thinking." Freire adds that since liberating action is dialogical in nature, dialogue cannot be *a posteriori* to the action but concomitant to it.

Specifically, dialogue empowers students because the teaching of inquiry skills can bring about individual self-awareness or empowerment, and empowered individuals can in turn confront oppressive social structures as catalysts for wider change. Indeed, David Hursh argues that critical social studies "can become a crucible within which students give voice to their own concerns and lives and connect with others."[53] When people engage in dialogue in a classroom, they participate actively in the learning process, and a democratic process develops because dialogue is the foundation of a true democracy.

By providing a challenging and engaging learning environment through dialogue, students are able to learn from one another. Accordingly they trust, respect and care for each other. As Juan Fernandez-Balboa and James Marshall put it, "Dialogue helps students and teachers relate on a more personal, trusting level and makes the classroom a more humane place in which to learn."[54] Importantly, Lilia I. Bartolomé argues that education should be a "process in which teacher and students mutually participate in the intellectually exciting undertaking we call learning."[55] She concludes that students should be active subjects in their own learning, instead of passive objects waiting to be filled with facts and figures by the teacher.

Some of the ways of initiating a class dialogue is by codification and conscientization, that is, problematizing everyday life and "learning to perceive social, political, and economic contradictions, and taking action against the oppressive elements of reality."[56] Codification means representation of an ordinary piece of reality. This means knowledge drawn from lived experiences or basing content on knowledge that students bring to school. It implies proceeding from the known to the unknown, connecting class activities and exercises to students' prior experiences. In codification, the facts presented in *real* life or concrete context are critically analyzed. Codification may take the form of a photograph, a videotape, an article or a sketch that represents a real existent or an existent constructed by the learner.

But Paulo Freire and Henry Giroux warn against a curriculum that takes on "the easy and sometimes sloppy demands of liberal pluralism," because such a curriculum works to silence, marginalize, control as well as construct forms of cultural containment, conformity, discrimination and socioeconomic inequality. They argue that education should engage "the power-sensitive relations that articulate between and among different groups. This means, we should see schools as places that produce not only subjects but subjectivities."[57] In other words, learning is as much about the acquisition of knowledge as it is about the social production of social practices that provide individuals with a sense of identity, self-worth, value and place. Educators should help students to overcome their voicelessness. Giroux advocates the type of education that is capable of preparing students to be active, critical and risk-taking citizens. He calls for what he describes as a "pedagogy of representation" or "pedagogy of the popular" or "critical pedagogy." He defines critical pedagogy as:

a form of cultural practice which does not simply tell the student how to think or what to believe, but provides the conditions for a set of ideological and social relations which engender diverse possibilities for students to produce rather than simply acquire knowledge, to be self-critical about both the positions they describe and the locations from which they speak, and to make explicit the values that inform their relations with others as a part of a broader attempt to produce conditions necessary for either the existing society or a new more democratic social order.[58]

According to Henry Giroux, critical pedagogy establishes more egalitarian relations among participants and enables those typically silenced by schooling to become subjects of the learning process. As he puts it, critical pedagogy lends itself to the demands and purposes of democracy because teachers should engage themselves in the production of knowledge that is transformative, relevant and emancipatory. Teachers should incorporate aspects of popular culture and bring into dialogue voices of those who have been marginalized, silenced and excluded. Freire and Giroux maintain: "Educational programs need to provide students with an understanding of how knowledge and power come together in various educational spheres to both enable and silence the voices of different [groups of] students."[59] This means, teachers should be involved in what Barry Kanpol calls cultural politics—those values that challenge dominant, oppressive ethos in society.

Furthermore, knowledge should include a perspective of history from the students' point of view and should be selected and constructed in relationship to the students' desires, visions, descriptions of reality and repertoires of action. Indeed, empowering education must provide students with "a curriculum and an instructional agenda that enable them to draw on their own histories, voices and cultural resources in developing new skills and knowledge."[60] According to Søren Kierkegaard, learning would be meaningful to every student if it takes "cognizance of the concrete and the temporal, the existential process, the predicament of the existing individual arising from his being a synthesis of the temporal and the eternal situated in existence."[61] This means educators should take seriously the strengths, experiences and goals of their students, because as Kierkegaard put it: "One must know oneself before knowing anything else. It is only after a man has understood himself that life acquires peace and significance."[62] Indeed, Johann Heinrich Pestalozzi summed up this point in the early part of the nineteenth century in the following words: "For it is my opinion that if public education does not take into consideration the circumstances of family life, and everything else that bears on a man's general education, it can only lead to an artificial and methodical dwarfing of humanity."[63]

Pestalozzi further argued that learning should be connected with personal belief systems and prior experiences. Paulo Freire makes the point that it is important that the "school system knows and values the knowledge of class, the experience-based knowledge the child brings to it,"[64] because if learning is not made relevant to students' real life experiences, school becomes a place where students learn only compliance to adult authority and consequently students experience subject matter that is boring. This is why Maxine Greene argues that "the life of reason develops against a background of perceived realities."[65] Hence, concepts should be related to events that are pertinent to the lives of students or to their cultural knowledge, for humanistic psychologists make the point that learning is likely to occur if students realize that the subject is related to the maintenance and enhancement of the self. In his book *Experience and Education*, John Dewey cogently defined educative experience as one in which students and teachers find meaning in their lives: "I have taken for granted the soundness of the principle that education in order to accomplish its ends both for the individual learner and for society must be based upon experience—which is always the actual life-experience of some individual."[66]

Critical theorists argue that the purpose of mass education (such as practiced in Africa) is to maintain the status quo. Under mass education, teachers are the transmitters of knowledge while students are the passive recipients of knowledge. This is what Paulo Freire calls *banking education* and Jean-Paul Sartre described as *philosophie alimentaire*.[67] Indeed, Lauren Resnick remarks as follows:

Mass education was, from its inception, concerned with inculcating routine abilities: simple computation, reading predictable texts, reciting religious or civic codes. It did not take as goals for its students the ability to interpret unfamiliar texts, create material others would want and need to read, construct convincing arguments, develop original solutions to technical or social problems. The political conditions under which mass education developed encouraged instead the routinization of basic skills as well as the standardization of teaching and education institutions.[68]

In mass education, dialogue is almost nonexistent because students look for correct answers from teachers who are considered depositories of knowledge. On the contrary, critical theorists maintain that a democratic view of education demands a relationship between teachers and students in which dialogue is an important means of learning because dialogue not only draws from and contributes to the education of the individual, but is the foundation of a true democratic society. Indeed, Bert Bower argues that when a subject is taught using an active dialogical approach, students not only remember their lessons, but they truly appreciate how the subject affects their lives.[69] Through the dynamics of dialogue then, students become active participants in the learning process because dialogue enables students to be active subjects of history rather than passive recipients of information, for to learn is to experience oneself as an empowered individual.

TEACHER EDUCATION AND CRITICAL CONSCIOUSNESS

As I have noted in the preceeding chapters in this book, critical citizenship is essential to democracy and teachers are essential to critical citizenship. To accomplish their tasks of creating critical citizens, schools should become "sites of social transformation where students are educated to become informed, active, and critical citizens."[70] In other words, schools in Africa should become sites where "citizenship and the politics of possibility are given serious consideration."[71] Teacher trainers in Africa, therefore, should begin to develop critical discourses that challenge kleptomania, civil service mentality, sexism, exploitation and inhumanity. Teacher programs should examine the ways in which Western education has been used as an effective instrument of domination and for silencing the poor majority in Africa. What I imply here is that teacher-education programs should have a sense of utmost mission—the mission being to produce the type of teachers who will take "seriously the imperatives of social critique and social change as part of a wider emancipatory vision."[72] These are the types of teachers who will recognize that education produces not only subjects but subjectivities. In other words, student teachers should be made to realize "the importance of educating students in the languages of critique and possibility; that is, providing teachers with the critical terminology and conceptual framework that will allow them not only to critically analyze the (intellectual) democratic, political and [economic] shortcomings of schools, but also to develop the knowledge and skills that will advance the possibilities for generating and cultivating a deep respect for a democratic and ethically-based community."[73]

What form should the type of teacher education advocated here take?

Giroux and McLaren answer that this type of teacher education programs should give students the "opportunity to learn the discourse of public association and civil responsibility," because "such a discourse," they argue, "seeks to recapture the idea of a critical democracy that commands respect for individual freedom and social justice."[74] Second, teachers need to be reskilled. This means, they should be able to intellectualize their functions as such functions relate to the curriculum, teaching methods, oppression and alienation, and they should be able to take absolute responsibility for the different phases of their work. Indeed, teachers should learn to become transformative intellectuals—those who would challenge dominant, oppressive, sexist and degenerate values in African society. Transformative intellectuals are those teachers who impute in their students a sense of morality; instill their students with practices that will enable them to engage in critical and intellectual analyses of competing views and understand competing knowledge. They are teachers who would have the political and ethical will to judge, critique and reject oppressive forces in African society—forces that silence teachers' and students' voices. Such teachers should be able to show the relationship between knowledge and power as they are used to constrain the poor in Africa. Such teachers should also be able to prepare students in Africa for economic self-sufficiency.

What should be the make-up of the type of teacher preparation advocated here? This type of teacher preparation calls for the linking of the critical analysis of economic vision, history, political power, culture and language to the practice of critical pedagogy.[75] It also means producing the type of teachers who value students' voices. It equally means producing teachers who understand that classrooms are "cultural terrains where a variety of interests and practices collide in a constant and often chaotic struggle for dominance."[76] This is to say, schools are not neutral sites that are devoid of politics, power and economic vision. Giroux and McLaren argue that teacher educators should take into account students' subjectivities or experiences as well as their self-constitution and empowerment. They define empowerment as the "process whereby students acquire the means to critically appropriate knowledge existing outside of their immediate experience in order to broaden their understanding of themselves, the world, and the possibilities for transforming the taken-for-granted assumptions about the way we live."[77] Empowering pedagogy, then, is one that respects students' histories, language, voices and cultural traditions. Similarly, teacher educators should develop the type of curriculum that would help their students to understand the relationship between knowledge and power, for as Benjamin R. Barber argues, "the missing term in most recent arguments on behalf of neutrality, impartiality is power . . . power skews theoretical neutrality and unbalances apparently symmetrical relationships."[78] (Also see chapter 4 in this book.) By this, Barber means that knowledge is linked to a particular construction and interests that can distort as well as uphold truth. Student teachers in Africa should be exposed to the relationships between knowledge and language because the use of former colonial languages as educational mediums in all African countries bars knowledge from a large majority of African children who are not endowed with the cultural capital. Language, as we know, is a medium through which knowledge is acquired. Therefore, in Africa, the use of foreign languages in schools has turned language into a medium of social stratification. Indeed, the use of former colonial languages in Africa disenfranchises children of the poor. This is because, as Basil Bernstein has stated, the elaborated or universalistic language patterns of the middle and upper-class predominate in schools. He notes that

Middle-class children are better able to participate in their own socialization processes because their language is similar to the language of the schools. Since [poor children] have less competence in the language of the school..., they often fail to understand exactly what is expected of them. They therefore respond inappropriately, perform more poorly, and reap fewer rewards for their efforts.[79]

Paulo Freire and Donaldo Macedo add that "while education in [a European language] provides access to positions of political and economic power for the high echelon of African society, it screens out the majority of the masses, who fail to learn the [European] language in question well enough to acquire the necessary literacy level for social, economic, and political advancement." "By offering a literacy program conducted in the language of the colonizers with the aim of reappropriating the African culture," they maintain, "these educators have, in fact, developed new manipulative strategies that support the maintenance of [European] cultural dominance."

On the contrary, teachers should listen to their students' real voices as a way of learning about their cultural, historical, social and economic situations because students' voices are "shaped by [their] owner's particular cultural history and prior experiences."[80] Listening to students' voices also helps teachers in understanding how cultural traditions evolve and how such traditions have constructed reality throughout history. It is also important for teachers to know the policies and practices that have served to silence some students' voices as well. Giroux and McLaren define the student's voice as "the various measures by which students and teachers actively participate in dialogue. It is related to the [way] students and teachers attempt to make themselves 'heard' and to define themselves as active authors of their worlds."[81] They argue that students' voices should be clearly heard in critical pedagogy because "the concept of voice represents the unique instances of self-expression through which students affirm their own class, cultural, . . . and gender identities."[82] It is important to understand that one's voice is shaped by environment, history, and culture. Through dialogue, therefore, we come to understand the individual, and students come to define themselves and their world in an attempt to change it. At stake here is a reconstruction of the democratic ideal of citizenship with schools as democratic public spheres that dignify and critically engage the different voices in Africa. This means affirming those histories, traditions, stories and events of the various groups in Africa who had hitherto been silenced. As Henry Giroux has convincingly argued, teachers have a "vital role in maintaining the structure of schools and transmitting the values needed to support the larger social order."[83] I agree. The larger social order in Africa today is the need for economic sufficiency. This demands a different type of consciousness and a different solution. Indeed, as the saying goes, "Desperate times demand desperate measures."

Notes

CHAPTER 1—INTRODUCTION

1. T. T. Solaru, *Teacher Training in Nigeria* (Ibadan, Nigeria: Ibadan University Press, 1964); J. F. Ade Ajayi, *Christian Missions in Nigeria 1841–1891: The Making of a New Elite* (Evanston, IL: Northwestern University Press, 1965); James S. Coleman, "Introduction: Education and Political Development," in James S. Coleman, ed., *Education and Political Development* (Princeton, NJ: Princeton University Press, 1965); Emmanuel A. Ayandele, *The Missionary Impact on Modern Nigeria 1842–1914: A Political and Social Analysis* (New York: Humanities Press, 1967); A. Babs Fafunwa, *History of Education in Nigeria* (London: George Allen and Unwin, 1974); Felix K. Ekechi, *Missionary Enterprise and Rivalry in Igboland 1857–1914* (London: Frank Cass, 1972).

2. Coleman, "Introduction," 36–37.

3. J. F. Ade Ajayi, "Nineteenth Century Origins of Nigerian Nationalism" *Journal of the Historical Society of Nigeria* 2, no. 2 (1961): 196–210, 197.

4. David B. Abernethy, *The Political Dilemma of Popular Education: An African Case* (Stanford, CA: Stanford University Press, 1969).

5. Ajayi Report, 1963, 23.

6. Peter C. Lloyd, ed., *The New Elites of Tropical Africa* (London: Oxford University Press, 1966), 57.

7. James S. Coleman, "Introduction to Part III" in James S. Coleman, ed., *Education and Political Development* (Princeton, NJ: Princeton University Press, 1965), 353.

8. Ibid.

9. See Abernethy, *The Political Dilemma*, 104.

10. Coleman, "Introduction," 26.

11. Lucian W. Pye, *Politics, Personality and Nation Building: Burma's Search for Identity* (New Haven: Yale University Press, 1962), 220.

12. Paulo Freire, *Cultural Action for Freedom* (Cambridge, MA: Harvard Educational Review, 1970).

13. Ibid.

14. Ibid.

15. Ibid.

16. Paulo Freire and Henry A. Giroux, "Pedagogy, Popular Culture and Public Life: An Introduction," in Henry A. Giroux, Roger I. Simon and Contributors, *Popular Culture: Schooling and Everyday Life* (Westport, CT: Bergin & Garvey, 1989), vii–xii.

17. Coleman, "Introduction," 38.

18. David Court, "Education as Social Control: The Response to Inequality in Kenya and Tanzania" in Victor C. Uchendu, ed., *Education and Politics in Tropical Africa* (New York: Conch Magazine Limited, 1979), 55.

19. John B. Knight and Richard H. Sabot, *Education, Productivity, and Inequality: The East African Natural Experiment* (New York: Oxford University Press, 1990), 48.

20. Barbara B. Lloyd, "Education and Family Life in the Development of Class Identification Among the Yoruba" in Peter C. Lloyd, ed., *The New Elites of Tropical Africa* (London: Oxford University Press, 1966), 164.

21. Ibid.

22. Ibid., 164–65.

23. Timothy Reagan, "Philosophy of Education in the Service of Apartheid: The Role of 'Fundamental Pedagogics' in South African Education," *Educational Foundations* 4, no. 2 (1990): 65.

24. Ibid.

25. Ibid., 66.

26. Ibid., 68.

27. Michel Foucault, "Truth and Power," in C. Gordon, ed., *Power/Knowledge: Selected Interviews and Other Writings, 1972–1977* (New York: Pantheon Books, 1980), 133.

28. Ibid., 131.

29. Michel Foucault, *The History of Sexuality: Volume 1: An Introduction* (New York: Vintage Books, 1978), 100.

30. Michel Foucault, *Discipline and Punish: The Birth of the Prison* (New York: Pantheon Books, 1977), 27.

31. Michel Foucault, "Question of Geography" in C. Gordon, ed., *Power/Knowledge: Selected Interviews and Other Writings, 1972–1977* (New York: Pantheon Books, 1980), 69.

32. Henry Giroux, *Theory and Resistance in Education: A Pedagogy for the Opposition* (South Hadley, MA: Bergin & Garvey, 1983), 157.

33. Abernethy, *The Political Dilemma*, 64.

34. Bonnie Cook Freeman, "Female Education in Patriarchal Power Systems," in Philip G. Altbach and Gail P. Kelly, eds. *Education and Colonialism* (New York: Longman, 1978), 212.

35. Ibid., 213.

36. Paulo Freire, *Pedagogy of Hope: Reliving Pedagogy of the Oppressed* (New York: The Continuum Publishing Company, 1994), 179.

37. Gail P. Kelly and Philip G. Altbach, "Introduction," in Philip G. Altbach and Gail P. Kelly, eds., *Education and Colonialism* (New York: Longman, 1978).

38. Audrey Thompson and Andrew Gitlin, "Creating Spaces for Reconstructing Knowledge in Feminist Pedagogy," *Educational Theory* 45, no. 2 (1995): 125.

39. Henry A. Giroux, *Teachers as Intellectuals: Toward a Critical Pedagogy of Learning* (Westport, CT: Bergin & Garvey, 1988), 101–102.

40. Ibid., 102.

41. Barry Kanpol, *Critical Pedagogy: An Introduction* (Westport, CT: Bergin & Garvey, 1994), 107.

42. Henry A. Giroux, "Rethinking Education Reform in the Age of George Bush," *Phi Delta Kappan* 70, no. 9 (1989): 728.

43. Bishop Shanahan cited in Abernethy, *The Political Dilemma*, 41.

44. See Abernethy, *The Political Dilemma*, 39.

45. Ekechi, *Missionary Enterprise*, 176.

46. Ibid.

47. Coleman, "Introduction," 37.

48. Freire and Giroux, "Pedagogy, Popular Culture"; Henry A. Giroux, *Living Dangerously: Multiculturalism and the Politics of Difference* (New York: Peter Lang, 1993).

49. Thompson and Gitlin, "Creating Spaces," 126.

50. Henry A. Giroux and Peter McLaren, "Teacher Education and the Politics of Engagement: The Case for Democratic Schooling," in Pepi Leistyna, Arlie Woodrum and Stephen A. Sherblom, eds., *Breaking Free: The Transformative Power of Critical Pedagogy* (Cambridge, MA: Harvard Educational Review-Reprint Series, no. 27, 1996), 311.

CHAPTER 2—TRADITIONAL AFRICAN EDUCATION

1. Cited in C. Tsehloane Keto, "Pre-Industrial Education Policies and Practices in South Africa," in Mokubung Nkomo, ed., *Pedagogy of Domination: Toward a Democratic Education in South Africa* (Trenton, NJ: Africa World Press, Inc., 1990), 19. See also Christopher J. Lucas, "The More Things Change . . ." *Phi Delta Kappan* (February 1980).

2. A. Babs Fafunwa, *History of Education in Nigeria* (London: George Allen and Unwin, 1974).

3. Ibid., 20.

4. Chuka Eze Okonkwo, "Education and the African Novel: Perceptions of a Culture in Crisis," *Journal of African Studies* 12, no. 2 (Summer 1985): 104.

5. Ibid.

6. Abdou Moumouni, *Education in Africa* (London: Andre Deutsch, 1968).

7. Okonkwo, "Education and the African Novel."

8. Moumouni, *Education in Africa*, 16.

9. Fafunwa, *History of Education*, 15.

10. Ibid., 15–16.

11. Kofi A. Opoku, "Education and Moral Values in Contemporary Africa: The Role of the Family in Education (The Akan of Ghana)," in Charles E. Nnolim,

ed., *The Role of Education in Contemporary Africa* (New York: Professors World Peace Academy, 1988).

12. K. A. Busia, *Purposeful Education for Africa* (The Hague: Mouton and Company, 1964), 16–17.

13. Opoku, "Education and Moral Values," 8.

14. Kenneth L. Little, "The Role of the Secret Society in Cultural Specialization," *American Anthropologist* 51, no. 2 (1949): 202.

15. See Francis X. Sutton, "Education and the Making of Modern Nations," in James S. Coleman, ed., *Education and Political Development* (Princeton, NJ: Princeton University Press, 1965).

16. Fafunwa, *History of Education*, 24.

17. Charles E. Nnolim, "The Implications of Education in the Humanities for Good Citizenship," in Charles E. Nnolim, ed., *The Role of Education in Contemporary Africa* (New York: Professors World Peace Academy, 1988), 100.

18. Opoku, "Education and Moral Values," 6.

19. Moumouni, *Education in Africa*, 22.

20. V. L. Crosson and J. C. Stailey, *Spinning Stories: An Introduction to Storytelling Skills* (Austin: Texas State Library, Department of Library Development, 1988), 3. ERIC Document Reproduction Service No. ED 301195.

21. Cited in Fafunwa, *History of Education*, 27.

22. Ibid.

23. Ibid., 32.

24. Interview with Bassey Umana, August 1986.

25. John S. Mbiti, *African Religions and Philosophy* (Garden City, NY: Anchor Books, 1970), 218–19.

26. Okonkwo, "Education and the African Novel," 106.

27. Cited in Dickson A. Mungazi and L. Kay Walker, *Educational Reform and the Transformation of Southern Africa* (Westport, CT: Praeger, 1997), 29.

28. Ibid., 30.

29. Dominic T. Ashley, "The Role of Education in Combating Violence in Sierra Leone," in Charles E. Nnolim, ed., *The Role of Education in Contemporary Africa* (New York: Professors World Peace Academy, 1988), 41.

30. Fafunwa, *History of Education*; Mungazi and Walker, *Educational Reform*; Ashley, *The Role of Education*; Magnus O. Bassey, *Missionary Rivalry and Educational Expansion in Nigeria, 1885–1945* (Lewiston, NY: The Edwin Mellen Press, 1999); Opoku, "Education and Moral Values"; Philip Foster, *Education and Social Change in Ghana* (Chicago: The University of Chicago Press, 1965).

31. Ibid.

32. K. A. Busia, *The Challenge of Africa* (New York: Praeger, 1962), 33.

33. Ibid.

34. Cited in Mungazi and Walker, *Educational Reform*, 31. See also Fafunwa, *History of Education*; Bassey, *Missionary Rivalry*; Opoku, "Education and Moral Values"; Foster, *Education and Social Change*.

35. Ibid.

36. Cited in Mungazi and Walker, *Educational Reform*, 29.

37. Busia, *Purposeful Education for Africa*, 17.

38. Ibid.

39. Opoku, "Education and Moral Values."

40. Mungazi and Walker, *Educational Reform*.
41. Cited in Mungazi and Walker, *Educational Reform*, 38.
42. See Fafunwa, *History of Education*, 15; see also Mungazi and Walker, *Educational Reform*, 38.
43. Ashley, "The Role of Education," 44.

CHAPTER 3—CHRISTIAN MISSIONARY/COLONIAL EDUCATION IN AFRICA

1. James S. Coleman, *Nigeria: Background to Nationalism* (Berkeley: University of California Press, 1958), 113.
2. Magnus O. Bassey, "Missionary Rivalry and Educational Expansion in Southern Nigeria, 1885–1932," *Journal of Negro Education* 60, no. 1 (Winter 1991).
3. Ibid.
4. Ibid.
5. Thomas Fowell Buxton, *The African Slave Trade and its Remedy* (1839; reprint, London: Frank Cass, 1976), 282.
6. Ibid.
7. Buxton, *The African Slave Trade*, 511.
8. Cited in James Bertin Webster, "The Bible and the Plough," *Journal of the Historical Society of Nigeria*, 2, no. 4 (1963): 420.
9. W. S. Naylor, *Daybreak in the Dark Continent* (New York: Young Peoples Missionary Movement, 1905); Roland Oliver, *The Missionary Factor in East Africa* (London: Longman, 1967).
10. Edward H. Berman, *African Reactions to Missionary Education* (New York: Teachers College Press, 1975); Oliver, *The Missionary Factor*.
11. Ibid.
12. Magnus O. Bassey, *Missionary Rivalry and Educational Expansion in Nigeria, 1885–1945* (Lewiston, NY: The Edwin Mellen Press, 1999).
13. Ibid.
14. David B. Abernethy, *The Political Dilemma of Popular Education: An African Case* (Stanford, CA: Stanford University Press, 1969), 46.
15. Remi Clignet, "Education and Elite Formation," in John N. Paden and Edward W. Soja, eds., *The African Experience, Vol. 1: Essays* (Evanston, IL: Northwestern University Press, 1970), 305.
16. Clignet, "Education and Elite Formation"; Dickson A. Mungazi and L. Kay Walker, *Educational Reform and the Transformation of Southern Africa* (Westport, CT: Praeger, 1997); Philip Foster, *Education and Social Change in Ghana* (Chicago: The University of Chicago Press, 1965).
17. Clignet, "Education and Elite Formation," 306.
18. Ibid., 308.
19. Ibid., 309.
20. Cited in Mungazi and Walker, *Educational Reform*, 34.
21. Ibid., 34–35.
22. Ibid., 35.
23. Ibid.
24. Ibid.
25. Ibid., 36.
26. Ibid.

27. Ibid., 36–37.
28. Ibid., 37.
29. Mungazi and Walker, *Educational Reform*, 36.
30. Cited in Mungazi and Walker, *Educational Reform*, 36.
31. Cited in Edward H. Berman, *African Reactions to Missionary Education* (New York: Teachers College Press, 1975), 61.
32. Ibid., 56.
33. Berman, *African Reactions*, 57.
34. Ibid.
35. Ibid., 56.
36. Ibid., 57.
37. Victor C. Uchendu, "Introduction," in Victor C. Uchendu, ed., *Education and Politics in Tropical Africa* (New York: Conch Magazine Limited Publishers, 1979), 5.
38. Cited in Uchendu, "Introduction," 5.
39. Uchendu, "Introduction," 2.
40. Cited in Uchendu, "Introduction," 2.
41. Paulo Freire and Donaldo Macedo, "Literacy and Critical Pedagogy," in Fred Schultz, ed., *Sources: Notable Selections in Education*, 2nd ed. (Guilford, CT: Dushkin/McGraw-Hill, 1998), 195.
42. Berman, *African Reactions*, 61.
43. Cited in Mungazi and Walker, *Educational Reform*, 39.
44. Ibid.
45. Uchendu, "Introduction," 1.
46. Ibid., 3.
47. See Berman, *African Reactions*, 8.
48. Ibid.
49. Ibid.
50. James S. Coleman, "Introduction: Education and Political Development," in James S. Coleman, ed., *Education and Political Development* (Princeton, NJ: Princeton University Press, 1965).
51. Foster, *Education and Social Change*, 8.
52. Mungazi and Walker, *Educational Reform*, 187.
53. Chinua Achebe, *Things Fall Apart* (London: Heinemann, 1965), 166.
54. Berman, *African Reactions*, 22.
55. Magnus O. Bassey, "The Politics of Education in Nigeria: The Case of Government Take-Over of Schools in the Cross River and Kano States," (Unpublished Doctoral Dissertation, Rutgers University, 1989); Bassey, "Missionary Rivalry and Educational Expansion."
56. Berman, *African Reactions*, 22.
57. P. Amaury Talbot, *The Peoples of Southern Nigeria*, Vol. 4 (London: Frank Cass, 1969), 124.
58. See Felix K. Ekechi, *Missionary Enterprise and Rivalry in Igboland, 1857–1914* (London: Frank Cass, 1972), 178.
59. Emmanuel A. Ayandele, *Nigerian Historical Studies* (London: Frank Cass, 1979), 169.
60. Cited in Clayton G. Mackenzie, "Demythologizing the Missionaries: A

Reassessment of the Functions and Relationships of Christian Missionary Education Under Colonialism," *Comparative Education* 19, no. 1 (1993), 46.

61. Ibid.
62. Ibid.
63. Ibid.
64. Ibid.
65. Ernest Emenyonu, *The Rise of the Igbo Novel* (Ibadan, Nigeria: Oxford University Press, 1978).
66. A. Babs Fafunwa, *History of Education in Nigeria* (London: George Allen and Unwin 1974), 81.
67. A. F. Leach cited in Fafunwa, *History of Education*, 81.
68. D. Westermann, *Africa and Christianity* (Oxford: Oxford University Press, 1937), 163.
69. A. E. Afigbo, "The Missions, the State and Education in South-Eastern Nigeria, 1956–1971," in Edward Fasholé-Luke et al., eds., *Christianity in Independent Africa* (Ibadan, Nigeria: Ibadan University Press, 1978), 182.
70. Abernethy, *The Political Dilemma*, 46–47.
71. Afigbo, "The Missions, the State and Education," 185.
72. Cited in Berman, *African Reactions*, 31.
73. Ibid.
74. Ibid.
75. Ibid., 31–32.
76. F. B. Welbourn, *East African Rebels* (London: London University Press, 1961), 171–172.
77. Berman, *African Reactions*, 31.
78. Ibid., 32.
79. Ibid.
80. Ibid.
81. Ibid.
82. Ayandele, *The Missionary Impact*, 5, 8.
83. Abernethy, *The Political Dilemma*, 32.
84. Cited in Ekechi, *Missionary Enterprise*, 1.
85. James S. Coleman, *Nigeria: Background to Nationalism* (Berkeley: University of California Press, 1958), 108.
86. Abernethy, *The Political Dilemma*, 38, 52.
87. Uchendu, "Introduction."
88. Coleman, "Introduction: Education and Political Development," 38.
89. Gail P. Kelly and Philip G. Altbach, "Introduction," in Philip G. Altbach and Gail P. Kelly, eds., *Education and Colonialism* (New York: Longman, 1978).
90. Peter Worsley, *The Third World* (Chicago: The University of Chicago Press, 1977), 56.
91. Ibid., 58.
92. Kelly and Altbach, "Introduction."
93. Ibid., 8.
94. Ibid., 15.
95. Ibid.
96. Emmanuel A. Ayandele, *The Missionary Impact on Modern Nigeria 1842–1914: A Political and Social Analysis* (New York: Humanities Press, 1967), 289.

97. James S. Coleman, Introduction, 36–37.
98. Kelly and Altbach, "Introduction."
99. Carter G. Woodson, *The Mis-Education of the Negro* (1933; reprint, Trenton, NJ: Africa World Press, 1993).
100. Ibid., xiii, x.
101. I. Kandel, *Comparative Education* (New York: Teachers College Press, 1933).
102. Vernon Mallinson, *An Introduction to the Study of Comparative Education* (New York: Heinemann, 1966).
103. Woodson, *The Mis-Education of the Negro*.
104. Abdou Moumouni, *Education in Africa* (London: Andre Deutsch, 1968).
105. Ibid., 146.
106. Ibid., 147.
107. Ibid.
108. Ibid., 148.
109. Ibid.
110. Ibid., 152.
111. Ibid., 270

CHAPTER 4—WESTERN EDUCATION AND THE RISE OF EDUCATED ELITES IN AFRICA

1. K. E. DeGraft-Johnson, "The Evolution of Elites in Ghana," in Peter C. Lloyd, ed., *The New Elites of Tropical Africa* (London: Oxford University Press, 1966).
2. Peter C. Lloyd, *Africa in Social Change: Changing Traditional Societies in the Modern World* (Baltimore, MD: Penguin Books, 1967); Emmanuel A. Ayandele, *The Missionary Impact on Modern Nigeria 1842–1914: A Political and Social Analysis* (New York: Hamanities Press, 1967); Peter C. Lloyd, ed., *The New Elites of Tropical Africa* (London: Oxford University Press, 1966); J. F. Ade Ajayi, *Christian Missions in Nigeria 1841–1891* (Evanston, IL: Northwestern University Press, 1965); David B. Abernethy, *The Political Dilemma of Popular Education: An African Case* (Stanford, CA: Stanford University Press, 1969).
3. Bishop Shanahan cited in David B. Abernethy, *The Political Dilemma*, 41.
4. Emmanuel A. Ayandele, "Traditional Rulers and Missionaries in Pre-Colonial West Africa," *Tarikh* 3, no. 1. (1969): 28–29; Edward H. Berman, *African Reactions to Missionary Education* (New York: Teachers College Press, 1975), 24–25.
5. Cited in Berman, *African Reactions*, 26.
6. Felix K. Ekechi, *Missionary Enterprise and Rivalry in Igboland, 1857–1914* (London: Frank Cass, 1972), 187.
7. Cited in Berman, *African Reactions*, 15.
8. Emmanuel A. Ayandele, *The Missionary Impact on Modern Nigeria*, 5.
9. Ekechi, *Missionary Enterprise*, 176.
10. Ibid.
11. Peter B. Clarke, "The Methods and Ideology of the Holy Ghost Fathers in Eastern Nigeria, 1885–1905," in O. U. Kalu, ed., *The History of Christianity in West Africa* (Essex, England: Longman, 1980), 51–52.

12. Otonti Nduka, "Background to the Foundation of Dennis Memorial Grammar School, Onitsha," *Journal of the Historical Society of Nigeria* 8, no. 3 (1976): 69, 73.

13. Abernethy, *The Political Dilemma*, 44.

14. Philip Foster, *Education and Social Change in Ghana* (Chicago: The University of Chicago Press, 1965).

15. Lloyd, *Africa in Social Change*, 141.

16. John B. Knight and Richard H. Sabot, *Education, Productivity, and Inequality: The East African Natural Experiment* (New York: Oxford University Press, 1990), 77.

17. Lloyd, *The New Elites*, 57.

18. James S. Coleman, "Introduction to Part 1," in James S. Coleman, ed., *Education and Political Development* (Princeton, NJ: Princeton University Press, 1965), 37.

19. Knight and Sabot, *Education, Productivity and Inequality*, 17.

20. Victor C. Uchendu, "Education and the Public Interest: The Politics of the Public Domain," in Victor C. Uchendu, ed., *Education and Politics in Tropical Africa* (New York: Conch Magazine Limited Publishers, 1979), 283.

21. Ibid.

22. Ibid.

23. Cited in Uchendu, "Education and the Public Interest," 285.

24. Uchendu, "Introduction," 1.

25. Ibid., 283.

26. Coleman, "Introduction to Part I," 38.

27. See Uchendu, "Education and the Public Interest," 289.

28. Cited in Peter B. Clarke, "Islam, Education and the Development Process in Nigeria," *Comparative Education* 14, no. 2 (1978): 134.

29. Ayandele, *The Missionary Impact on Modern Nigeria*; Emmanuel A. Ayandele, "The Missionary Factor in Northern Nigeria, 1870–1918," in O. U. Kalu, ed., *The History of Christianity in West Africa* (Essex, England: Longman, 1980).

30. A. R. I. Doi, "Islam in Nigeria: Changes Since Independence," in Edward Fasholé-Luke et al., eds., *Christianity in Independent Africa* (Ibadan, Nigeria: Ibadan University Press, 1978), 334.

31. Ayandele, "The Missionary Factor," 147.

32. Clarke, "Islam, Education and the Development Process," 134.

33. Ibid.

34. Ibid.

35. A. Babs Fafunwa, *History of Education in Nigeria* (London: George Allen and Unwin, 1974), 100.

36. C. K. Meek, *The Northern Tribes of Nigeria* (New York: Negro Universities Press, 1969), 263.

37. M. Bray, *Universal Primary Education in Nigeria: A Study of Kano State* (London: Routledge & Kegan Paul, 1980), 17.

38. Foster, *Education and Social Change*, 117.

39. Cited in Berman, *African Reactions*, 26.

40. Ibid.

CHAPTER 5—WESTERN EDUCATION AND POLITICAL SOCIALIZATION IN AFRICA

1. T. J. Bowen, *Adventures and Missionary Labors in Several Countries in Africa from 1849 to 1856*, 2nd ed. (1857; reprint, London: Frank Cass, 1968), 322–23.

2. Emmanuel A. Ayandele, "Introduction," in T. J. Bowen, ed., *Adventures and Missionary Labors in Several Countries in Africa from 1849 to 1856* (London: Frank Cass, 1968/1857), xxxv.

3. Thomas Fowell Buxton, *The African Slave Trade and its Remedy* (1839; reprint, London: Frank Cass, 1976), 282.

4. Ibid., 511.

5. Cited in James Bertin Webster, "The Bible and the Plough," *Journal of the Historical Society of Nigeria* 2, no. 4 (1963): 420.

6. J. F. Ade Ajayi, "Nineteenth Century Origins of Nigerian Nationalism," *Journal of the Historical Society of Nigeria* 2, no. 2 (1961): 199.

7. Ibid.

8. Edward H. Berman, *African Reactions to Missionary Education* (New York: Teachers College Press, 1975), 42.

9. Ibid.

10. Ibid.

11. James S. Coleman, "Introduction: Education and Political Development," in James S. Coleman, ed., *Education and Political Development* (Princeton, NJ: Princeton University Press, 1965).

12. James S. Coleman, "Introduction"; Robert D. Grey, "Education and Politicization," in Victor C. Uchendu, ed., *Education and Politics in Tropical Africa* (New York: Conch Magazine Limited Publishers, 1979); Victor C. Uchendu, "Introduction," in Victor C. Uchendu, ed., *Education and Politics in Tropical Africa* (New York: Conch Magazine Limited Publishers, 1979); Victor C. Uchendu, "Education and the Public Interest: The Politics of the Public Domain," in Victor C. Uchendu, ed., *Education and Politics in Tropical Africa* (New York: Conch Magazine Limited Publishers, 1979); Philip Foster, *Education and Social Change in Ghana* (Chicago: The University of Chicago Press, 1965).

13. Grey, "Education and Politicization."

14. Ayo Ogunsheye, "Nigeria," in James S. Coleman, ed., *Education and Political Development* (Princeton, NJ: Princeton University Press, 1965), 130.

15. Ibid.

16. Ibid., 131.

17. David B. Abernethy, *The Political Dilemma of Popular Education: An African Case* (Stanford, CA: Stanford University Press, 1969), 51–52.

18. Ibid., 52.

19. T. T. Solaru, *Teacher Training in Nigeria* (Ibadan, Nigeria: Ibadan University Press, 1964), 45–46.

20. Ogunsheye, "Nigeria."

21. Ajayi, "Nineteenth Century Origins," 203.

22. Ibid., 205.

23. Ibid.

24. Abernethy, *The Political Dilemma*, 67.

25. William Tordoff, *Government and Politics in Africa* (Bloomington: Indiana University Press, 1991), 54.
26. Ibid., 55.
27. Thomas Hodgkin, *Nationalism in Colonial Africa* (London: Frederick Muller, 1956), 99.
28. Cited in Berman, *African Reactions*, 20.
29. Berman, *African Reactions*, 40.
30. Ibid.
31. Ibid.
32. Cited in Berman, *African Reactions*, 40.
33. Berman, *African Reactions*, 40.
34. Ibid.
35. Ibid.
36. Tordoff, *Government and Politics in Africa*, 57.
37. Ibid., 58.
38. Ibid., 61.
39. Ibid., 63.
40. Ibid., 65–66.
41. Ajayi, "Nineteenth-Century Origins," 197.
42. Coleman, "Introduction," 4.
43. Robert D. Grey, "Education and Politicization," 161; see also Gabriel A. Almond and Sidney Verba, *The Civic Culture* (Princeton, NJ: Princeton University Press, 1963); Lester Milbraith, Gabriel A. Almond and Sidney Verba, *Political Participation* (Chicago: Rand-McNally, 1965).
44. Grey, "Education and Politicization," 161.
45. Ibid.
46. Ibid.
47. James S. Coleman, "Introduction to Part I," in James S. Coleman, ed., *Education and Political Development* (Princeton, NJ: Princeton University Press, 1965), 36–37.
48. Ibid., 45.

CHAPTER 6—EDUCATED ELITES AND POLITICAL DOMINATION IN AFRICA

1. Patrick Chabal, *Power in Africa: An Essay in Political Interpretation* (New York: St. Martin's Press, 1994), 5.
2. Cited in Seth Kreisberg, *Transforming Power: Domination, Empowerment and Education* (Albany: State University of New York Press, 1992), 41.
3. Ibid., 40.
4. Ibid., 41.
5. Ibid., 45.
6. Ibid.
7. Ibid.
8. Seth Kreisberg, *Transforming Power*, 37.
9. Cited in Kreisberg, *Transforming Power*, 37.
10. Ibid.
11. See Kreisberg, *Transforming Power*, 29–54.
12. Michael Korda cited in Kreisberg, *Transforming Power*, 32.

13. Ibid., 31.

14. Michel Foucault, "Truth and Power," in C. Gordon, ed., *Power/Knowledge: Selected Interviews and Other Writings 1972–1977* (New York: Pantheon Books, 1980), 133.

15. Ibid., 131.

16. Michel Foucault, *Discipline and Punish: The Birth of the Prison* (New York: Pantheon Books, 1977), 187.

17. David Nyberg, cited in Kreisberg, *Transforming Power*, 35.

18. Kreisberg, *Transforming Power*, 11.

19. Ibid.

20. Foucault, "Truth and Power," 132.

21. Ibid.

22. Foucault, *Discipline and Punish*, 27.

23. Michel Foucault, "Questions on Geography," in C. Gordon, ed., *Power/Knowledge: Selected Interviews and Other Writings 1972–1977* (New York: Pantheon Books, 1980), 69.

24. William Tordoff, *Government and Politics in Africa* (Bloomington: Indiana University Press, 1991), 5.

25. Ibid., 7.

26. Ibid., 7–8.

27. Kenneth Prewitt, "Dilemma of Higher Education in Africa: A Comment," in Victor C. Uchendu, ed., *Education and Politics in Tropical Africa* (New York: Conch Magazine Limited, Publishers, 1979), 191–93.

28. See Tunde Adeleke, "Africa and Pan-Africanism: Betrayal of a Historic Cause," *The Western Journal of Black Studies* 21, no. 2 (1997): 109.

29. Ibid.

30. Ibid.

31. Ibid.

32. Ibid., 110.

33. Ibid.

34. Ibid.

35. Ibid.

36. Cited in Kreisberg, *Transforming Power*, 39.

37. Kreisberg, *Transforming Power*, 39.

38. Ibid.

39. Adeleke, "Africa and Pan-Africanism," 110.

40. Chabal, *Power in Africa*, 82.

41. Victor T. LeVine, "Role Ambiguity and Corruption: Bureaucrat and Apparatchik in African Political Systems," *Philippine Journal of Public Administration* 38, no. 1 (1994).

42. See ibid., 31.

43. Ibid., 31–32.

44. Cited in Ernest N. Emenyonu, "Education and the Contemporary Malaise in Nigeria," in Charles E. Nnolim, ed., *The Role of Education in Contemporary Africa* (New York: Professors World Peace Academy, 1988), 33–34.

45. Ibid., 30.

46. Ibid.

47. Ibid., 32.

48. Ibid.
49. Chabal, *Power in Africa*, 213.
50. Ibid.
51. Ibid., 216.
52. Ibid., 214.
53. Kreisberg, *Transforming Power*, 11.
54. Ibid.
55. Adeleke, "Africa and Pan-Africanism," 112.
56. Chabal, *Power in Africa*, 214–15.
57. Abernethy, *The Political Dilemma*, 243.

CHAPTER 7—SCHOOLS IN AFRICA AS SITES OF CULTURAL AND STRUCTURAL INEQUALITIES, DISEMPOWERMENT, SEXISM, DOMINATION AND HEGEMONY

1. Paulo Freire, *Pedagogy of the Oppressed* (1970; reprint, New York: The Continuum Publishing Company, 1994). See also Paulo Freire, *Cultural Action for Freedom* (Cambridge, MA: Harvard Educational Review, 1970); Paulo Freire, *Education for Critical Consciousness* (New York: The Continuum Publishing Company, 1973); Paulo Freire, *The Politics of Education: Culture, Power, and Liberation* (South Hadley, MA: Bergin & Garvey, 1985); Paulo Freire and Donaldo Macedo, *Literacy: Reading the Word and the World* (South Hadley, MA: Bergin & Garvey, 1987); Paulo Freire, *Pedagogy of the City* (New York: The Continuum Publishing Company, 1993).

2. Remi Clignet, "Damned If You Do, Damned If You Don't: The Dilemmas of Colonizer-Colonized Relations," in Philip G. Altbach and Gail P. Kelly, eds., *Education and Colonialism* (New York: Longman, 1978), 131.

3. Ibid.
4. Freire and Macedo, *Literacy*, 143.
5. Ibid.
6. Ibid., 143–144.
7. Ibid., 143.
8. Ibid.
9. Audrey Thompson and Andrew Gitlin, "Creating Spaces for Reconstructing Knowledge in Feminist Pedagogy," *Educational Theory* 45, no. 2 (1995). See also Freire, *Cultural Action*; Freire, *Education for Cultural Consciousness*; Freire, *Pedagogy of the Oppressed*; Freire, *The Politics of Education*; Freire, *Politics of the City*; Freire and Macedo, *Literacy*; Henry Giroux, *Teachers as Intellectuals: Toward a Critical Pedagogy of Learning* (New York: Bergin & Garvey, 1988); Henry Giroux, "Rethinking Education Reform in the Age of George Bush," *Phi Delta Kappan* 70, no. 9 (1989); Henry Giroux, *Living Dangerously: Multiculturalism and the Politics of Difference* (New York: Peter Lang, 1993); Seth Kreisberg, *Transforming Power: Domination, Empowerment and Education* (Albany: State University of New York Press, 1992); Peter McLaren, *Life in Schools: An Introduction to Critical Pedagogy in the Foundations of Education* (New York: Longman, 1994); Barry Kanpol, *Critical Pedagogy: An Introduction* (Westport, CT: Bergin & Garvey, 1994).

10. Anedeto Gaspar, "Assimilation and Discrimination: Catholic Education in Angola and the Congo," in Edward H. Berman, *African Reactions to Missionary Education* (New York: Teachers College Press, 1975), 65.

11. Ibid.
12. Freire, *Pedagogy of the Oppressed*, 54.
13. Ibid., 52.
14. Michel Foucault, "Truth and Power," in C. Gordon, ed., *Power/Knowledge: Selected Interviews and Other Writings 1972–1977* (New York: Pantheon Books, 1980), 133.
15. Adhiambo Odaga and Ward Heneveld, *Girls and Schools in Sub-Saharan Africa: From Analysis to Action* (Washington, DC: The World Bank, 1995).
16. Kanpol, *Critical Pedagogy*, 20.
17. Ibid.
18. Kreisberg, *Transforming Power*, 8.
19. Pepi Leistyna and Arlie Woodrum, "Context and Culture: What is Critical Pedagogy?" in Pepi Leistyna, Arlie Woodrum and Stephen A. Sherblom, eds., *Breaking Free: The Transformative Power of Critical Pedagogy* (Cambridge, MA: Harvard Educational Review Reprint Series, no. 27, 1996), 4.
20. Ibid.
21. Kreisberg, *Transforming Power*, 8.
22. Freire, *Pedagogy of the Oppressed*, 52.
23. Ibid., 54.
24. Ibid., 54–55.
25. Ibid., 55.
26. Ibid.
27. Henry Giroux, "Theories of Reproduction and Resistance in the New Sociology of Education," *Harvard Educational Review* 53 (1983): 258.
28. Kanpol, *Critical Pedagogy*, 39.
29. Basil Bernstein, *Class, Codes and Control, Vol. III: Towards a Theory of Educational Transmission* (London: Routledge & Kegan Paul, 1977); Pierre Bourdieu, "Cultural Reproduction and Social Reproduction," in R. K. Brown, ed., *Knowledge, Education and Cultural Change: Papers in the Sociology of Education* (London: Tavistock, 1973); David Swartz, "Pierre Bourdieu: The Cultural Transmission of Social Inequality," *Harvard Educational Review* 47, no. 4 (1977); McLaren, *Life in Schools*; Freire, *Pedagogy of the City*.
30. Freire, *Pedagogy of the City*; Bernstein, *Class, Codes and Control*; Bourdieu, *Cultural Reproduction*.
31. Y. I. Rubanza, "Can A Three-Tier Language Policy Model Work in Tanzania? A New Perspective," *Ufahamu* 24, no. 1 (1996): 84.
32. Peter C. Lloyd, "Introduction: The Study of the Elite," in Peter C. Lloyd, ed., *The New Elites of Tropical Africa* (London: Oxford University Press, 1966), 57.
33. John B. Knight and Richard H. Sabot, *Education, Productivity, and Inequality: The East African Natural Experiment* (Oxford University Press, 1990).
34. Freire and Macedo, *Literacy*, 142.
35. Giroux, *Living Dangerously*, 25.
36. Timothy Lintner, "Learning a New Language—Reframing the Discourse on African Education" *Ufahamu* 24, no. 1 (1996): 7.
37. Odaga and Heneveld, *Girls and Schools*.
38. Ibid., 9.
39. Ibid., 10.
40. Ibid., 11.

41. Cited in Odaga and Heneveld, *Girls and Schools*, 8.
42. Ibid., 12.
43. Ibid.
44. Ibid.
45. Ibid., 13.
46. Ibid., 16.
47. Ibid., 34.
48. Ibid., 35.
49. Ibid., 34–35.
50. Ibid., 31.
51. Ibid., 33.
52. Ibid., 34.

CHAPTER 8—EDUCATION IN THE SERVICE OF APARTHEID IN SOUTH AFRICA, 1802–1993

1. Walton R. Johnson, "Education: Keystone of Apartheid," *Anthropology & Education Quarterly* 13, no. 3 (1982): 216.
2. Ibid.
3. Cited in Dickson A. Mungazi and L. Kay Walker, *Educational Reform and the Transformation of Southern Africa* (Westport, CT: Praeger, 1997), 34.
4. Johnson, "Education: Keystone," 216.
5. Ibid.
6. Mokubung Nkomo, "Introduction," in Mokubung, Nkomo, ed., *Pedagogy of Domination: Toward a Democratic Education in South Africa* (Trenton, NJ: Africa World Press, 1990).
7. Ibid.
8. Ibid., 2.
9. Johnson, "Education: Keystone," 217.
10. See ibid., 218.
11. Ibid.
12. Ibid.
13. Timothy Reagan, "Philosophy of Education in the Service of Apartheid: The Role of 'Fundamental Pedagogics' in South African Education," *Educational Foundations* 4, no. 2 (1990): 62.
14. Cited in Mungazi and Walker, *Educational Reform*, 35.
15. Michael Cross and Linda Chisholm, "The Roots of Segregated Schooling in Twentieth Century South Africa," in Mokubung Nkomo, ed., *Pedagogy of Domination: Toward a Democratic Education in South Africa* (Trenton, NJ: Africa World Press, 1990), 56.
16. Reagan, "Philosophy of Education," 62.
17. Nkomo, "Introduction," 1.
18. Reagan, "Philosophy of Education," 66.
19. See ibid., 62–63.
20. Nkomo, "Introduction," 2.
21. Johnson, "Education: Keystone," 221.
22. Ibid.
23. Penny Enslin, "Science and Doctrine: Theoretical Discourse in South African Teacher Education," in Mokubung Nkomo, ed., *Pedagogy of Domination:*

Toward a Democratic Education in South Africa (Trenton, NJ: Africa World Press, 1990), 77–78.

24. Mark Mathabane, *Kaffir Boy in America* (New York: Collier Books, 1989), 41.

CHAPTER 9—EDUCATION OF MOST WORTH FOR AFRICA IN THE TWENTY-FIRST CENTURY

1. Paulo Freire and Donaldo Macedo, *Literacy: Reading the Word and the World* (South Hadley, MA: Bergin & Garvey, 1987), 143–144.

2. Philip Foster, *Education and Social Change in Ghana* (Chicago: The University of Chicago Press, 1965), 136.

3. Ibid.

4. William Tordoff, *Government and Politics in Africa* (Bloomington: Indiana University Press, 1991); Patrick Chabal, *Power in Africa: An Essay in Political Interpretation* (New York: St. Martin's Press, 1994); Victor T. LeVine, "Role Ambiguity and Corruption: Bureaucrat and Apparatchik in African Political Systems," *Philippine Journal of Public Administration* 38, no. 1 (1994).

5. See LeVine, "Role Ambiguity and Corruption."

6. Cited in David B. Abernethy, *The Political Dilemma of Popular Education: An African Case* (Stanford, CA: Stanford University Press, 1969), 104.

7. A. E. Afigbo, "The Missions, the State and Education in South-Eastern Nigeria, 1956–1971," in Edward Fasholé-Luke et al., eds., *Christianity in Independent Africa* (Ibadan, Nigeria: University of Ibadan Press, 1978), 182.

8. Ibid.

9. Victor C. Uchendu, "Introduction," in Victor C. Uchendu, ed., *Education and Politics in Tropical Africa* (New York: Conch Magazine Limited Publishers, 1979), 1.

10. Ibid.

11. David Court, "Education as Social Control: The Response to Inequality in Kenya and Tanzania," in Victor C. Uchendu, ed., *Education and Politics in Tropical Africa* (New York: Conch Magazine Limited Publishers, 1979), 27.

12. Michael Omolewa, "London University's Earliest Examinations in Nigeria, 1887–1931," *West African Journal of Education* 20, no. 2 (1976): 352.

13. Abernethy, *The Political Dilemma*, 38, 52.

14. Victor P. Diejomaoh, "The Economics of Nigerian Conflict," in Joseph Okpaku, ed., *Nigeria: Dilemma of Nationhood: An African Analysis of the Biafran Conflict* (New York: The Third Press, 1972), 321.

15. Ibid., 318–20.

16. Sir Alhaji Ahmadu Bello, *My Life* (Cambridge, England: Cambridge University Press, 1962), 110–11.

17. Cited in James S. Coleman, *Nigeria: Background to Nationalism* (Berkeley. University of California Press, 1958), 362.

18. A. R. Thompson, *Education and Development in Africa* (London: Macmillan Press, 1983), 56.

19. Ibid, 120.

20. Cited in Thomas J. Fiala, "William T. Harris: Rationalizing Public Education in the American State" *Educational Foundations*, Fall 1998, 35.

21. Cited in Thompson, *Education and Development*, 201.

22. Ibid., 113.
23. Cited in John D. Pulliam and James J. Van Patten, *History of Education in America*, seventh edition (Upper Saddle River, NJ: Prentice-Hall, 1999), 17.
24. Cited in Henry A. Giroux, *Living Dangerously: Multiculturalism and the Politics of Difference* (New York: Peter Lang, 1993), 20.
25. Ibid., 24.
26. Ibid.
27. Ibid.
28. Ibid., 23.
29. Ernest Emenyonu, "Education as a Cooperative Venture: Towards Increased Parental Participation in the Educational Process in Nigeria," in Charles E. Nnolim, ed., *The Role of Education in Contemporary Africa* (New York: Professors World Peace Academy, 1988), 94.
30. Ernest Emenyonu, "Education and the Contemporary Malaise in Nigeria," in Charles E. Nnolim, ed. *The Role of Education in Contemporary Africa* (New York: Professors World Peace Academy, 1988), 34.
31. Ibid.
32. Ibid.
33. Cited in Afigbo, *The Missions, the State and Education*, 181.
34. See Henry J. Perkinson, *The Imperfect Panacea: American Faith in Education, 1865–1990* (New York: McGraw-Hill, Inc., 1991), 8.
35. Ibid.
36. Ibid., 121.
37. Carol Rolheiser and Carl D. Glickman, "Teaching for Democratic Life," *Educational Forum* 59, no. 2 (1995): 198.
38. Seth Kreisberg, *Transformative Power: Domination, Empowerment and Education* (Albany: State University of New York Press, 1992), 6.
39. Paulo Freire, *Pedagogy of the Oppressed* (1970; reprint, New York: The Continuum Publishing Company, 1994), 54.
40. Ibid.
41. Ibid., 74.
42. Henry Giroux, "Rethinking Education Reform in the Age of George Bush," *Phi Delta Kappan* 70, no. 9 (1989): 728–30.
43. Paulo Freire, *Education for Critical Consciousness* (New York: The Continuum Publishing Company, 1973).
44. Richard Paul, *Critical Thinking: What Every Person Needs to Survive in a Rapidly Changing World* (Rohnert Park, CA: Center for Critical Thinking and Moral Critique, 1990).
45. John McPeck, *Teaching Critical Thinking: Dialogue and Dialectic* (New York: Routledge, 1990).
46. Ibid., 30.
47. Ibid.
48. Paul, *Critical Thinking*.
49. Freire, *Education for Critical Consciousness*; Freire, *Pedagogy of the Oppressed*; Henry Giroux, *Teachers as Intellectuals: Toward a Critical Pedagogy of Learning* (New York: Bergin & Garvey, 1988); Peter McLaren, *Life in Schools: An Introduction to Critical Pedagogy in the Foundations of Education* (New York: Longman, 1994); Barry Kanpol, *Critical Pedagogy: An Introduction* (Westport, CT: Bergin & Garvey, 1994).

50. Juan-Miguel Fernandez-Balboa and James P. Marshall, "Dialogical Pedagogy in Teacher Education: Toward an Education for Democracy," *Journal of Teacher Education* 45, no. 3 (May/June 1994): 172–82.

51. Ibid.

52. Ibid., 174.

53. David Hursh, "Multicultural Social Studies: Schools as Public Arenas for Understanding Diversity," *Social Science Record* 29, no. 1 (Spring 1992): 31–42.

54. Fernandez-Balboa and Marshall, "Dialogical Pedagogy," 175.

55. Lilia I. Bartolomé, "Beyond the Methods Fetish: Toward a Humanizing Pedagogy," *Harvard Educational Review* 64, no. 2 (Summer 1994): 173–94.

56. Freire, *Education for Critical Consciousness*: Freire, *Pedagogy of the Oppressed*.

57. Paulo Freire and Henry Giroux, "Pedagogy, Popular Culture, and Public Life: An Introduction," in Henry A. Giroux, R. I. Simon and Contributors, *Popular Culture: Schooling and Everyday Life* (New York: Bergin & Garvey, 1989), vii–xii.

58. Henry A. Giroux, *Living Dangerously*.

59. Freire and Giroux, "Pedagogy, Popular Culture," ix.

60. Giroux, "Rethinking Education," 729.

61. Søren Kierkegaard, *Concluding Unscientific Postscript*, trans. and ed. D. F. Swenson and W. Lowrie (Princeton, NJ: Princeton University Press, 1944), 267.

62. Søren Kierkegaard, *The Journals of Kierkegaard*, ed. and trans. A. Dru (New York: Harper, 1959), 46.

63. See Johanna Nel and Donald S. Seckinger, "Johann Heinrich Pestalozzi in the 1990s: Implications for Today's Multicultural Classrooms," *The Educational Forum* 57, no. 4 (1993): 396.

64. Paulo Freire, *Pedagogy of the City* (New York: The Continuum Publishing Company, 1993), 41.

65. Maxine Greene, *Landscapes of Learning* (New York: Teachers College Press, 1978), 2.

66. John Dewey, *Experience and Education* (1938; reprint, New York: Collier Books, 1963), 89.

67. Paulo Freire, *Pedagogy of the Oppressed*; Jean-Paul Sartre, *Situations 1* (Paris: Librairie Gallimard, 1947).

68. Lauren Resnick, *Education and Learning to Think* (Washington, DC: National Academy Press, 1987), 5.

69. Bert Bower, "History Alive! An Alternative Program for Engaging Diverse Learners," *The Educational Forum* 58, no. 3 (1994): 315–22.

70. Henry A. Giroux and Peter McLaren, "Teacher Education and the Politics of Engagement: The Case for Democratic Schooling" in Pepi Leistyna, Arlie Woodrum and Stephen A. Sherblom, eds., *Breaking Free: The Transformative Power of Critical Pedagogy* (Cambridge, MA: Harvard Educational Review-Reprint Series, no. 27, 1996), 309.

71. Ibid., 308.

72. Ibid., 311.

73. Ibid.

74. Ibid., 312.

75. Ibid.

76. Ibid., 316.

77. Ibid., 318.

78. Benjamin R. Barber, *An Aristocracy of Everyone: The Politics of Education and the Future of America* (New York: Oxford University Press, 1992), 103.

79. See Kathleen Bennett de Marrais and Margaret D. LeCompte, *The Way Schools Work: A Sociological Analysis of Education* (New York: Longman, 1995), 15.

80. McLaren, *Life in Schools*, 227.

81. Giroux and McLaren, "Teacher Education," 324.

82. Ibid.

83. Giroux, *Teachers as Intellectuals*, 33.

Bibliography

Abernethy, David B. *The Political Dilemma of Popular Education: An African Case*. Stanford, CA: Stanford University Press, 1969.
Achebe, Chinua. *No Longer At Ease*. London: Heinemann, 1965.
———. *Things Fall Apart*. London: Heinemann, 1965.
———. *A Man of the People*. London: Heinemann, 1966.
Adeleke, Tunde. "Africa and Pan-Africanism: Betrayal of a Historic Cause." *The Western Journal of Black Studies* 21, no. 2 (1997): 106–16.
Afigbo, A. E. "The Mission, the State and Education in South-Eastern Nigeria, 1956–1971." In E. Fasholé-Luke, R. Gray, A. Hastings, and G. Tasie, eds., *Christianity in Independent Africa* (176–92). Ibadan, Nigeria: Ibadan University Press, 1978.
Ajayi, J. F. Ade. "Nineteenth Century Origins of Nigerian Nationalism." *Journal of the Historical Society of Nigeria* 2, no. 2 (1961): 196–210.
———. *Christian Missions in Nigeria 1841–1891: The Making of a New Elite*. Evanston, IL: Northwestern University Press, 1965.
Akinfeleye, Ralph A. "The Youth, Education, Mass Media and Nation Building." In Charles E. Nnolim, ed., *The Role of Education in Contemporary Africa* (117–33). New York: Professors World Peace Academy, 1988.
Akpan, N. U. *The Struggle for Secession, 1966–1970*. London: Frank Cass, 1972.
Almond, Gabriel A., and Sidney Verba. *The Civic Culture*. Princeton, NJ: Princeton University Press, 1963.
Altbach, Philip G. "The Distribution of Knowledge in the Third World: A Case Study in Neocolonialism." In Philip G. Altbach and Gail P. Kelly, eds., *Education and Colonialism* (301–30). New York: Longman, 1978.

Altbach, Philip G., and Gail P. Kelly, eds. *Education and Colonialism*. New York: Longman, 1978.

Apple, Michael W. *Cultural Politics & Education*. New York: Teachers College Press, 1996.

Arcilla, René Vincente. "For the Stranger in My Home: Self-Knowledge, Cultural Recognition, and Philosophy of Education." In Wendy Kohli, ed., *Critical Conversations in Philosophy of Education* (159–72). New York: Routledge, 1995.

Aronowitz, Stanley, and Henry A. Giroux. *Education Under Seige: The Conservative, Liberal and Radical Debate Over Schooling*. South Hadley, MA: Bergin & Garvey, 1985.

Ashley, Dominic T. "The Role of Education in Combating Violence in Sierra Leone." In Charles E. Nnolim, ed., *The Role of Education in Contemporary Africa* (41–52). New York: Professors World Peace Academy, 1988.

Awoonor, Kofi. *The Breast of the Earth: A Survey of the History, Culture, and Literature of Africa South of the Sahara*. Garden City, NY: Anchor Press/Doubleday, 1975.

Ayandele, Emmanuel A. *The Missionary Impact on Modern Nigeria 1842–1914: A Political and Social Analysis*. New York: Humanities Press, 1967.

———. "Introduction." In Emmanuel A. Ayandele, ed., *Adventures and Missionary Leaders in Several Countries in Africa from 1849 to 1856*. London: Frank Cass, 1968.

———. "Traditional Rulers and Missionaries in Pre-Colonial West Africa." *Tarikh* 3, no. 1 (1969): 23–37.

———. *Nigerian Historical Studies*. London: Frank Cass, 1979.

———. "The Missionary Factor in Northern Nigeria, 1870–1918." In O. U. Kalu, ed., *The History of Christianity in West Africa*. Essex, England: Longman, 1980.

———, ed. *Adventures and Missionary Leaders in Several Countries in Africa from 1849 to 1856*. 1857. Reprint, London: Frank Cass, 1968.

Barber, Benjamin R. *An Aristocracy of Everyone: The Politics of Education and the Future of America*. New York: Oxford University Press, 1992.

Barkan, Joel D. "African University Students and the Dilemmas of Development." In Victor C. Uchendu, ed., *Education and Politics in Tropical Africa* (176–90). New York: Conch Magazine, 1979.

Bartolomé, Lilia I. "Beyond the Methods Fetish: Toward a Humanizing Pedagogy." *Harvard Educational Review* 64, no. 2 (Summer 1994): 173–94.

Bassey, Magnus O. "The Politics of Education in Nigeria: The Case of Government Take-Over of Schools in the Cross River and Kano States." Unpublished Doctoral Dissertation, Rutgers University, 1989.

———. "Missionary Rivalry and Educational Expansion in Southern Nigeria, 1885–1932." *Journal of Negro Education* 60, no. 1 (Winter 1991): 36–46.

———. "Multicultural Education: Its Unexplored Philosophical Themes." *Western Journal of Black Studies* 17, no. 4 (1993): 202–08.

———. "The Place of Dialogical Pedagogy in the Academy." *College at Oneonta Teaching Notes* 1, no. 6 (1995): 1–2.

———. "Teachers as Cultural Brokers in the Midst of Diversity." *Educational Foundations* 10, no. 2 (1996): 37–52.

———. "Preparing Teachers for the 21st Century: Connecting Preservice Teachers with Community." *Educational Change* (Spring 1997): 29–37.
———. "Multicultural Education, Philosophy, Theory and Practice." *Western Journal of Black Studies* 21, no. 4 (1997).
———. *Missionary Rivalry and Educational Expansion in Nigeria, 1885–1945*. Lewiston, NY: The Edwin Mellen Press, 1999.
Bello, Sir Alhaji Ahmadu. *My Life*. Cambridge: Cambridge University Press, 1962.
Berman, Edward H. *African Reactions to Missionary Education*. New York: Teachers College Press, 1975.
Bernstein, Basil. *Class, Codes and Control, Vol. III: Towards a Theory of Educational Transmission*. London: Routledge & Kegan Paul, 1977.
Beshir, Mohamed Omer. *Educational Development in the Sudan, 1898–1956*. London: Oxford University Press, 1969.
Beti, Mongo. *Mission to Kala*. London: Heinemann, 1965.
Bourdieu, Pierre. "Cultural Reproduction and Social Reproduction." In R. K. Brown, ed., *Knowledge, Education and Cultural Change: Papers in the Sociology of Education*. London: Tavistock, 1973.
Bowen, T. J. *Adventures and Missionary Labours in Several Countries in Africa from 1849–1856*. 2nd ed. 1857. Reprint, London: Frank Cass, 1968.
Bower, Bert. "History Alive! An Alternative Program for Engaging Diverse Learners." *The Educational Forum* 58, no. 3 (1994): 315–22.
Bowman, M. J., and C. A. Anderson. "Concerning the Role of Education in Development." In C. Greertz, ed., *Old Societies and New States: The Quest for Modernity in Asia and Africa*. New York: Free Press, 1963.
Boyd, W. *The History of Western Education*. New York: Barnes and Noble, 1965.
Bray, M. *Universal Primary Education in Nigeria: A Study of Kano State*. London: Routledge & Kegan Paul, 1981.
Brown, Leon Carl. "Tunisia." In James S. Coleman, ed., *Education and Political Development* (144–68). Princeton, NJ: Princeton University Press, 1965.
Burns, Sir Alan. *History of Nigeria*. London: George Allen and Unwin Ltd., 1958.
Busia, K. A. *The Challenge of Africa*. New York: Praeger, 1962.
———. *Purposeful Education for Africa*. The Hague: Mouton and Company, 1964.
Buxton, Thomas Fowell. *The African Slave Trade and its Remedy*. 1839. Reprint, London: Frank Cass, 1976.
Callaway, B. *Muslim Hausa Women in Nigeria: Tradition and Change*. Syracuse, NY: Syracuse University Press, 1987.
Carlson, Dennis. "Teachers as Political Actors: From Reproductive Theory to the Crisis of Schooling." In Pepi Leistyna, Arlie Woodrum and Stephen A. Sherblom, eds., *Breaking Free: The Transformative Power of Critical Pedagogy* (273–300). Cambridge, MA: Harvard Educational Review-Reprint No. 27, 1996.
Chabal, Patrick. *Power in Africa: An Essay in Political Interpretation*. New York: St. Martin's Press, 1994.
Cherkaoui, Mohamed. "Bernstein and Durkheim: Two Theories of Change in Educational Systems." *Harvard Educational Review* 47, no. 4 (1977): 556–64.
Clarke, Peter B. "Islam, Education and the Development Process in Nigeria." *Comparative Education* 14 no. 2 (1978): 133–41.
———. "The Methods and Ideology of the Holy Ghost Fathers in Eastern Ni-

geria, 1885–1905." In O. U. Kalu, ed., *The History of Christianity in West Africa* (36–62). Essex, England: Longman, 1980.

———. *West Africa and Islam: A Study of Religious Development from the 8th to the 20th Century*. London: Edward Arnold, 1982.

Clignet, Remi. "Education and Elite Formation." In John N. Paden and Edward W. Soja, eds., *The African Experience, Vol. 1: Essays* (304–58). Evanston, IL: Northwestern University Press, 1970.

———. "Damned If You Do, Damned If You Don't: The Dilemmas of Colonizer-Colonized Relations." In Philip G. Altbach and Gail. P. Kelly, eds., *Education and Colonialism* (122–45). New York: Longman, 1978.

Clignet, Remi, and Philip Foster. *The Fortunate Few: A Study of Secondary Schools and Students in the Ivory Coast*. Evanston, IL: Northwestern University Press, 1966.

Cohen, Ronald. "Traditional Society in Africa." In John N. Paden and Edward W. Soja, eds., *The African Experience, Vol. 1: Essays* (37–60). Evanston, IL: Northwestern University Press, 1970.

Coleman, James S. *Nigeria: Background to Nationalism*. Berkeley: University of California Press, 1958.

———. "Introduction: Education and Political Development." In James S. Coleman, ed., *Education and Political Development* (3–32). Princeton, NJ: Princeton University Press, 1965.

———. "Introduction to Part I." In James S. Coleman, ed., *Education and Political Development* (35–50). Princeton, NJ: Princeton University Press, 1965.

———. "Introduction to Part III." In James S. Coleman, ed., *Education and Political Development* (353–71). Princeton, NJ: Princeton University Press, 1965.

———, ed. *Education and Political Development*. Princeton, NJ: Princeton University Press, 1965.

Court, David. "Education as Social Control: The Response to Inequality in Kenya and Tanzania." In Victor C. Uchendu, ed., *Education and Politics in Tropical Africa* (20–62). New York: Conch Magazine Limited Publishers, 1979.

Cramer, John, and George Browne. *Contemporary Education: A Comparative Study of National Systems*. New York: Harcourt, Brace and World, 1956.

Cross, Michael, and Linda Chisholm. "The Roots of Segregated Schooling in Twentieth-Century South Africa." In Mokubung Nkomo, ed., *Pedagogy of Domination: Toward a Democratic Education in South Africa* (43–74). Trenton, NJ: Africa World Press, 1990.

Crosson, V. L., and J. C. Stailey. *Spinning Stories: An Introduction to Storytelling Skills*. Austin: Texas State Library, Department of Library Development 1988. ERIC Document Reproduction Service No. ED 301195.

Crowder, Michael. *A Short History of Nigeria*. New York: Praeger, 1962.

———. *West Africa Under Colonial Rule*. Evanston, IL: Northwestern University Press, 1968.

———. "The Impact of Colonialism." In John N. Paden and Edward W. Soja, eds., *The African Experience, Vol. 1: Essays* (233–75). Evanston, IL: Northwestern University Press, 1970.

Debeauvais, Michel. "Education in Former French Africa." In James S. Coleman, ed., *Education and Political Development* (75–91). Princeton, NJ: Princeton University Press, 1965.

DeGraft-Johnson, K. E. "The Evolution of Elites in Ghana." In Peter C. Lloyd, ed., *The New Elites of Tropical Africa* (104–17). London: Oxford University Press, 1966.
DeMarrais, Kathleen Bennett, and Margaret D. LeCompte. *The Way Schools Work: A Sociological Analysis of Education*. New York: Longman, 1995.
Dewey, John. *Experience and Education*. 1938. Reprint, New York: Collier Books, 1963.
———. *Democracy and Education*. New York: Free Press, 1966.
Diejomaoh, Victor P. "The Economics of the Nigerian Conflict." In Joseph Okpaku, ed., *Nigeria: Dilemma of Nationhood: An African Analysis of the Biafran Conflict* (318–65). New York: The Third Press, 1972.
Dillard, Mary. "Objectivity and Opportunism: The Social Power of Mental Measurement in Anglophone West Africa." *Ufahamu* 24, no. 1. (1996): 22–41.
Doi, A.R.I. "Islam in Nigeria: Changes Since Independence." In Edward Fasholé-Luke et al., eds., *Christianity in Independent Africa*. Ibadan, Nigeria: Ibadan University Press, 1978.
Ekechi, Felix K. *Missionary Enterprise and Rivalry in Igboland, 1857–1914*. London: Frank Cass, 1972.
Emecheta, Buchi. *Second-Class Citizen*. Glasgow: William Collins Sons, 1974.
———. *The Bride Price*. Glasgow: William Collins Sons, 1982.
Emenyonu, Ernest N. *The Rise of the Igbo Novel*. Ibadan, Nigeria: Oxford University Press, 1978.
———. "Education and Contemporary Malaise in Nigeria." In Charles E. Nnolim, ed., *The Role of Education in Contemporary Africa* (31–40). New York: Professors World Peace Academy, 1988.
———. "Education as a Cooperative Venture: Towards Increased Parental Participation in the Educational Process in Nigeria." In Charles E. Nnolim, ed., *The Role of Education in Contemporary Africa* (91–97). New York: Professors World Peace Academy, 1988.
Enslin, Penny. "Science and Doctrine: Theoretical Discourse in South African Teacher Education." In Mokubung Nkomo, ed., *Pedagogy of Domination: Toward a Democratic Education in South Africa*. Trenton, NJ: Africa World Press, 1990.
Erese, W. I. "Equality of Educational Opportunity in Nigeria." In Nduka Okoh, ed., *Professional Education: A Book of Readings* (32–51). Benin City, Nigeria: Ethiope Publishing Corp., 1983.
Fafunwa, A. Babs. *History of Education in Nigeria*. London: George Allen and Unwin, 1974.
Fajana, A. "Missionary Educational Policy in Nigeria: 1842–1882." *West African Journal of Education* 14, no. 2 (1970).
Fasholé-Luke, Edward et al., eds. *Christianity in Independent Africa*. Ibadan, Nigeria: Ibadan University Press, 1978.
Fernandez-Balboa, Juan-Miguel, and James P. Marshall. "Dialogical Pedagogy in Teacher Education: Toward an Education for Democracy." *Journal of Teacher Education* 45, no. 3 (May/June 1994): 172–82.
Fiala, Thomas J. "William T. Harris: Rationalizing Public Education in the American State." *Educational Foundations* 12, no. 4 (Fall 1998).

Foster, Philip. *Education and Social Change in Ghana*. Chicago: The University of Chicago Press, 1965.

Foucault, Michel. *Discipline and Punish: The Birth of the Prison*. New York: Pantheon Books, 1977.

———. *The History of Sexuality: Volume 1: An Introduction*. New York: Vintage Books, 1978.

———. "Questions on Geography." In C. Gordon, ed., *Power/Knowledge: Selected Interviews and Other Writings, 1972–1977*. New York: Pantheon Books, 1980.

———. "Truth and Power." In C. Gordon, ed., *Power/Knowledge: Selected Interviews and Other Writings, 1972–1977*. New York: Pantheon Books, 1980.

Freeman, Bonnie Cook. "Female Education in Patriarchal Power Systems." In Philip G. Altbach and Gail P. Kelly, eds., *Education and Colonialism* (207–42). New York: Longman, 1978.

Freire, Paulo. *Cultural Action for Freedom*. Cambridge, MA: Harvard Educational Review, 1970.

———. *Pedagogy of the Oppressed*. 1970. Reprint, New York: The Continuum Publishing Company, 1994.

———. *Education for Critical Consciousness*. New York: The Continuum Publishing Company, 1973.

———. *The Politics of Education: Culture, Power, and Liberation*. South Hadley, MA: Bergin & Garvey, 1985.

———. *Pedagogy of the City*. New York: The Continuum Publishing Company, 1993.

———. *Pedagogy of Hope: Reliving Pedagogy of the Oppressed*. New York: The Continuum Publishing Company, 1994.

———. *Letters to Cristina: Reflections on My Life and Work*. New York: Routledge, 1996.

Freire, Paulo, and Henry A. Giroux. "Pedagogy, Popular Culture, and Public Life: An Introduction." In Henry A. Giroux, Roger I. Simon and Contributors, *Popular Culture: Schooling and Everyday Life*. (vii–xii). New York: Bergin & Garvey, 1989.

Freire, Paulo, and Donaldo Macedo. *Literacy: Reading the Word and the World*. South Hadley, MA: Bergin & Garvey, 1987.

———. "A Dialogue: Culture, Language, and Race." In Pepi Leistyna, Arlie Woodrum and Stephen A. Sherblom, eds., *Breaking Free: The Transformative Power of Critical Pedagogy* (199–228). Cambridge, MA: Harvard Educational Review-Reprint Series, no. 27 1996.

Giarelli, James M. "Education for Public Life." In Wendy Kohli, ed., *Critical Conversations in Philosophy of Education* (201–16). New York: Routledge, 1995.

Giroux, Henry A. "Theories of Reproduction and Resistance in the New Sociology of Education." *Harvard Educational Review* 53 (1983): 257–93.

———. *Theory and Resistance in Education: A Pedagogy for the Opposition*. South Hadley, MA: Bergin & Garvey, 1983.

———. *Teachers as Intellectuals: Toward a Critical Pedagogy of Learning*. New York: Bergin & Garvey, 1988.

———. "Rethinking Education Reform in the Age of George Bush." *Phi Delta Kappan* 70, no. 9 (1989): 728–30.

———. *Border Crossings: Cultural Workers and the Politics of Education.* New York: Routledge, 1992.

———. *Living Dangerously: Multiculturalism and the Politics of Difference.* New York: Peter Lang, 1993.

———. "Teaching in the Age of Political Correctness." *The Educational Forum* 59, no. 2 (1995): 130–39.

———. "Doing Cultural Studies: Youth and the Challenge of Pedagogy." In Pepi Leistyna, Arlie Woodrum and Stephen A. Sherblom, eds., *Breaking Free: The Transformative Power of Critical Pedagogy* (83–107). Cambridge, MA: Harvard Educational Review, 1996.

Giroux, Henry A., and Peter McLaren, eds. *Between Borders: Pedagogy and the Politics of Cultural Studies.* New York: Routledge, 1994.

Giroux, Henry A., and Peter McLaren. "Teacher Education and the Politics of Engagement: The Case for Democratic Schooling." In Pepi Leistyna, Arlie Woodrum and Stephen A. Sherblom, eds., *Breaking Free: The Transformative Power of Critical Pedagogy* (301–31). Cambridge, MA: Harvard Educational Review-Reprint Series no. 27, 1996.

Giroux, Henry A., Roger I. Simon, and Contributors. *Popular Culture: Schooling & Everyday Life.* New York: Bergin & Garvey, 1989.

Gordon, C., ed. *Power/Knowledge: Selected Interviews and Other Writings, 1972–1977.* New York: Pantheon Books, 1980.

Greene, Maxine. *Landscapes of Learning.* New York: Teachers College Press, 1978.

———. "Multiple Voices and Multiple Realities: A Reviewing of Educational Foundations." *Educational Foundations* 4, no. 2 (1990): 5–19.

———. "In Search of a Critical Pedagogy." In Pepi Leistyna, Arlie Woodrum and Stephen A. Sherblom, eds., *Breaking Free: The Transformative Power of Critical Pedagogy* (13–30). Cambridge, MA: Harvard Educational Review, 1996.

Grey, Robert D. "Education and Politicization." In Victor C. Uchendu, ed., *Education and Politics in Tropical Africa* (152–71). New York: Conch Magazine Publishers, 1979.

Gutteridge, William F. "Education of Military Leadership in Emergent States." In James S. Coleman, ed., *Education and Political Development* (437–62). Princeton, NJ: Princeton University Press, 1965.

Hanna, William John. "University Students and African Politics: A Research Review and Preview." In Victor C. Uchendu, ed., *Education and Politics in Tropical Africa* (126–47). New York: Conch Magazine Limited Publishers, 1979.

Harrington, H. "Teaching and Knowing." *Journal of Teacher Education* 45, no. 3 (1994): 190–98.

Hodgkin, Thomas. *Nationalism in Colonial Africa.* London: Frederick Muller, 1956.

Hooks, Bell. *Teaching to Transgress: Education as the Practice of Freedom.* New York: Routledge, 1994.

Hoselitz, Bert F. "Investment in Education and its Political Impact." In James S. Coleman, ed., *Education and Political Development* (541–65). Princeton, NJ: Princeton University Press, 1965.

Hursh, David. "Multicultural Social Studies: Schools as Public Arenas for Un-

derstanding Diversity." *Social Science Record* 29, no. 1 (Spring 1992): 31–42.
Johnson, Walton R., "Education: Keystone of Apartheid." *Anthropology & Education Quarterly* 13, no. 3 (1982): 214–37.
Kaba, Brahima D. "The Role of Education in Combating Violence." In Charles E. Nnolim, ed., *The Role of Education in Contemporary Africa* (53–57). New York: Professors World Peace Academy, 1988.
Kalu, O. U., ed., *The History of Christianity in West Africa*. Essex: Longman, 1980.
Kandel, I. *Comparative Education*. New York: Teachers College Press, 1933.
Kanpol, Barry. *Critical Pedagogy: An Introduction*. Westport, CT: Bergin & Garvey, 1994.
Kelly, Gail P., and Philip G. Altbach. "Introduction." In Philip G. Altbach and Gail P. Kelly, eds., *Education and Colonialism* (1–49). New York: Longman, 1978.
Kerr, Malcolm H. "Egypt." In James S. Coleman, ed., *Education and Political Development* (169–94). Princeton, NJ: Princeton University Press, 1965.
Keto, C. Tsehloane. "Pre-Industrial Education Policies and Practices in South Africa." In Mokubung Nkomo, ed., *Pedagogy of Domination: Toward a Democratic Education in South Africa* (19–42). Trenton, NJ: Africa World Press, 1990.
Kierkegaard, Søren. *Concluding Unscientific Postscript*. Edited and translated by D. F. Swenson and W. Lowrie. Princeton, NJ: Princeton University Press, 1944.
———. *The Journals of Kierkegaard*. Edited and translated by A. Dru. New York: Harper, 1959.
Kincheloe, Joe L., and Shirley R. Steinberg. "A Tentative Description of Post-Formal Thinking: The Critical Confrontation with Cognitive Theory." In Pepi Leistyna, Arlie Woodrum and Stephen A. Sherblom, eds., *Breaking Free: The Transformative Power of Critical Pedagogy* (167–95). Cambridge, MA: Harvard Educational Review-Reprint Series, no. 27, 1996.
Knight, John B., and Richard H. Sabot. *Education, Productivity, and Inequality: The East African Natural Experiment*. New York: Oxford University Press, 1990.
Kreisberg, Seth. *Transforming Power: Domination, Empowerment and Education*. Albany: State University of New York Press, 1992.
Lankshear, Colin, and Peter McLaren, eds. *Critical Literacy: Politics, Praxis, and the Postmodern*. Albany: State University of New York Press, 1993.
Laye, Camara. *The African Child*. London: Fontana/Collins, 1959.
Leistyna, Pepi, and S. Sherblom. "A Dialogue with Noam Chomsky." In Pepi Leistyna, Arlie Woodrum and Stephen A. Sherblom, eds., *Breaking Free: The Transformative Power of Critical Pedagogy* (109–28). Cambridge, MA: Harvard Educational Review-Reprint Series, no. 27, 1996.
Leistyna, Pepi, and Arlie Woodrum, "Context and Culture: What is Critical Pedagogy?" In Pepi Leistyna, Arlie Woodrum and Stephen A. Sherblom, eds., *Breaking Free: The Transformative Power of Critical Pedagogy* (1–7). Cambridge, MA: Harvard Educational Review-Reprint Series, no. 27, 1996.
Leistyna, Pepi, Arlie Woodrum, Stephen A. Sherblom, eds., *Breaking Free: The Transformative Power of Critical Pedagogy*. Cambridge, MA: Harvard Educational Review-Reprint Series, no. 27, 1996.

LeVine, Victor T. "Role Ambiguity and Corruption: Bureaucrat and Apparatchik in African Political Systems." *Philippine Journal of Public Administration* 38, no. 1 (1994).

Lewis, Magda, and Roger I. Simon "A Discourse Not Intended for Her: Learning and Teaching within Patriarchy." In Pepi Leistyna, Arlie Woodrum and Stephen A. Sherblom, eds., *Breaking Free: The Transformative Power of Critical Pedagogy* (253–71). Cambridge, MA: Harvard Educational Review-Reprint Series, no. 27, 1996.

Lintner, Timothy. "Learning A New Language—Re-Framing the Discourse on African Education." *Ufahamu* 24, no. 1 (1996): 4–8.

Lipman, M., A. M. Sharp and F. S. Oscanyan. *Philosophy in the Classroom*. Philadelphia: Temple University Press, 1980.

Little, Kenneth L. "The Role of the Secret Society in Cultural Specialization." *American Anthropologist* 51, no. 2 (1949): 199–212.

Lloyd, Barbara B. "Education and Family Life in the Development of Class Identification among the Yoruba." In Peter C. Lloyd, ed., *The New Elites of Tropical Africa* (163–81). London: Oxford University Press, 1966.

Lloyd, Peter C. "Introduction." In Peter C. Lloyd, ed., *The New Elites of Tropical Africa*. (1–65). London: Oxford University Press, 1966.

———. *Africa in Social Change: Changing Traditional Societies in the Modern World*. Baltimore, MD: Penguin Books, 1967.

———, ed. *The New Elites of Tropical Africa*. London: Oxford University Press, 1966.

Lucas, Christopher J. "The More Things Change . . ." *Phi Delta Kappan* (February 1980).

Lugard, L. *The Dual Mandate in British Tropical Africa*. 5th ed. London: Frank Cass, 1965.

Lukhero, M. B. "The Social Characteristics of an Emergent Elite in Harare." In Peter C. Lloyd, ed., *The New Elites of Tropical Africa* (126–37). London: Oxford University Press, 1966.

Macedo, Donaldo P. "Literacy for Stupidification: The Pedagogy of Big Lies." In Pepi Leistyna, Arlie Woodrum and Stephen A. Sherblom, eds., *Breaking Free: The Transformative Power of Critical Pedagogy* (31–57). Cambridge, MA: Harvard Education Review-Reprint Series, no. 27, 1996.

Mackenzie, Clayton G. "Prisoners of Fortune: Commonwealth African Universities and Their Political Masters." *Comparative Education* 22, no. 2 (1986): 111–20.

———. "Demythologizing the Missionaries: A Reassessment of the Functions and Relationships of Christian Missionary Education Under Colonialism." *Comparative Education* 19, no. 1 (1993).

Madike, F. U. "Aims in Education: Nature & Effects of External Imposition of Aims." In Nduka Okoh, ed., *Professional Education: A Book of Readings* (52–57). Benin City, Nigeria: Ethiope Publishing Corporation, 1983.

———. "Humanism in Education: A Brief Historical Survey." In Nduka Okoh, ed., *Professional Education: A Book of Readings* (7–15). Benin City, Nigeria: Ethiope Publishing Corp., 1983.

———. "State Control of Education: A Critical Philosophical Analysis." In

Nduka Okoh, ed., *Professional Education: A Book of Readings* (58–63). Benin City, Nigeria: Ethiope Publishing Corp., 1983.

Makulu, H. F. *Education, Development and Nation Building in Independent Africa.* London: SCM Press, 1991.

Mallinson, Vernon. *An Introduction to the Study of Comparative Education.* New York: Heinemann, 1966.

Marshall, James D. "Needs, Interests, Growth and Personal Autonomy: Foucault on Power." In Wendy Kohli, ed., *Critical Conversations in Philosophy of Education* (364–78). New York: Routledge, 1995.

Marvick, Dwaine. "African University Students: A Presumptive Elite." In James S. Coleman, ed., *Education and Political Development* (463–97). Princeton, NJ: Princeton University Press, 1965.

Mathabane, Mark. *Kaffir Boy in America.* New York: Collier Books, 1989.

Mathews, Kay. "Some Reflections on Education and National Development in Africa." In Charles E. Nnolim, ed., *The Role of Education in Contemporary Africa* (71–89). New York: Professors World Peace Academy, 1988.

Mbata, J. Congress. "Race and Resistance in South Africa." In John N. Paden and Edward W. Soja, eds., *The African Experience, Vol. I: Essays* (210–32). Evanston, IL: Northwestern University Press, 1970.

Mbiti, John S. *African Religions and Philosophy.* Garden City, NY: Anchor Books, 1970.

McCarthy, Cameron. "Rethinking Liberal and Radical Perspectives on Racial Inequality in Schooling: Making the Case for Nonsynchrony." In Pepi Leistyna, Arlie Woodrum and Stephen A. Sherblom, eds., *Breaking Free: The Transformative Power of Critical Pedagogy* (149–66). Cambridge, MA: Harvard Education Review-Reprint Series, no. 27, 1996.

McLaren, Peter. *Life in Schools: An Introduction to Critical Pedagogy in the Foundations of Education.* New York: Longman, 1994.

McLaren, Peter, and Rhonda Hammer. "Critical Pedagogy and Postmodern Challenge: Towards a Critical Postmodernist Pedagogy of Liberation." *Educational Foundations* 3, no. 3 (1989): 29–62.

McPeck, John. *Teaching Critical Thinking: Dialogue and Dialectic.* New York: Routledge, 1990.

McQueen, Albert J. "Urban Youth on the Margins of Nigerian Society: Research and Theoretical Perspectives." In Victor C. Uchendu, ed., *Education and Politics in Tropical Africa* (87–115). New York: Conch Magazine Publishers, 1979.

Meek, C. K. *The Northern Tribes of Nigeria.* New York: Negro Universities Press, 1969.

Meier, Kenneth J., Joseph Stewart Jr. and Robert E. England. *Race, Class, and Education: The Politics of Second-Generation Discrimination.* Madison: The University of Wisconsin Press, 1989.

Milbraith, Lester, Gabriel A. Almond, and Sidney Verba. *Political Participation.* Chicago: Rand-McNally, 1965.

Moumouni, Abdou. *Education in Africa.* London: Andre Deutsch, 1968.

Mungazi, Dickson A., and L. Kay Walker. *Educational Reform and the Transformation of Southern Africa.* Westport, CT: Praeger, 1997.

Naylor, W. S. *Daybreak in the Dark Continent*. New York: Young Peoples Missionary Movement, 1905.

Nduka, O. "Background to the Foundation of Dennis Memorial Grammar School, Onitsha." *Journal of the Historical Society of Nigeria* 8, no. 3 (1976): 69–92.

Nel, Johanna, and Donald S. Seckinger. "Johann Heinrich Pestalozzi in the 1990s: Implications for Today's Multicultural Classrooms." *The Educational Forum* 57, no. 4 (1993): 396–401.

Nkomo, Mokubung. "Introduction." In Mokubung Nkomo, ed., *Pedagogy of Domination: Toward a Democratic Education in South Africa* (1–15). Trenton, NJ: Africa World Press, 1990.

———, ed. *Pedagogy of Domination: Toward a Democratic Education in South Africa*. Trenton, NJ: Africa World Press, 1990.

Nnoli, Okwudiba. "Education and Ethnic Politics in Nigeria." In Victor C. Uchendu, ed., *Education and Politics in Tropical Africa* (63–81). New York: Conch Magazine Publishers, 1979.

Nnolim, Charles E. "The Implications of Education in the Humanities for Good Citizenship." In Charles E. Nnolim, ed., *The Role of Education in Contemporary Africa* (99–108). New York: Professors World Peace Academy, 1988.

———. "Moral Values in the Nigerian Novel." In Charles E. Nnolim, ed., *The Role of Education in Contemporary Africa* (21–29). New York: Professors World Peace Academy, 1988.

———, ed. *The Role of Education in Contemporary Africa*. New York: Professors World Peace Academy, 1988.

Nwamuo, Chris I. "Youth Education Through the Theatre." In Charles E. Nnolim, ed., *The Role of Education in Contemporary Africa* (109–16). New York: Professors World Peace Academy, 1988.

Obichere, Boniface I. "Politicians and Educational Reform in French-Speaking West Africa: A Comparative Study of Mali and the Ivory Coast." In Victor C. Uchendu, ed., *Education and Politics in Tropical Africa* (196–201). New York: Conch Magazine Limited Publishers, 1979.

Odaga, Adhiambo, and Ward Heneveld. *Girls and Schools in Sub-Saharan Africa: From Analysis to Action*. Washington, DC: The World Bank, 1995.

Ognibene, Richard. "Social Foundations and School Reform Networks: The Case against E. D. Hirsch." *Educational Foundations* 12, no. 4 (Fall 1998): 5–27.

Ogunsheye, Ayo. "Nigeria." In James S. Coleman, ed., *Education and Political Development* (123–43). Princeton, NJ: Princeton University Press, 1965.

Okoh, Nduka, ed. *Professional Education: A Book of Readings*. Benin City, Nigeria: Ethiope Publishing Corp., 1983.

Okoli, Ekwueme F. "Education Policies and Moral Values in Nigeria." In Charles E. Nnolim, ed., *The Role of Education in Contemporary Africa* (59–69). New York: Professors World Peace Academy, 1988.

Okonkwo, Chuka Eze. "Education and the African Novel: Perceptions of a Culture in Crisis." *Journal of African Studies* 12, no. 1 (Summer 1985): 103–10.

Okpaku, Joseph, ed. *Nigeria: Dilemma of Nationhood: An African Analysis of the Biafran Conflict*. Westport, CT: Greenwood, 1972.

Oliver, Roland. *The Missionary Factor in East Africa*. London: Longman, 1967.

Omolewa, Michael. "London University's Earliest Examinations in Nigeria, 1887–1931." *West African Journal of Education* 20, no. 2 (1976).

Opoku, Kofi A. "Education and Moral Values in Contemporary Africa: The Role of the Family in Education (The Akan of Ghana)." In Charles E. Nnolim, ed., *The Role of Education in Contemporary Africa* (1–11). New York: Professors World Peace Academy, 1988.

Oyono, Ferdinand. *Boy*. New York: Collier Books, 1974.

Paden, John N. "African Concepts of Nationhood." In John N. Paden and Edward W. Soja, eds., *The African Experience, Vol. I: Essays* (403–33). Evanston, IL: Northwestern University Press, 1970.

Paden, John N., and Edward W. Soja, eds. *The African Experience, Vol. I: Essays*. Evanston, IL: Northwestern University Press, 1970.

Paul, Richard. *Critical Thinking: What Every Person Needs to Survive in a Rapidly Changing World*. Rohnert Park, CA: Center for Critical Thinking and Moral Critique, 1990.

Perkinson, Henry J. *The Imperfect Panacea: American Faith in Education 1865–1990*. New York: McGraw-Hill, 1991.

Platt, William J. "Conflicts in Educational Planning." In James S. Coleman, ed., *Education and Political Development* (566–82). Princeton, NJ: Princeton University Press, 1965.

Pulliam, John D., and James J. Van Patten, *History of Education in America*, seventh edition (Upper Saddle River, NJ: Prentice-Hall, 1999), 17.

Pye, Lucian W. *Politics, Personality and Nation Building: Burma's Search for Identity* (New Haven: Yale University Press, 1962).

Reagan, Timothy. "Philosophy of Education in the Service of Apartheid: The Role of 'Fundamental Pedagogics' in South African Education." *Educational Foundations* 4, no. 2 (1990): 59–71.

Resnick, Lauren. *Education and Learning to Think*. Washington, DC: National Academy Press, 1987.

Rolheiser, Carol, and Carl D. Glickman. "Teaching for Democratic Life." *The Educational Forum* 59, no. 2 (1995): 196–206.

Rubanza, Y. I. "Can a Three-Tier Language Policy Model Work in Tanzania? A New Perspective." *Ufahamu* 24, no. 1 (1996): 82–97.

Sartre, Jean-Paul. *Situations 1*. Paris, Librairie Gallimard, 1947.

Schultz, Fred, ed. *Sources: Notable Selections in Education*. 2nd ed. Guilford, CT: Dushkin/McGraw-Hill, 1998.

Shapiro, Svi. "Towards a Language of Educational Politics: The Struggle for a Critical Public Discourse of Education." *Educational Foundations* 3, no. 3 (1989): 79–100.

———. "Postmodern Dilemmas." In Wendy Kohli, ed., *Critical Conversations in Philosophy of Education* (298–309). New York: Routledge, 1995.

Shor, Ira. *Critical Teaching & Everyday Life*. Chicago: The University of Chicago Press, 1987.

———. *Empowering Education: Critical Teaching for Social Change*. Chicago: The University of Chicago Press, 1992.

Shor, Ira, and Paulo Freire. *A Pedagogy for Liberation: Dialogues on Transforming Education*. New York: Bergin and Garvey, 1987.

Shultz, T. W. "Investment in Man: An Economist's View." *Social Science Review* 33 (1959): 309–17.

———. "Investment in Human Capital." *American Economic Review* 51 (1961): 1–17.
Smith, A. *The Wealth of Nations*. 1760. Reprint, London: Dent.
Soja, Edward W. "Introduction to the African Experience." In John N. Paden and Edward W. Soja, eds., *The African Experience, Vol. I: Essays* (3–19). Evanston, IL: Northwestern University Press, 1970.
Soja, Edward W., and John N. Paden. "The African Setting." In John N. Paden and Edward W. Soja, eds., *The African Experience, Vol. I: Essays* (20–36). Evanston, IL: Northwestern University Press, 1970.
Solaru, T. T. *Teacher Training in Nigeria*. Ibadan, Nigeria: Ibadan University Press, 1964.
Spencer, David. "Transitional Bilingual Education and the Socialization of Immigrants." In Pepi Leistyna, Arlie Woodrum and Stephen A. Sherblom, eds., *Breaking Free: The Transformative Power of Critical Pedagogy* (59–82). Cambridge, MA: Harvard Educational Review-Reprint Series, no. 27, 1996.
Sutton, Francis X. "Education and the Making of Modern Nations." In James S. Coleman, ed., *Education and Political Development* (51–74). Princeton, NJ: Princeton University Press, 1965.
Swartz, David. "Pierre Bourdieu: The Cultural Transmission of Social Inequality." *Harvard Educational Review* 47, no. 4 (1977): 545–55.
Talbot, P. Amaury. *The Peoples of Southern Nigeria*. Vol. 4. London: Frank Cass, 1969.
Thompson, A. R. *Education and Development in Africa* (London: Macmillan, 1983).
Thompson, Audrey, and Andrew Gitlin. "Creating Spaces for Reconstructing Knowledge in Feminist Pedagogy." *Educational Theory* 45, no. 2 (1995): 125–50.
Tierney, William G. "Academic Freedom and the Parameters of Knowledge." In Pepi Leistyna, Arlie Woodrum and Stephen A. Sherblom, eds., *Breaking Free: The Transformative Power of Critical Pedagogy* (129–48). Cambridge, MA: Harvard Educational Review-Reprint Series, no. 27, 1996.
Tordoff, William. *Government and Politics in Africa*. Bloomington: Indiana University Press, 1991.
Ubah, C. N. "Problems of Christian Missionaries in the Muslim Emirates of Nigeria." *Journal of African Studies* 3, no. 3 (1976): 351–71.
Uchendu, Victor C. "Education and the Public Interest: The Politics of the Public Domain." In Victor C. Uchendu, ed., *Education and Politics in Tropical Africa* (280–94). New York: Conch Magazine Limited Publishers, 1979.
———. "Introduction." In Victor C. Uchendu, ed., *Education and Politics in Tropical Africa* (1–17). New York: Conch Magazine Limited Publishers, 1979.
Uzoigwe, Godfrey N., and Onyewuchi S. Chimezie. "The Role of the Family in Education: An African Perspective." In Charles E. Nnolim, ed., *The Role of Education in Contemporary Africa* (13–19). New York: Professors World Peace Academy, 1988.
Van den Berghe, Pierre L. "Major Themes in Social Change." In John N. Paden and Edward W. Soja, eds., *The African Experience, Vol. 1: Essays* (252–75). Evanston, IL: Northwestern University Press, 1970.
———. "Education, Class, and Ethnicity in Southern Peru: Revolutionary Colo-

nialism." In Philip G. Altbach and Gail P. Kelly, eds., *Education and Colonialism* (270–98). New York: Longman, 1978.

Webster, James Bertin. "The Bible and the Plough." *Journal of the Historical Society of Nigeria* 2, no. 4 (1963): 418–34.

Weis, Lois, ed. *Class, Race and Gender in American Education*. Albany: State University of New York Press, 1988.

Weis, Lois, and Michelle Fine, eds. *Beyond Silenced Voices: Class, Race and Gender in United States Schools*. Albany: State University of New York Press, 1993.

Welbourn, F. B. *East African Rebels*. London: London University Press, 1961.

Westermann, D. *Africa and Christianity*. Oxford: Oxford University Press, 1937.

Woodson, Carter G. *The Mis-Education of the Negro*. 1933. Reprint, Trenton, NJ: Africa World Press, 1990.

Worsley, Peter. *The Third World*. Chicago: The University of Chicago Press, 1977.

Young, Crawford. "Political Systems Development." In John N. Paden and Edward W. Soja, eds., *The African Experience, Vol. I: Essays* (452–72). Evanston, IL: Northwestern University Press, 1970.

Zolberg, Aristide. "Patterns of Nation-Building." In John N. Paden and Edward W. Soja, eds., *The African Experience, Vol. I: Essays* (434–51). Evanston, IL: Northwestern University Press, 1970.

Index

't' indicates a table

Abacha, Sani, 78, 79
Abdu, Muhammad, 45
Abernethy, David B., 6, 9, 30, 41, 43–44, 54, 56, 64, 82, 107
Accra Baptist School (Ghana), 67
Achebe, Chinua, 38, 80
Achimota College (Ghana), 64
Action Group (AG), 69
"Adapted" schools, 45
Adeleke, Tunde, 77–78, 79, 81
Adjaye, Nana Annor, 42
Administrative state, in Africa, 77
African boys: fishing education, 20–21; hardships in traditional society, 17; modern education of, 87
African education: characteristics of post-colonial, 84–98; characteristics of traditional, 22–25; traditional, 11, 15–22
African elites: characteristics of, 2, 51; children of, 6–7; creation of, 1, 29, 44, 62–63, 70, 71; educational interest of, 106; French colonial policy, 30; institutional control by, 2; intellectual discourse, control of, 3–4
African girls: modern education of, 9, 87, 91–93, 92t; traditional education of, 21
African Inland Mission, 52
African men, status of, 6
African political elites: creation of, 1–2, 3, 12, 46, 68–71; political domination by, 1, 3, 12–13
African Slave Trade and Its Remedy, The, 28, 62
African state, development of, 76–82
African women, education of, 9
Agbebi, Mojola, 67
Age-grades, role in traditional education, 16
Agricultural education, in traditional education, 19, 20
Ahidjo, Ahmadou, 69
Ahuma, Attoh, 68
Ajayi, J. F. Ade, 2, 63, 66, 70
Ajayi Commission, on education, 2

Algeria: ethnic crises in, 6; political developments in, 78
Alienation, in school system, 83–84
Alliance of Protestant Missionary Societies, anticolonial view, 67–68
Altbach, Philip G., 45, 46
Amin, Idi, 78–79, 82
Angola: political developments in, 78, 79; Portuguese educational policy in, 33–35
Apartheid: education, aims of, 102–103; in South Africa, 8, 9, 101–4
Apprenticeship, traditional education, 20–21
Apter, D. E., 59
Army, ethnic representation in, 5–6, 44
Ashanti, missionary activity among, 52, 59
Ashby, Eric, 1
Ashley, Dominic T., 22, 24
Asians, education in Africa, 59
Assimilado, 33–34, 36
Ayandele, Emmanuel A., 43, 44, 46, 53, 58

Babalola, A., 19
Babangida, Ibrahim, 78, 82
Balewa, Mallam Abubakar Tafawa, 109
Banana, Canaan, 24
Banda, Hastings Kamuzu, 68, 82
"Banking" education, 4, 85–89, 114–15, 119
Bantu Education Act, South Africa, 32, 101, 102
Baptists, missionary society of, 28
Barber, Benjamin R., 121–25
Barre, Siad, 78, 79
Bartolomé, Lilia I., 117
Basel Mission Society, 28, 39
Becker, G. S., 56
Belgian Congo (Zaire): Belgian educational policy in, 35; colonial education in, 29; independent church movement, 67
Belgium, educational policy in Africa, 35, 37

Bello, Alhaji Ahmadu, 109
Bennett, P. A., 39
Berlin Conference, partition of Africa, 29
Berman, Edward H., 38, 43, 63, 68
Bernstein, Basil, 90, 122
Bierstadt, Robert, 73
Blau, Peter, 74
Blyden, Edward Wilmont, 42–43, 66
Boigny, Félix Houphouet, 77, 82
Bokassa, Jean Badel, 78, 82
Bourdieu, Pierre, 90
Bourgeois education, 48
Bowen, T. J., 61–62
Bower, Bert, 120
Boy Scouts, in Africa, 64
Boyd, William, 40
Bride price, 96
Brown, George, 84
Buber, Martin, 85
Buganda: colonial education in, 3, 29, 54; missionary activity in, 52; nationalist activists in, 68; status in, 59
Bureaucracy: African elites in, 106, 108, 109; ethnic representation in, 5–6, 44. *See also* Civil service
Busia, K. A., 17, 23, 24
Buxton, Thomas Fowell, 28, 62

Cameroons: colonial education in, 39; independent church movement, 67; political developments in, 76
Cape Education Act (1866), South Africa, 99
Cape Verde, lack of corruption in, 79–80
Carnegie, Andrew, 114
Casely-Hayford, J. E., 42, 68
Catholic Church Congress for Overseas territories, on work, 34
Catholic College (Uganda), 64
Central African Republic, political developments in, 78, 79
Chabal, Patrick, 73, 81
Chad: ethnic crises in, 6; political developments in, 78, 79
Character-building: in Boy Scouts, 64; traditional education, 17–18

Chiefs, pre-colonial leadership, 51
Chilembwe, John, 66
Christian National Education (CNE), South Africa, 101
Christian Philosophy of Life, 7
Church Missionary Society (CMS), 27, 28, 29, 38, 39, 41, 52, 53, 62, 68; revolt against, 66
Circumcision ceremonies, traditional education, 17
Civil service, and African elites, 107, 108. *See also* Bureaucracy
Clan, expected behavior toward, 16
Clans, education abroad, 3
Clapham Sect, 28
Class structure, reproduction of, 6, 8
Clerical workers, children's education, 4
Clignet, Remi, 6
Codification, concept of, 117
Coker, J. K., 66
Coleman, James S., 1, 2, 12, 27, 37, 38, 43, 46, 55, 56, 70, 71
Colonial era: attitude of elites during, 9; creation of modern elites, 2, 55–56, 62; European educational policies, 30–38, 55; missionary rivalry, 29–30, 38, 53, 66; residential patterns, 7; traditional leadership during, 51
Colonial regimes: missionary support for, 43; need for educated Africans, 54, 63
Colonization, 4
Community: education abroad, 3; traditional education, 17
Competition, class advantages, 4
Conscientization, concept of, 117
Contempt, missionary attitude toward Africans, 42–43
Conversion, missionary role, 11, 52
Corruption, in Africa, 13, 79–82, 106
Court, David, 6, 107
Crafts, traditional education for, 21
Cramer, John, 84
Critical citizenship, 14, 120

"Critical consciousness," goal of education, 111, 115
"Critical pedagogy," 118, 122–23
Critical social studies, role of, 117
Critical subjects, 13, 118
Critical theory, role of, 112
Critical thinking: skills, development of, 116–20; value of, 115–16
Crosson, V. L., 19
Crowther, Samuel Ajayi, 63, 66
Crozier, D.J.S., 57
Cultural capital, 90, 91
"Cultural politics," 11, 13, 118
Cultural values, educational transmission of, 7
"Culture of silence," 4
Curriculum: colonial regulation of, 7, 83; critical theory criticism of, 117–18; language of, 90, 122; post-colonial, 86–87; revising colonial, 14, 49
Custom, role in traditional education, 18

Dahomey, political developments in, 78
Dawodu, T. B., 66
De Graft-Johnson, J. W., 68
Deculturalization, 45, 84
Democracy: definition of, 113–14; in education, 14; goal of education, 111, 113, 123; in traditional education, 25
Denominational rivalry, in Africa, 30, 38, 53
Dewey, John, 111, 119
Dialogue, critical theory, 116–17, 120, 123
Diejomaoh, Victor P., 107–8
Distance, impact on girl's education, 97
Dodds, F. W., 53
Doe, Samuel, 78, 79, 81–82
Doi, A.R.I., 57
Domingo, Charles, 68
Dropout rate, African girls, 93
Dube, John L., 67
Dutch Reformed Church, missionary activity, 38–39

Economic development: role of education in, 109–11, 112, 113; skills of, 111

Education: characteristics of traditional, 22–25; colonial legacy, 47–50, 83–84, 105; as commodity, 3, 106; Islamic, 57–58; missionary bait, 12; missionary role in African, 27, 30–39, 70–71; for modern Africa, 111–13, 115–23; role of, 4, 47, 108; role in Africa, 112; social mobility, 3, 55; sub-Saharan expenditures per student, 10t; traditional African, 15–22; value in traditional society, 16

Education Committee of the Privy Council, educational policy in Africa, 31

Educational costs: for African girls, 95–96; in African schools, 4

Educational opportunity: and inequality, 6, 10, 13, 54–57, 59, 107, 108–9; traditional education, 22

Educational philosophy: control by elites, 3–4; in South Africa, 7–8, 100–104

Educational system, post-colonial reforms in, 106–7

Efik people, missionary activity among, 52

Ekechi, Felix, 12, 52–53

Elementary school: earning levels, 55; enrollment by gender, 92t

Elite codes, 13

Emancipatory theory, educational leadership, 111–12

Emenyonu, Ernest N., 40, 113

Employment opportunities, for African women, 93–94, 96–97

Empowerment, definition of, 121

Ensino de adaptação, 34

Ensino oficial, 34

Enslin, Penny, 103

Equality, concept of, 113

Equatorial Guinea, political developments in, 79

Ethiopia: colonial education in, 29; independent church movement, 67; political developments in, 78

Ethnic groups, educational opportunity among, 5, 44, 46, 56–57, 107

Evenson, John, 40

Experience and Education, 119

Extension services, political socialization, 65

Extra-mural department. *See* Extension services

Fafunwa, A. Babs, 16–17, 24, 40

Family: background, educational opportunity, 6, 54–55, 90–91; concept of African, 22–23; education abroad, 3; educational investment decisions, 96–97; expected behavior toward, 16, 17; role in traditional education, 16, 22; sex role transmission, 9

Fanti people, role in Ghana, 68

Farmers, children's education, 6

Fernandez-Balboa, Juan-Miguel, 117

Fishing, traditional education for, 20–21

Folklore, role in traditional education, 18, 19

Foster, Philip, 6, 38, 54, 55, 59, 105–6

Foucault, Michel, 8, 75, 76, 87, 104

Fourah Bay College (Sierra Leone), 68

France: colonial educational policy in Africa, 30–31, 37; educational legacy of, 48–49

Freeman, Bonnie Cook, 9

Freire, Paulo, 4, 9–10, 36, 83, 84, 85, 86, 88, 90, 91, 105, 112, 114–15, 116, 117–18, 119, 122

French language, in Africa, 31

Functionalism, in traditional education, 16, 24

Fundamental pedagogics, 7–8

Gabon, political developments in, 78

Gambia, political developments in, 78

Gaskiya Ta Fi Kwabo, on self-government, 109

Gaspar, Anedeto, 33–34, 36, 85–86

Gelfand, Michael, 22, 23

Gender gap, African education, 91–93

Geography, role in traditional education, 19

Germany, educational policy in Africa, 35–36
Ghana (Gold Coast): missionary activity in, 59; nationalist activists, 67, 68; political developments in, 76, 77, 78; political domination in, 12–13; secondary school entrance, 54
Giroux, Henry, 8, 11, 88, 91, 111–12, 115, 117–18, 120–21, 122, 123
Great Britain: colonial educational policy in Africa, 31–33, 37, 58; educational legacy of, 49
Greene, Maxine, 119
Grey, Earl, 32–33
Grey, Robert D., 63–64, 70
Guinea: elite domination in, 12–13; political developments in, 76, 77, 78, 79

Hanson, J. W., 57
Harris, William Wade, 67, 110, 112
Hartzell, Bishop James Crane, 36–37
Hausa people, cultural organization, 69
Hawiye people, genocide in Somalia, 79
Hayford, Mark, 67, 68
Heneveld, Ward, 92
Herbstein, Denis, 40
Hirji, Karim, 40
Hobbes, Thomas, 74
Hodgkin, Thomas, 35, 67
Holy Ghost Fathers, 53
Hope Waddell Training Institute, 64
Hursh, David, 117
Hutchinson, T. J., 37

Ibos, missionary activity among, 52–53
Ideology: elite control of, 3–4; reproduction of, 6
"Ijala," oral poetry, 19
Illiteracy, in African women, 95
Independence church movement, in African churches, 66, 67–68
Independent West African University, 66

Inequality: in African education, 10, 13, 54–57, 59, 107, 108–9; Kenyan educational, 6
Intellectual training, traditional education, 19
Intelligentsia, 51
Interdenominational International Missionary Council, attack on traditional religion, 42
Interdepartmental Committee on Native Education, South Africa, 100–101
International Missionary Council, anticolonial views, 68
Isaaqs, genocide in Somalia, 79
Islam: education for girls in, 97; in Africa, 57–58; resistance to Christian missionaries, 40, 57–58
Ismail, Khedive, 45
Ita, Eyo, 67
Ivory Coast: educational opportunity, 55; elite domination in, 12–13; French colonial educational policies, 31; political developments in, 77

Jamiyyar Mutanen Arewa, 69
Jefferson, Thomas, 113–14
Jesuits, missionary activity, 28, 29
Jibowu, S. S., 66
Johnson, George William, 66
Johnson, Henry, 43
Johnson, James, 66
Johnson, Walton R., 100
Jollie, Ethel Tawse, 33

Kakwa, genocide in Uganda, 78–79
Kalibala, Ernest, 67
Kandel, I., 47
Kanpol, Barry, 11, 87, 89, 118
Kaplan, A., 73
Kearney, Richard, 111
Kelly, Gail P., 45, 46
Kenya: earning levels in, 55; educational inequality in, 6, 59; elites in, 12–13, 107; independent church/school movement, 66; missionary activity in, 52, 67; political developments in, 76, 78, 79

Kenya Federation of Labor (KFL), 69
Kenyan African National Union (KANU), 69
Kierkegaard, Søren, 118–19
Kikuyu Independent School Association (Kenya), 66
Kimbangu, Simon, 67
King's College (Nigeria), 64
King's College (Uganda), 68
Kiwia, Jerome, 40
Knight, John B., 6, 55, 91
Knowledge, construction of, 8, 87
Korda, Michael, 74–75
Krapf, Johann, 29
Kreisberg, Seth, 74, 76, 81, 88
Kruger, Paul, 32

Labor productivity, and education, 56
Lagos Daily News, establishment of, 2
Lagos Weekly Record, establishment of, 2
Lakeru, J. A., 66
Langerin, Paul, 50
Language, formal instruction, 9, 13, 89–90, 122
Language codes, 90
Language of critique, 11, 13, 113, 120
Languages, African national, 12
Larson, B., 93
Lasswell, H., 73
Leach, A. F., 40
Leistyna, Pepi, 87
LeVine, Victor T., 80
Liberia: corruption in, 81–82; elite domination in, 12–13; ethnic crises in, 6; political developments in, 78, 79
Liberty, definition of, 113
Libya: elite domination in, 12–13; political developments in, 78
Lintner, Timothy, 91
Little, Kenneth L., 17
Livingstonia Institute (Nyasaland), 68
Lloyd, Barbara B., 6, 7
Lloyd, Peter C., 2, 6, 54, 55, 90
London University Examinations, 107
Loveridge, F. G., 23

Lugard, Lord, 35
Lutfi-al-Sayyid, Ahmad, 45
Lutheran Berlin Mission, missionary activity of, 28, 29, 39

Macaulay, Zachary, 28
Macedo, Donaldo, 36, 84, 91, 105, 122
Mackay, Alexander M., 29, 68
Mahdist uprising, 58
Makulu, H. F., 112
Malawi, political developments in, 77, 79
Mallamai class, 57–58
Mallinson, Vernon, 47
Managers, children's education, 6, 54
Marginality: creation of, 6, 46–47; definition of, 4; educational opportunity, 3
Mariam, Mengistu Haile, 78, 79
Marshall, James D., 117
Marx, Karl, 4
Masai, missionary activity among, 52
Mass education, criticism of, 119–20
Mathabane, Mark, 104
Mathematics, traditional education, 20
Mbiti, John S., 21
Mboya, Tom, 69
McLaren, Peter, 120–21, 122
McPeck, John, 115
Medicine-men, education of, 21
Mende people, professional education, 68
Methodist High School (Nigeria), 65
Methodist Missionary Society, 68
Middle class, creation of African, 63
Military dictatorships, 3, 13, 78–79
Ministry of Education, role of, 84, 85
Missionaries; African reception of, 12, 52–53; in Islamic Africa, 40, 57–58; role of, 2, 11, 29, 38–39; training of Africans abroad, 63
Missionary/colonial education: contemporary African view of, 39–47; limits of, 45–47
Missionary movement: in Africa, 28–29, 30–38, 61–63; African independence from, 65–68; anticolonial views

of, 65–66, 67–68; denominational rivalry, 30, 38, 53; origins of, 27–28
Morality, traditional education, 16, 23–24
Moravian Mission, missionary activity, 39
Morocco, ethnic crises in, 6
Mort, E. L., 65
Moumouni, Abdou, 18, 48–50
Mozambique: political developments in, 76; Portuguese educational policy in, 35
Mumba, Levi, 68
Mungazi, Dickson A., 24, 33, 38

Namibia, German educational policy in, 35
Names, in African tradition, 17–18
Narrative education, 4
National Council of Nigeria and the Cameroons (NCNC), 67, 69
National Education Policy Act, South Africa, 103
National Party (South Africa), educational policy, 32, 101–4
Nationalism, in Africa, 1, 2, 12, 63, 70, 109–10
Nation-states, creation of African, 12, 70
Native laws, role in traditional education, 18
Ndilula, Nghidi, 40, 53
"Neo-bourgeoisie" education, 49
Neocolonialism, emergence of, 77–78
Nguema, Macias, 79
Niger Delta Pastorate, 66
Niger, political developments in, 78
Nigeria: colonial education in, 30, 38; corruption in, 80–81; elite domination in, 12–13; ethnic crises in, 6; ethnic educational opportunity, 5; independent church/school movement, 66–67; missionary activity in, 52–53, 58–59; nationalism in, 2, 67; political developments in, 78, 79; social mobility, 2–3
Nkomo, Mokubung, 102

Nnoli, Okwudiba, 44
Northern People's Congress (NPC), 69
Northern Rhodesia African Congress, 69
Nyasaland, nationalist activists in, 68
Nyasaland African Congress, 68
Nyberg, David, 75
Nyerere, Julius, 111

Obadina, A. A., 66
Odaga, Adhiambo, 92
Odinga, Oginga, 42
Oduduwa, Egbe Omo, 69
Ogundijo, Matthew, 20
Ogunsheye, Ayo, 64
Ohlange Institute (South Africa), 67
Ojike, Mbonu, 42
Okafor, R.B.K., 80
Okonkwo, Chuka Eze, 16, 21–22
Okpara, M. I., 113
Oldham, J. H., 68
Olympio, Sylvanus, 78
Omolewa, Michael, 107
Opoku, Kofi A., 18, 24
Oral history, role in traditional education, 19
Ordinance Number 133, 33

Parents, role in traditional education, 18
Paris Evangelical Missionary Society, 52
Parti Démocratique de Côte d'Ivoire (PDCI), 69
Parti Démocatique de Guinée (PDG), 69
Pestalozzi, Johann Heinrich, 119
Petit-bourgeois class, creation in Africa, 36, 84, 105
Philosophie alimentaire, 119
Physical training, traditional education, 17, 18–19
Platonism, Belgian education philosophy, 35
Poetry, role in traditional education, 19–20

Police force, ethnic representation in, 5–6, 44
Political parties: abolition of, 76; ethnic representation in, 5–6, 44; origins of, 68, 69–70
Political repression, by elites, 3
Political socialization, of Africans, 64–67
Poor, educational disadvantages of, 4, 9, 13, 54–55, 89–90
Portugal, educational policy in Africa, 33–35, 37
Portuguese Colonial Act, 34
Portuguese language, 34–35
Post-colonial period: colonial legacy in education, 47–50, 84–85, 105; traditional leaders in, 51
Power: in Africa, 75–76; concept of, 73–75, 79; knowledge, relationship to, 8, 104; truth, relationship to, 75, 76, 87
Pre-colonial period: African education in, 15–22; characteristics of African education, 22–25; traditional leaders, 51
Presbyterian Church of Scotland, missionary society, 28, 68
Presidency, divine rights of, 76–77
Primitive Methodist Mission, 53
Printing presses, 2, 63
Professionals: children's education, 54; in traditional society, 19–20, 21
Professions, modern careers in, 6–7
"Protestant Awakening," 28
Protestant King's College (Uganda), 64
Proverbs, role in traditional education, 18, 19
Providence Industrial Mission, 66
Pye, Lucian W., 3

Rassemblement Démocratique Africain (RDA), 69
Reagan, Timothy, 8
"Recruiters," missionary, 61
Regulation of 1899, on work, 34
Religion, elite control of, 3–4
Repetition rate, African girls, 93
Residential patterns, 7

Resnick, Lauren, 119
Review of the Educational System of Eastern Nigeria, 41
Rhodes, Cecil John, 32, 100
Rhodesian Herald, on African education, 33
Rickert Commission, South Africa, 103
Royal Commission to West Africa, report of, 31–32, 37
Ruperti, M., 15
Rural areas, educational inequality in, 56, 107
Russell, Bertrand, 73
Rwanda: ethnic crises in, 6; ethnic educational opportunity, 5; political developments in, 79

Sabot, Richard H., 6, 55, 91
Sarbah, John Mensah, 68
Sartre, Jean-Paul, 119
Scholars, Islamic, 57
Scholarships, social mobility, 3
School enrollment, in sub-Saharan countries, 94–95t
School subject areas, enrollment by gender, 92–93, 98, 98t
School system: inequality in African, 6, 10, 13, 54–57, 59, 107; role of, 4
Schools: concept of schooling, 11; detachment from African culture, 44–45, 83–84; elite control of, 3–4; establishment of missionary, 53–54; ideological production of, 3; Islamic in Africa, 57–58; mission-run, 2, 52–53; political socialization in, 64–67; self-government in, 64; sex role transmission, 9, 97; status quo reinforcement, 88–89; in Third World, 4
Schweitzer, Albert, 37
Scorification, traditional education, 17
Secondary schools: earning levels, 55; enrollment by gender, 92t, 92–93; entrance exams, 54; girls enrolled in sub-Saharan countries, 96t; role of, 2
Secret-societies, role in traditional education, 16, 17

Segregation, missionary movement, 42
Seko, Mobutu Sese, 78, 79, 81
Self-development, educational, 111
Self-government, in missionary schools, 64
Senegal, political developments in, 76, 77
Sex roles, transmission of, 9, 98
Sexism, in African schools, 13, 91–93, 92t, 94–95t, 95–98, 96t, 98t
Sexual harassment, in African schools, 97
Sharp, Granville, 28
Sierra Leone: elite domination in, 12–13; ethnic crises in, 6; nationalist movement, 68; political developments in, 78
Sierra Leone Organization Society, 69–70
Sierra Leone People's Party, 69–70
Single-party state, in Africa, 76–77
Slave trade, European advocacy against, 28, 62
Social class, educational competition, 4
Social mobility: colonial education, 46; role of education in, 2–3, 55, 63
Social privilege, education and, 56
Social responsibility, traditional education, 16, 23
Social sensitivity, traditional education, 17
Social status, education and, 6, 63
Socialism, in Africa, 77
Society of African Missions, Catholic missionary society, 28, 38, 41, 53
Somalia: ethnic crises in, 6; political developments in, 79
South Africa: apartheid in, 8, 9, 32, 101–4; education in, 13, 100–104; educational philosophy of, 7–8, 32, 100–104; independent church movement, 67; nationalist activists, 67; origin of educational system, 99–101
St. Andrew's College (Nigeria), 64

St. Kizito Mixed Secondary School, mass rape at, 97
Stailey, J. C., 19
Stone, M. L., 67
Storytelling, role in traditional education, 18
Strasser, Valentine, 78
Students, sub-Saharan: expenditures on, 10t; school attendance, 5t
Sudan: colonial education in, 29, 38; ethnic crises in, 6; political developments in, 79
Sutton, Francis X., 17, 38
Symes, Stewart, 29

Talbot, P. Amaury, 39
Tanganiyka African National Union (TANU), 69, 70
Tanzania (Tanganyika): colonial education in, 39; educational inequality in, 59; elites in, 107; political developments in, 76
Teacher education, 13, 14; reform of, 120–23; South Africa, 103–4
Teachers: attitude toward girl students, 97–98; de-skilling of, 89; role of, 10–11, 13–14, 111–12
Teaching methods: in African schools, 7–8, 114–15; post-colonial school system, 85, 87; traditional education, 16–19
Technical education, promotion of, 106–7
Technology, and Western education, 39, 54, 55–56, 63
Things Fall Apart, 38
Thompson, A. R., 110
Togo, political developments in, 78
Tordoff, William, 69, 76–77
Toro College (Nigeria), 65
Touré, Sékou, 69, 77, 79
Trade unions: African nationalism, 69; education abroad, 3
Trades, traditional education for, 21
Traditional order, missionary movement's attack on, 42
Traditional religion: Christian attack on, 42; role in Africa, 41–42

Traditional rulers, loss of power by, 1, 13
Traditional rules, power of, 51
Transformative intellectual, teacher as, 11, 13, 121
Triumphant Democracy, 114
Truth, construction of, 8, 75, 76, 87
Tunisia, political developments in, 76
Tyler, J. W., 52

Uchendu, Victor, 35, 37, 44, 55, 56, 107
Uganda: elite domination in, 12–13; nationalist activist, 67; political developments in, 78–79
Union Camerounaise, 69
Union Générale des Travailleurs d'Afrique Noire (UGTAN), 69
United Free Church of Scotland, 68
United Gold Coast Convention (UGCC), 69
United Native Church (Cameroons), 67
Universities: earning levels, 55; enrollment by gender, 92t, 93; role of, 2
Upper Volta, political developments in, 76, 78
Urban areas, education in, 56, 59, 83–84, 107

Venn, Henry, 29, 62
Verwoerd, Hendrik, 32, 101
Vocational education: in Africa, 9; promotion of, 106–7; traditional education, 16, 20–21

Walker, L. Kay, 24, 33, 38
Wallerstein, Immanuel, 69, 77

Weber, Max, 79
Weekly Star, on Nigerian corruption, 80
Welbourn, F. B., 42
Wesley, John, 28
Wesleyan Methodist Missionary Society (WMMS), 28, 38, 68
West African People's Institute (Nigeria), 67
Westermann, D., 40–41
Western education: advantages of, 39, 54–56; Africa, impact on, 1–2, 36–39; missionary role, 11–12, 27, 30–38, 70–71
Western languages, in African schools, 9–10, 31, 34–35, 91, 122
Western liberal tradition: elitism of, 2; role of, 1
White Fathers, missionary activity, 29
Wilberforce, William, 28
William Ponty school (Senegal), 64
Williams, F. E., 66
Williams, H.L.O., 65
Williams, Hugh, 33
Woodrum, Arlie, 87
Woodson, Carter G., 47–48

Yorubaland, missionary activity in, 52
Youth movements, African nationalism, 69

Zaire, 78, 79; colonial education in, 29; corruption in, 81; ethnic crises in, 6
Zambia, political developments in, 76
Zimbabwe, British educational policy in, 32–33
Zolberg, Aristide, 77
Zulus, missionary activity among, 53

About the Author

MAGNUS O. BASSEY is Assistant Professor in the Department of Secondary Education and Youth Services at Queens College, The City University of New York. Dr. Bassey has published several academic articles. His forthcoming book, *Missionary Rivalry and Educational Expansion in Nigeria, 1885–1945*, will be published in 1999. Dr. Bassey also taught in the New York City Public Schools and at SUNY-Oneonta.